# A BOYHOOD DREAM REALIZED:
## Half a Century of Texas Culture, One Newspaper Column at a Time

# A BOYHOOD DREAM REALIZED:
## Half a Century of Texas Culture, One Newspaper Column at a Time

by
*BURLE PETTIT*

Edited by
Kenneth L. Untiedt

Texas Folklore Society Extra Book Number 27

University of North Texas Press

Denton, Texas

Permissions:
University of North Texas Press
1155 Union Circle #311336
Denton, TX 76203-5017

The paper used in this book meets the minimum requirements of the American
National Standard for Permanence of Paper for Printed Library Materials,
z39.48.1984. Binding materials have been chosen for durability.

Library of Congress Cataloging-in-Publication Data

Names: Pettit, Burle, 1934- author. | Untiedt, Kenneth L., 1966- editor.
Title: A boyhood dream realized : half a century of Texas culture, one newspaper
    column at a time / by Burle Pettit ; edited by Kenneth L. Untiedt.
Other titles: Texas Folklore Society extra book ; no. 27.
Description: Denton, TX : University of North Texas Press, [2019] | Series:
    Texas folklore society extra book ; number 27 | Includes index.
Identifiers: LCCN 2019024285 | ISBN 9781574417708 (cloth) | ISBN
    9781574417807 (ebook)
Subjects: LCSH: Pettit, Burle, 1934- | Pettit, Burle, 1934---Childhood and
    youth--Anecdotes. | Sportswriters--Texas--Biography. | Newspaper
    editors--Texas Biography. | Newspapers--Sections, columns, etc. | Moran
    (Tex.)--Social life and customs--20th century--Anecdotes. |
    Texas--Social life and customs--20th century--Anecdotes. | LCGFT:
    Autobiographies.
Classification: LCC PN4874.P456 A3 2019 | DDC 070.4/49796--dc23
LC record available at https://lccn.loc.gov/2019024285

*A Boyhood Dream Realized: Half a Century of Texas Culture, One Newspaper Column
at a Time* is Texas Folklore Society Extra Book Number 27

The electronic edition of this book was made possible by the support of the Vick
Family Foundation.

# DEDICATION

Not only was it her constant insistence that I gather a group of my columns and publish them in a book, it was my beloved wife Frances who put me in a position to write the columns to begin with.

When she came into my life, I not only had seen my boyhood dream turn into a fantasy but had watched willingly from the seat of a bulldozer or the derrick of a drilling rig as it faded off into a hazy future ahead. She changed that by making college a condition of our marriage.

There were others taking her side: special friends such as Carlton Stowers, an accomplished author; Morris Knox, a sidekick who appeared in more than a few of those columns; and my three sons, Kevin, Kyle and Scott. The youngest of those, Scott, followed up by asking (nagging?) daily for a progress report.

Yet the catalytic force behind it all was Frances Hill Pettit, whom a part of me believes that, from somewhere above, she is smiling and nodding her approval.

# CONTENTS

# PREFACE

I first met Burle Pettit in the early 1990s; although I don't recall the date, I know that it was in Hodges Chapel at First Christian Church in Lubbock, Texas. I had read his columns in the *Lubbock Avalanche-Journal* for years, and I always enjoyed his wit and clever use of language. I discovered that he was a member of Kenneth Davis's Sunday school class, and Kenneth—my mentor, and one of the Texas Folklore Society's few members who have ever achieved the status of Fellow—often shared humorous stories from or about Burle. By chance, more than twenty years later, Fran Vick suggested that I contact Burle to see about doing a TFS Extra Book featuring his columns. This book is the result.

Some may wonder about classifying editorial newspaper columns as folklore. If you think about what folklore really is, it makes perfect sense. These columns represent decades of observations of local lore—customs, traditions, legends, beliefs, and folkways of West Texas. Even the fact that these columns appeared in newspapers is, in many ways, folkloric. Although the newspaper industry has changed a great deal from the time Burle Pettit first began his career, newspapers still reflect what is most important to a group of people. They are, in a way, the heartbeat of a region, and they serve as a record of people's livelihoods and losses, their triumphs and tragedies, and their musings and memories.

These columns do not appear in chronological order, nor do they feature the dates of their original publication— unless it was part of the column's title. Not all of them have titles, but some of the formatting has been retained to give the pieces the same newsprint "feel," such as the capitalization of first words of paragraphs that begin new sections. Otherwise, they've been selectively chosen and grouped into chapters of various topics. You'll recognize some of the people and places and events recalled in these pages, but some you won't. While they were editorial columns in a newspaper with a sizeable readership—and are the result of a career that spanned half a century—they are also quite personal, referencing friends, family, and life events that are relevant to anyone who read them at the time of their first publication, and even to people reading them today.

What's interesting about editorial columns is that they can capture the general attitude of a group of people, and over time they show how the moral climate may begin to evolve as the people grow and experience new and difficult challenges. These columns recorded momentous events that often altered how we live and interact with one another—for a specific region in West Texas, and for an entire nation. They also confess boyhood dreams . . . and foolishness. They tell stories, and tell about telling stories. All reveal what was—and for many, still is—important. You don't have to be an avid reader of the *Lubbock Avalanche Journal*, or even be from Lubbock, or know where Moran is to relate to the subjects covered in these pieces.

The Texas Folklore Society's annual publication is most often a miscellany of articles from multiple authors over a wide range of topics; the articles originate as papers that have been given at our annual meetings, and the series of books is called the Publications of the Texas Folklore Society. In addition to the 72 books published in that series, the TFS has also supported more than two dozen "Extra Books," which are single-author books written on a particular topic. I am excited that this is Extra Book #27; I hope you find it entertaining—and also a valuable source of West Texas lore.

My special thanks to everyone at the UNT Press, especially Ron Chrisman and Karen DeVinney; their professionalism and support always simplifies the process of putting together the TFS books and getting them in our members' hands each year. As always, I am extremely grateful for the ongoing support provided by Stephen F. Austin State University, which has supported the TFS for nearly fifty years in our efforts to fulfill the mission of collecting, preserving, and presenting the folklore of Texas and the Southwest. As always, I extend my most heartfelt thanks to Charlotte Blacksher, our Office Secretary and Treasurer; you are appreciated more than I can say.

Kenneth L. Untiedt

Stephen F. Austin State University

Nacogdoches, Texas

May 3, 2019

# INTRODUCTION

*Lubbock Avalanche-Journal* Building

## THE TOWN, THE TIMES, THE CHARACTERS

It is not the Panhandle or even El Paso; in fact, it is definable neither by boundaries created by mapmakers nor landmarks laid out by nature. West Texas was more about attitude than geography, more about feel than grasp. Yet its citizens knew exactly where it was. Its capital could have been Lubbock or Abilene, or perhaps Midland or Odessa, or any point in between.

West Texas was about oilfields and ranches, and small towns and the people espoused by both. It was about all the elements of which Texas Folklore was born and nurtured.

But, for me, that West Texas was about a particular community where the scrub oaks and rolling hills begin to give way to flatter lands and intrusive mesquites. Moran was at the point of that separation. Cisco, to the south, and Albany, to the north, offered noticeable change in flora and fauna but shared a common culture unique to the times and the spaces. That period immediately followed the end of WWII and faded into a marked cultural change in the late 1950s. That evolution seemed to follow the musical trends of that era, and that area, as the Hank Williams country (nee Hillbilly) sound would be replaced by Elvis Presley and Bill Haley and Rock and Roll.

It was during those times that much of my writings were based. Moran, whose population was 1,000 or, as we said back then, "purt near," was self-contained to the point five grocery stores and seven "fillin' stations" were able to exist—some to thrive, others to survive. The habit of "shopping at home" was sustained more by habit than civic loyalty. Even after the automobile became a fixture in the majority of driveways, mobility was curtailed by limited funds and, later, by wartime rationing of gasoline and tires. Even after the war ended, financial prudence held strong. It was well into the 1950s before locals began to realize that the forty-mile round trip to Cisco's Piggly Wiggly would more than account for the gasoline consumption involved.

Although the columns featured herein cover a wide variety of topics reflecting history of the times, my favorites clearly are those involving the period of my life marked by the carefree days of boyhood and the characters with whom I was cast. Attesting to the indelibility of those memories is that not a one of the incidents described was a figment of a wistful memory. The characters were real.

Cuz was my first cousin, a lifelong partner in mischief if not mayhem. Ray was my lifelong best friend, from pre-school until his death in the year 2001. Charley D., Jackie, John, Bill, and Danny were real people. Then there was Rabbit, the most outrageous member of the lot. Whatever Rabbit did, he carried to the extreme. He would be worthy of a book unto himself. But getting a publisher to consider any part of him as believable would be the challenge.

Those were easily my favorites among all my columns. Partially, I suppose, because they were so easy to write; in fact, they had written themselves years ago. But mainly because they reflected on a life that, sadly, will never again be available to American boyhood.

Regrettably, the West Texas that was their setting is no longer a region, or even an attitude.

## The *A-J*: A Funny Name with a Colorful Cast

Unlike the challenges that were the daily life of most newspapers, the *Lubbock Avalanche-Journal* was more often required to explain its name than to defend its purpose. It was founded in 1900 by John J. Dillard; his choice of the name "Avalanche" obviously had naught to do with the flat terrain upon which Lubbock rests. Despite the various versions of the stories, they all agree that Dillard referenced an intended "avalanche of news."

Despite its having gone through several owners and scores of personalities during its 119-year history, Charles Armor Guy remains the face of the newspaper, even though he retired as editor and publisher in 1972, shortly after it sold to Morris Communications. Although he was known as "Charlie (or Cholly) Guy," the name on the masthead was "Chas. A. Guy." Even today, the *A-J* style honors that application.

To me, even after his retirement, he was always Mister Guy. I couldn't have brought myself to call him "Charlie" if he had invited me to (which he didn't).

A description of Guy would have to begin with his stature as a journalism pioneer, beginning with his arriving in Lubbock early in the 20th century and immediately involving himself in the newspaper craft. When he and his partner, Dorrance Roderick, bought the established Lubbock Avalanche and combined it with their afternoon *Journal*, the resulting *Lubbock Avalanche-Journal* became a commanding voice of the Plains. Its influence never waned; in fact, it picked up steam as the country town morphed into an infant city.

Meanwhile, the name Chas. A. Guy gained in significance, as his prominence, driven by a colorful persona and outspoken nature, spread onto the statewide stage and beyond. A staunch conservative, he broke with his normal GOP leanings to endorse his close friend, Lyndon B. Johnson, in the 1964 Presidential race. Yet he took Johnson to task for LBJ's strong support for Civil Rights legislation.

Back home, his influence was both cussed and saluted. As head of a small circle of men known as "The King Makers," he, his A-J cohort Parker F. Prouty, and three other community leaders, had almost unrestricted power. It was they who decided who would hold all public offices, determined the direction of the city's growth, and—of greatest import—authored the city charter which is still in effect today.

He was, among all other things, unique in a sense that would make his persona impossible to emulate. Not only did he wind a trail that stretched through six decades of Texas journalism, that path left scores of indelible footprints. As with all legendary characters of Texas lore, CAG's antics and accomplishments are recalled with the contradictions of respect and resentment. Those hundreds of us who toiled beneath his scrutinous nature have responded in a wide variety of ways. One, the late Freda McVay, wrote a book about him and titled it perfectly: "The Paradoxical Plainsman." On the cover was the sketch that ran above his daily column, "The Plainsman."

Freda's work blended his professional philosophy and anecdotal examples to aptly describe his complex persona. Perhaps the most revealing part of the importance he placed on his position was his belief that "the success of a newspaper is built around the personality of its editor . . . he might be hated or he might be loved, but he has to be respected."

Among the anecdotes Freda used involved one that represented what was perhaps the most uncomfortable thirty seconds of my life at that juncture. Mister Guy was given to moods that often affected not only his approachability but his decisions. I, at the time of Freda's reference, carried the title Executive Sports Editor. I had learned that if he was in a good mood, Mister Guy was amenable to almost any reasonable request. But if he was out of sorts . . . well, don't even ask permission to go to the bathroom. Accordingly, if I had an important request, I would check with his secretary before asking.

On that day, I was wanting to get an unscheduled raise for one of my sports writers. So I leaned into Arlene's office and asked, "What kind of mood is the old buzzard in today?" Before she could respond, an all-too familiar voice behind me growled, "Grouchy as hell! What do you want?"

"In that case, nothing," I more wheezed than uttered, and trotted off hastily for my desk where the phone was already ringing. He beckoned me back to his corner office and opined that I must have wanted something or I wouldn't have asked. I thought of something of little or no significance, he said no, and I headed back to my office, thankful that I still had one.

## Parker Prouty Influenced My Most Critical Decision

Guy and Parker F. Prouty, the company president, had lateral authority. That they worked "in harness" was probably due not only to their mutual respect but because of their division of duties. As editor and publisher, Guy had total control over the news product and its production. Prouty oversaw the business end, which included the accounting, advertising, and circulation aspects. But when it came to Texas Tech athletics, Prouty was by far the more enthusiastic of the two. In fact, during the Depression years, it was Prouty whose fund-raising skills and personal contributions kept the Red Raider Club afloat. And even though as sports editor I reported to Guy, it was Prouty's support that led to my spending my entire career at the *Avalanche-Journal*.

Because of an endorsement from Blair Cherry, whose legendary career included coaching such immortals as Bobby Layne and Tom Landry at the University of Texas, I gained lasting favor with Prouty. When I took over the Tech beat in 1962, J. T. King was beginning his second year as head football coach. One of King's staunchest supporters was Cherry. Prouty first knew Cherry when he was coaching the Amarillo High Sandies. The two men developed a close friendship that lasted a lifetime. To Prouty, if Cherry said it, it was not open to challenge. By then, Cherry had retired and moved to Lubbock and renewed friendships with King, one of his assistants back at UT, and Prouty. It was my great fortune that Cherry liked my writing and, more importantly, told Prouty, "You'd better hold onto that kid; he's a great one." That endorsement served me well at the time. A few years later, it was directly responsible for perhaps the most significant professional decision I would make.

## A DREAM FORGOTTEN AND THE GIRL WHO REVIVED IT

When I arrived at the *A-J* on Aug. 29, 1960, I was realizing a boyhood dream that had finally come true. During good times or bad a constant in our household was the *Fort Worth Star-Telegram*. I was intrigued by that newspaper and imagined what it would be like to be a reporter. It started with my mother reading the comics to me when I was a toddler. Then, after I learned to read, I was a daily follower of the sports writers. It turned out that it wasn't merely a childhood fantasy. I knew that if I ever went to college, journalism would be my major.

Then, when I got the chance, I blew it. After graduating from high school, I had a full scholarship to college. But, as I was finalizing my plans, buddies of mine were taking roughnecking jobs, buying cars, and partying. Intrigued by the thought of a high-paying oilfield job, having my own car and the resulting amenities, I dropped out (actually, I left before classes had begun), headed to the Permian Basin, and got hired immediately. It's important to mention that neither my parents nor siblings were in on my change of plans. It was only when my oldest brother (I was the youngest of seven kids) drove up to the college to take me to dinner did he learn that I had packed up and left two days before. To say I was in the family doghouse would be a gross understatement. Then, a couple of years later, I was drafted into the Army where I trained in heavy equipment. After being discharged I took a job in highway construction. From time to time, that fleeting newspaper fantasy would resurface . . . but only as a boyhood dream that took a long time to become reality.

FLYING BACK from Houston where I had just been offered the position as sports editor of the *Post*, I looked at my wife who was seated beside me. We both had been wined and dined. Ed Hunter, the editor, introduced us to Oveta Culp Hobby and her son Bill, two of the most influential individuals in Texas. Ed—who previously had tried to hire me at two of his previous stops, the *San Angelo Standard Times* and the *Galveston News*—pressured me to accept the job before I left town. I declined, saying my wife and I needed time to privately consider the decision.

Frances, to whom this book is dedicated, was the sole reason I was in position to make such a choice. When I began dating her, she was in her fourth semester at North Texas State. Her folks had moved to Moran while I was in the army. Before she would agree to marry me (Note: our elopement is described in one of the columns included in this volume) I had to vow to join her church and enroll in college. The former was easy; the latter, not so much.

That I agreed and followed through with both conditions provided the journalism degree and a route-paver to my lifelong dream . . . and now this life-changing professional decision we were about to face.

When I walked into the *A-J* building the next morning, I soon learned that my intent to keep the Houston offer from my bosses was not an option. For sports writers, the grapevine always operates at full buzz. And by the time we left Hobby Airport, a Dallas sports writer had called Guy to apply for my "vacant" position. As I walked in the newsroom, the switchboard operator said, "Mr. Guy wants to see you the instant you arrive."

Our visit was short. And his expression made me thankful. He only said that he knew about the Houston deal "and Parker wants to talk to you right now!"

The short version of a long visit is that Prouty's opening sentence was, "You're not going anywhere and we're about to decide why." That I liked his eventual decision is attested by all the years that followed.

Only once did I think I might have made a bad choice. That came three years later when, while I was on the Southwest Conference press tour the newspaper sold to Morris Communications. The tour was at its Austin stop and, after a number of tries, I gave up on attempting to reach anyone in authority at the *A-J*. Blackie Sherrod, then at the *Dallas News*, quipped, "When you send your copy and they refuse charges, you'll know you're in trouble." (During those days of Western Union filings, copy was sent Night Press Rates [NPR] collect).

Prouty's convincing me not to go to Houston was not the first time he had influenced my decisions. About three years before, a managing editor's job had been offered to me. I was beckoned to Guy's office where he and a couple of other newsroom executives were assembled to encourage me to accept the position. A few minutes into the conversation, Prouty wandered in. He listened quietly as the others spoke, often convincingly. He hadn't said a word so, rather boldly, I said, "Mr. Prouty, what are your thoughts on this?" He looked at me then back at Guy and, before turning and walking out the door, said, "I see nothing wrong with having a damned good sports editor."

I declined the offer. And, mysteriously, my next paycheck validated that decision . . . and the relative importance Prouty placed on the two positions. I'll never know what conversations, if any, transpired between those two in the aftermath. I was pleased that it had no effect on my relationship with Guy.

Not long after Morris bought the paper I was faced with the same decision. This time there was nothing to deliberate. In my "farewell" sports column I observed that writing sports for Parker Prouty was akin to being a photographer for Hugh Hefner; this new outfit eyed sports as just another department.

Even though my lifelong dream had come true in a roundabout manner, I believe the path worked out for the best. Journalism is a profession that encompasses a breadth of knowledge, honed instincts, and an appreciation for the diversity of personalities. Accordingly, I believe my experiences in the West Texas oilfields, the U. S. Army, and highway construction were functional complements to my academic work at both the undergrad and graduate levels. It's almost as destiny directed the route I had taken. Only in the storybooks of yore would the perfect romance lead to the resurrection and fulfillment of a lifetime dream long forgotten.

# MORAN AND OTHER
# SPECIAL PLACES

Burle's boyhood home in Moran

## GINS

THIS GUY FROM *Newsday* must have thought Roby was really a swinging place when he arrived in town, along with scores of other journalists, to capture the essence of a community suddenly smitten with millionaires. He wanted to talk to the lady that had got the pool together, the one that led to 42 locals winning a lottery worth $42 million.

"I was told she worked at this gin mill right on the edge of town," he explained to a native whom he was asking for directions. "They said I'd know it because there would be a number of strippers parked right there on the lot . . ."

What a letdown he must have felt when, upon finally finding the Terry Gin, that the strongest drink available there was warmed-over coffee, and not a single stripper stalking the place would be available for a lap dance.

In all its history, Roby—heavily populated by Baptists and members of the Church of Christ—ain't your father's party town. Its penchant for sobriety ranked right up there with quail hunting as its claim to fame before the $40 million lottery brought worldwide fame to that town of 600 folks.

THAT ANECDOTE, which happened eleven years ago on Thanksgiving Eve, may have other applications. But its point right here is to illustrate that just because a town is small doesn't necessarily make it an easy place in which to find your way around. Given his assumptions, that *Newsday* guy might never have found the building he was looking for had it not borne a large sign across its cor-rugated carcass.

Just since I have been sitting here has it occurred to me to wonder how a stranger ever found what he may have been looking for back where I grew up.

Back when Moran was more than thrice the size it is today, there was nary a street sign to be found on any corner within the city limits. Now, there were roads that connected it directly to five other towns—Albany, Cisco, Baird, Breckenridge and Putnam—and only one, the U.S. highway that connected Albany to Cisco, was paved when I left to accept a job that my draft board had found for me.

All the streets had names, mind you, but few people knew what they were. I was aware that our house was on Fisher Street, and the one we always referred to as Main Street was actually the east end of Fisher. I had learned that one night when several of us guys grew tired of hang-ing out at the ice house and decided to go over to City Hall and see how much noise it would take to wake up the night watchman.

If he had dozed off with his hearing aid lying out on the desk, it would take several decibels. Anyway, while shuffling through some of the stuff Miz Chambers, the city secretary and one of two paid city employees (the water superintendent was the other), had left out on the counter, I came across an actual map of Moran, the city.

That my initial exclamation of "Wow, looky here" did not awake the dozing gendarme meant that my buddies and I would have lots of time to pore over my find.

Now the night watchman drew a check from the city, but it came mainly from fees that were paid by the downtown merchants in return for having their doors checked periodically throughout the night. The city kicked in just enough to justify his title of City Marshall, which he vocally preferred over "Night Watchman." We sometimes called him Night Watchman just to hear his emphatic correction.

But I digress.

THE NEXT DAY when I mentioned to my dad that I had discovered that we lived on a street that had an actual name, I was surprised that he already knew that.

Now my father had lived in the Moran area since 1895, so he'd had ample time to learn about such things. And he had. He told me the name of dern near all the streets, begging me to wonder why it was such a big secret. With some indignation, I asked him why we had no street signs.

He gave me sort of a puzzled look and a short answer: "Why?"

His point was that nobody needs them. I suspect that his longer answer would have been that he'd rather see that money spent grading the streets we already have. Moran streets, then as now, were mainly graveled.

While I was in the army, the state built FM 576 right through the heart of town, connecting Moran with Baird to the west, Breckenridge to the east. That sent it right in front of our house. I was delighted to return home and find that ol' Fisher Street might not have a sign, but it was the only paved street in a residential area not fronting the Albany-Cisco highway. At homecoming a few weeks ago, I was proud to see it now has both . . .

SOMETIME DURING the years since I left there, the streets in Moran have been designated by actual signs.

I found it strange, perhaps a bit morbidly ironic, that a town whose population had dwindled to a fifth the size it was in the '50s suddenly needed signs to designate each and every street. Then it occurred to me that even though many of the houses and other structures no longer existed, the streets themselves had remained the same in length, location and even in number.

Having not had even a glimpse of a Moran map since that night in the city hall—the watchman was still asleep when we left, despite Rabbit's having yelled goodnight at the top of his considerable lungs—I enjoyed driving all over town and reading the names.

I was also pleased to find my dad proven right. I heard a visitor ask a native how to get to the high school gym. He was given vivid and clear directions, and not a single street name was mentioned.

When I left Moran to head home, I decided to drive out the old Albany highway. En route, it occurred to me as I was passing Ed Mohon's tank that I was driving down Gin Road.

I wonder what that *Newsday* guy would've made of that . . .

## GRACE'S STATION

WHEN I PICKED up my old hometown weekly a while back and read where Albert Grace's station was being torn down, I got a lump right between my tonsils.

It had become an eyesore, the item explained, so the decision was made to remove it.

Now, had that been any of the other remaining fillin' stations, I probably wouldn't have given it a second thought. But this one had a bit of history with me and others of my ilk and era . . . boys who may not have invented mischief but who certainly did hone it into something that fit somewhere in between mayhem and decorum.

It was what we called in those days a hangout, a place where you went to immediately because that's where everybody was. "Everybody," of course, meant Rabbit and Cuz and Danny and Jackie and Bill and John and this new kid from Ranger, Tommy Wilson, whom Mr. Grace had hired to run it so he could retire, at least for the summer. Tommy's folks had moved to Moran where his dad worked for the Texas Company, and he was attending Ranger Junior College for at least another year.

I had finally gotten over a similar removal several years ago of John Gardner's Magnolia station, just across the street, which was our nighttime gathering place all through high school and beyond. It was also the ice house, and its popularity rested in part by the fact we could get into the locked soda pop box without doing any damage or, of equal import, leaving any clues.

We were a pretty noisy lot, and Mr. Brooks, who owned the hotel across the street, would sometimes step outside and urge us to quieten down or else he'd have to call Emory, the local sheriff. Mr. Brooks was the only man I ever saw who actually wore a nightcap.

But I digress.

TOMMY WAS a fun kid, probably less ornery than the rest of us, but tolerant of our water fights, and our need to play with the hot patch machine and the little deal they used to hammer the dates onto new batteries. He did insist that we pay for our sodas and candy and anything else in the inventory that might wind up as a debit to his own paycheck.

Mr. Grace trusted Tommy to the point that he seldom showed up at the station. And, when he did pop in, you never saw a quieter, more polite bunch of Moran boys. I was probably the nicest and quietest of them all, being as the Graces lived right across the street from us and our parents were good friends.

Being a ranching community, the Moran of that day was a bustling little town that supported six "fillin' stations"—seven if you counted the one on the south edge of town that Lydle Weir operated now and then.

LOOKING BACK ON it, those stations were a big part of Moran's culture, gathering places during the day and especially on Saturdays, when entire families would leave their farms and come into town to shop. Only the pool hall and barbershop drew bigger crowds.

The pool hall was popular because there were some very good snooker players to watch, and the barbershop was nice and cool and ol' Garland always had today's paper and a lot of magazines to read.

But at some point, everybody made it to one of the stations to gas up, and to sit awhile to see what strangers might stop off with news from elsewhere. Nobody was ever hesitant in asking one of them where he was from and where was he going and were they getting any rain where he lived.

Two of the stations, Jim Tom Brooks' Humble and Carroll Loudder's Texaco, also were garages that did everything from minor tune-ups to major overhauls. A couple of stations employed boys to do full-service car washes, complete with whisk broom interior cleaning and an overall wipe-down with a real chamois.

One might think that such competition would build ill will among the proprietors, but it never happened. For one thing, there was enough business to go around. In those days, the sprawling Moran school district was populated by enough rural homes to require five bus routes.

Jim Tom and Carroll were very friendly competitors. They loaned each other parts when necessary and, I suspect, were available for consultation if and when consultation was needed.

AT ALBERT'S Texaco, there was out behind the building a large container where the oil drained from cars was poured. I don't remember what happened to the contents once the big tank was filled, but I suspect it was picked up by the Cottles, who owned the Texaco distributorship.

Being as the EPA and Moran were mutual strangers, people could dispose of things as they saw fit.

Anyway, when Tommy was running the station, that's where a kid named James Young, who also had just moved to town, got oil for his aged Chevy. It burned so much oil that putting new stuff in its crankcase would have been financially inadvisable. There was a petcock at the bottom of the tank, but that's where the sludge all settled. We'd help him dip it out, using a tin can tied to a piece of fishing cord, in exchange for a ride to Round Hole, the best of several good swimming holes on Deep Creek or Battle Creek.

THE DECISION TO remove the old station makes sense to a community that does actually care about its appearance. Buster and Julie Cottle have for years headed an annual cleanup of a town where vacant lots have flourished as homes and businesses disappear.

I remember many years ago, when my parents were both living, I went home right after the old Brooks Hotel had been demolished. I parked my car and walked among the rubble, fondly remembering Mr. Brooks, his tolerance of our noise, and his nightcap with the pointy top. I picked up one of the bricks the contractor had left behind and put it in the trunk of my car.

I still have it today.

For reasons I don't even understand, when I go back to homecoming every other year I am more bothered by the voids than I am by the aging structures, no matter how dilapidated they have become. I think it's because when a building is swept away, many fond memories are whisked away in the wake.

Right now, though, the sights and sounds from Albert Grace's old station still ring loudly in my mind . . . and in my heart.

Somehow, I think they will linger in both places . . .

## BARBERS

I HOPE MY friend Avis, who has been doing my hair now for a quarter-century or purt near it, doesn't take this personally, but I sure do miss those old barbershops of yore.

Now, Avis is in a league of her own when it comes to styling my coif, sculpturing around the cowlicks and sticking down all those little strands that tend to jump up in clumps as the day wears on. Aided by her deft touch and warming gusts from a hand held dryer, the kinky nature of my hair lies down and behaves nicely.

So, then, what's there to bi . . . , er, gripe about?

Absolutely nothing, if getting my hair brought back into its proper length while engaging in intelligent conversation was all there was to it. I never leave there that I'm not looking nice and feeling somewhat enlightened.

I'm not just talking haircuts here. I am lamenting the passing of a culture.

WHERE AND WHEN I grew up, the barbershop was a social setting, one of the top gathering places in all of downtown Moran. Those that you couldn't find in the pool hall, the domino shack, or sitting on the bench at John Gardner's service station would most likely be gathered at Garland Shelton's barbershop.

A few would actually be there to get a haircut. Most, though, were there to catch up on the gossip, read that day's newspaper, or just watch Garland ply his trade while reviewing last night's football game and what the Bulldogs could do even better.

If anything was as close to ol' Garland's heart as the Moran Bulldogs, it would be those Baylor Bears or the Chicago White Sox. His brother-in-law, Brit, was a diehard Yankee fan, but they remained close friends in spite of it.

Man and boy, I loved to go into the barbershop, if for no other reason than the way it smelled in there. Lined up along the countertop in front of the mirror that spanned the entire room was bottle after bottle of tonics and lotions. When Garland finished your hair, he punctuated the job by applying a few drops that felt cool and smelled wonderful.

I was always puzzled by the ones that said "Toilet Water," but I never asked. I guess I may have been fearful of the answer.

GARLAND'S SHOP was typical of the time and the culture. Most all shops back then had a shine stand, where you could get your shoes polished by another artist in his own right. I was always amazed at how those guys could make a rag pop as loud as a gunshot. Most were as adept as the barbers themselves when it came to talking sports, politics, or how bad we needed a rain.

When I first came to Lubbock, I hung out quite a bit at a barbershop on (then) College Avenue. What I liked about it was that it reminded me in many ways of ol' Garland's shop back home. There were the same style of chairs, people actually would come in to get a shave, and all those aromatic bottles were lined up the same way. Also, the talcum-filled brush drifted across the nape of your neck to tell you to hop down, the job was done.

I had one problem with that place. At the time, I was a sports writer covering Tech football and basketball. Among those barbers and all their clients, no topic ever strayed far away from Red Raider athletics, its strengths, its problems and, alas, all the rumors surrounding them both. After spending too much of my time chasing down false leads spawned in that storehouse of misinformation, I found another shop much farther from the campus where rumors and hearsay were directed at some entity in which I had no concern.

Besides that, even in those days most things you heard about City Hall were probably true . . .

But I digress.

THE ANNALS OF rural medical history are rife with tales of patients who bartered for their treatment by paying off the doc with everything from live chickens and pigs to sacks of pintos, and even butter and eggs and probably some cracklings.

To bring that practice even closer to home, my very own dad forked over a .12 gauge Ithaca side-by-side, complete with inlays and engraving, to pay for my birthing. Seems it was the doc's own choice to take that in lieu of the $10 fee he normally charged for such a delivery.

That vintage shotgun would be worth a lot more than that in today's market. But then, nowadays you can hardly find a doc who'll deliver a baby for ten bucks— even though the HMOs and PPOs haven't given up on it. They're still lookin' . . .

Bartering, though, is still alive and well among some doctors—at least, it's a normal procedure for one of 'em whom I know quite well. To protect his identity, I'll just call him "Morris."

And, quite conveniently, that story will tie me right back into the topic I started out on, which is barbershops.

JUST DOWN THE road apiece, on the town square of Brownfield, there remains a barber who operates a shop that would do justice to either Norman Rockwell or Garland Shelton himself.

This barber, whose name escapes me, still barters with his long-time doctor, Morris. The difference is, it ain't the barber who trades merchandise to the doc for treatment. It's the doctor who uses "stuff" to pay his barber for haircuts . . .

I learned about this when Morris was chiding me for having my own hair styled instead of just cut, mentioning that it must "cost you a bundle."

"I haven't been out any cash for a haircut in years," he boasted, probably still stinging from the time his boyhood barber in Archer City upped his price to four bits.

Although Morris has no chickens or pigs or other negotiable produce, he pays for his haircuts with such things as drivers, putters and, occasionally, a jug of, uh, liquefied fruit of the fermented grape.

None of which is "tender," and that one part may not even be "legal."

I've never approached Avis about what she might take in lieu of cash. But, knowing where her outside interests lie, I don't think she wants anything she can't drop into a dollar slot. Garland also preferred cash, although everybody's credit was good there.

I wonder how many haircuts I could have got for that shotgun . . .

## CAFES

I'M SURE, WHAT with the number of barbecue restaurants around town and the quality of meals they all produce, that Lubbock diners with a hankering for that fare have never had it better. You could say pretty much the same about steaks. Scattered all across town are eateries that serve all cuts and, in many instances, do it well.

This city has probably the best selection of restaurants, per capita, of any place in the country. That's especially fortunate, being as how a recent survey showed that this city leads the country in the number of people, per capita, who eat out on any given evening.

Looking back, as we're all tending to do nowadays when the nostalgic urges of the entire community are being stirred by the approaching Centennial observation, two drastic changes have occurred during my residency here which, come to think of it, covers purt near half of that hundred years.

One has to do with the lifestyles of the city. The other concerns its eating out habits. Turns out, each is influenced by the other, sort of a Chicken v. Egg situation.

When I first came here, in the late summer of 1960, there were only a handful of restaurants that even bothered to serve the evening meal. That was because nearly everybody ate supper at home.

Only a limited number of restaurants could survive by waiting around for somebody's birthday or anniversary to drive them away from their own dinner table. Other than those special occasions, people generally ate supper at home because Mama was there to fix it. Nowadays, practically every Mom has stopped slaving inside the house and joined the work force outside it.

Consequently, by the time Mr. and Mrs. Lubbock arrive home at the end of a hard day at the office, it's already dinner time. The restaurant industry has thrived accordingly. A friend of mine insists that you should never eat in any place you can get into on Friday—unless you want to eat dinner at 4:00 p.m., that is.

But I digress.

GETTING BACK around to the barbecue joints and steak houses that got me onto this subject to begin with:

While I am greatly impressed by the places now available for both those very Texan entrees, there is one of each that I really miss. One is the original Gridiron. The other is the old Underwoods.

While it was probably Lester's Hickory Inn that introduced fine steaks to Lubbock, it was undoubtedly the late Jerrell Price who defined the business. For a guy who sort of swung into the restaurant craft out of nowhere, Jerrell—ably assisted by his wife Wanda—took over a building at 50th and Quaker that had seen one failure after another.

By not joining the list of failures on that lot—I believe a place called "Charolais" was the last one—he not only beat the odds, but went on to literally change the eating habits of an entire region. In a very short time, people who had never considered dining on prime steaks were stacking into the Gridiron lobby, waiting to be seated. What had happened?

The Prices focused on two things: quality meat and customer care.

They proved, that in the presence of both, people are attracted to upscale dining. The Prices made that introduction to a region whose culinary tastes had previously focused on chicken fried steak, potatoes, and lots of gravy. Enhancements such as blueberry muffins cooked on site from an old family recipe and served piping hot, and a little dish of garnishments on each table made up for any lack of ambiance. The quality of the steaks—all choice cuts—did the rest.

Jerrell, a former football star for the Raiders, also benefited from his Tech connections. But, in a steak house, only the quality of the meat can retain the business.

What the Gridiron lacked in romantic atmosphere, it made up for in personal attention. The Prices and their wait staff made it a point to learn their customers by name, then to connect them to their choices. By your third trip there, you not only were family, your personal preferences were being immediately attended.

THE GRIDIRON became the restaurant of choice from the sports writing corps that came in from all over the country to cover games at Tech.

Each year, at the end of the old Southwest Conference press tour, the writers voted on the best of everything they had encountered . . . best interview, best facilities, best one-liner, etc. Every year the best restaurant was the Gridiron in Lubbock.

The Prices enjoyed the same sort of success through the same formula when they opened the 50 Yard Line. I loved that place, too. But, to me, the Gridiron will always be special. I think I was influenced by a couple of unlikely aspects of it all. One was the aforementioned failures at that same location, which should have been choice, given that Lubbock was growing in that direction. Another was the way Jerrell Price, almost overnight, went from being a virtual novice as a restaurateur to becoming arguably the best steakhouse proprietor in the business, both locally and statewide.

Perhaps that is especially impressive to me, being as just a year or two earlier, he was selling cars at the old Lubbock Auto. Sold me the first new car I ever bought in Lubbock and, here he was, before I had made my last payment, selling me the best ribeye I had ever eaten . . .

Some success story, that of the Prices.

WHILE THE SUCCESS story of the Price family has somewhat of a continuing legacy—the 50 Yard Line is still operating, albeit with a different set of owners—that sadly is not the case with Underwoods Cafeteria.

Back when it was located on 34th Street, just off Avenue H, it was a favorite spot for everybody in town, but especially so for young families and hungry college kids. Everything about it had a unique flavor—the sauce-drenched beef, the spicy pinto beans, the huge yeast rolls and the cherry cobbler—and the atmosphere itself. It was all-you-can-eat dining on all items except the entrée, which was dished up in a serving sufficiently generous to begin with.

I don't know what influenced the decision by the Underwoods to vacate that area and build a new building in Southwest Lubbock, just off 50th Street. It may have been that the area around them had begun to deteriorate. At the time they located there, Avenue H was one of the main traffic arteries. Next door was the Wayfarer Inn which, at that time, was one of the city's most popular motels.

But, after investing in the new building, the Underwoods business began to drop off. Competition, perhaps, or maybe the new menu reflected a change in price structure. Whatever it was, the new place failed fairly soon. Not all that many years ago, one of the family members tried a comeback, opening a restaurant on Avenue Q. It went under almost immediately. There is an Underwoods still operating successfully in Brownwood, where the organization originated. I tried it fairly recently. The food was . . . well, all right.

But it was not the same, not nearly the same.

In all the years that have passed since the days of the old Gridiron and the original Lubbock Underwoods, many restaurants have come and gone and, fortunately, some have even achieved enviable heights in both quality and service.

Much of their present success can be attributed to the Underwoods and the Prices. They taught an entire region how to eat out.

## GROCERS

WHEN I SAY that I am a lifetime student of grocery stores, I'm not just blowin' smoke. I've got the body to prove it . . .

This is from a guy who, despite having grown up in a town that had one grocery store for every 200 residents, didn't see an actual Super Market until I had started combing my hair without being told to. Recently, while plodding my way around in the new Market Street, ghosts of Grocery Stores Past cropped up and perched right there on the handle bar of my shopping cart.

Back in Moran all those years ago, we had five grocery stores. And, even though the personalities of Jinks Raymond, Ed Hess, Mote Freeman, Edd Collinsworth and Ford Green varied greatly, their operations were much the same. There wasn't a grocery cart in the bunch. You simply gave ol' Jinks or whoever your grocery list, and he went from shelf to shelf, filling your order. Bananas hung from the ceiling, still attached to the very stalk they grew up on. And lunch meat—your choices were baloney, pressed ham and goose liver—was sliced and weighed as you watched.

Like most other families of the era, we bought our groceries on credit. I can still see my mom watching closely as Jinks wrote the amount in this little book with our name handwritten across its top.

All the stores purchased eggs and butter from local individuals, whose names were handwritten on the containers. For some reason, my mom always called for Mrs. Anderson's butter.

But I digress.

I KNOW THAT Super Market had been in Cisco for a good while. But even though it was only twenty miles down the road, a war had been fought and won before I ever saw it.

The reasons that all those grocers in Moran—and a similar number of them in Albany—could stay in business with that sort of competition were twofold. For starters, each of their owners had a lot of kinfolks. But the main reason had to do with transportation. In those days, folks didn't just jump into the car and head out for Cisco or Breckenridge to buy a bill of groceries.

Anyway, the initial excitement of seeing that first Super Market was short-lived. That's because it looked and behaved like every one I would see anywhere for many years to come. It was only when I arrived in Lubbock that similar excitement would be rekindled.

SEVERAL COMPANIES were doing grocery business in Lubbock that August in 1960, but the number of stores was relatively few. If memory serves correctly, only one among them opened on Sunday. It was located on the west end of the Five Point Shopping Center. I don't remember its name. The first store that followed the 7-11 concept wouldn't open for another three to four years later when Clendon Kerr built a bona fide convenience store on 50th Street.

But already operating and effectively commanding the industry was a store like no other I had ever seen. It was the spacious and comprehensive Furr's Family Center on 34th Street just off Quaker. Here was a virtual shopping center that happened to sell groceries. It also had a jewelry department and a wide variety of clothing. Its sporting goods area sold all sorts of fishing, hunting, and camping equipment.

Never before had I seen a place where you could arrive at the checkout register with a shotgun, pistol, engagement ring, fishing rod, eggs, coffee, pumpernickel, and a pair of drawers all in one cart.

I loved it.

THOSE WERE the days of Green Stamps and Blue Laws, the former coming at the rate of one for each dime spent. The latter made it illegal to sell on Sunday most any merchandise that couldn't be eaten, drunk, pinned around a baby's butt, or taken for a headache.

Eventually, the Family Center started opening on Sundays. And to be in compliance, areas of goods not legal to sell were roped off much the way police tape off a crime scene.

And, for the record, Furr's didn't give Green Stamps. They had their own brand, Frontier Stamps, which was a part of this highly diversified family business. Roy Furr, Sr. was the company patriarch and one of the leaders of a rapidly growing community and the university that was bustling along with it. Although the Family Center was but one of several grocery stores the Furrs operated, it clearly was the most impressive and memorable.

DURING THOSE same early-to-mid 1960s, Piggly Wiggly opened a huge store on 29th Drive that it chris-tened, "Piggly Wiggly Continental." It presented a concept totally new to Lubbock. It sold gourmet food, had its own deli, and carried a large number of exotic delicacies.

Pig Continental was an exciting store that, unfortunate for its owners, was ahead of its time. Lubbock people had not yet developed a taste for smoked eel, canned calf brain, or ants pickled in their own special sauce.

Still, Continental sold regular bread, milk from ordinary cows, and lunch meat of known descent.

I had a special affection for that store for a very definite reason. Among its other innovations, it ran its own contests that paid off in cash. And, just as my third son was about to be born, my wife won $300 in a scratch-off game offered by the store.

In those days, three C-notes would've purt near delivered two kids . . .

WHICH BRINGS me back to the newest Market Street. There is about the Market Streets something of a blend of the old Family Center and the Continental of yore, only bigger and better. While you can neither arm yourself nor pick up a nice bracelet for the wife, there are many delicacies (I never did find the calf brains or the gnu milk) not generally available elsewhere. And the Snells, who founded United, have provided the same sort of community activism and benevolence as the Furrs contributed before them.

But back to the topic of how the grocery business has changed.

I finally made it all the way through the new Market Street, having paused for a moment to look at the bananas stacked individually in clusters of five or six. I suddenly wondered what happens to all those stalks.

At the register, I watched the young woman scan my items and place them in the plastic bag and thought of how things had changed since those days at Jinks's store. I swiped my card through the reader, signed the ticket, and headed to the truck.

Then I smiled as I was struck by something that took me all the way back to those many days of yore.

I'm still buying my groceries on credit . . .

## Lake Cisco and Patriotism and Memories Revived

MAYBE IT wasn't actually the greatest recreation area on the universe, but it sure seemed to be. Perhaps Lake Cisco isn't what I miss but, rather, the carefree life that also was mine to enjoy during a time before the sophistication of elegance had smeared the purity of simplicity.

Lake Cisco was much more than a body of water. It was, among many other things, a breeding ground for memories. There was the mystique of what we believed at the time to be the largest hollow dam on the planet. It separated millions of gallons of water from a playground of many acres, including what—again—we believed to be the largest concrete swimming pool on the universe.

It was easy for me to believe, mainly because at that time Lake Cisco was near the outer reaches of the world of which I had personal experience.

It was a time when patriotism had no political bounds. And thoughts of a war raging on every front could be, at least temporarily, set aside—not lost, but shrouded by a respite of carefree play.

THAT HOLLOW dam also served as a highway bridge that was long and narrow but unavoidable to all who travelled between Moran and Cisco. A rite of passage was, in fact, a fright of passage. A fledgling driver couldn't enjoy the trip between the two towns for the dread of possibly meeting another car on that bridge, or, even more bothersome, a truck of any genre.

It also was a time when "The Fourth" was a holiday on par with Thanksgiving, or maybe even Christmas itself.

Even before the war, my family—quite a large clan—would be joined by aunts and uncles and cousins galore at a picnic area on the banks of Deep Creek. Bud Brooks, the land-owner, actually created the area for public consumption. The only admission I know of was to wave at him and Florence as you passed their house.

But Lake Cisco was, in later "Fourths," the place one needed to be. I especially remember the celebrations of 1942 and 1944 for reasons only distantly connected.

But I digress.

THE LAKE CISCO area was a playground like no other for miles and miles around. The swimming area itself covered several acres, beginning with a kiddie pool abutting the dam to an earthen pond whose twenty-foot depth and a diving tower with four levels were topped off by a platform forty-four feet above the water.

Beyond it was the first miniature golf course I ever saw. It was situated amid a virtual sea of picnic tables. Other amenities included a large skating rink situated atop a large concession stand and dressing rooms for swimmers. Because of the rural clientele it attracted—hey, creek-swimming was a way of life for country boys— bathing suit rental was a thriving business.

That hollow dam was a story unto itself. It had three levels through which you could walk from one end to the other. One was well below water level and had no lighting, real or artificial. That it was a haven for young lovers would be an understatement.

It was along that murky trail that I got my first serious, down-to-business kiss. Ah, for the memories . . .

THOSE WERE times when "The Fourth" was celebrated for its own cause, its own significance. The omnipresent flags were a contiguous part of décor expressing the solemn meaning of the holiday. No one dare dream that someday the flags would become nothing more than props for holiday sales events.

As mentioned earlier, The Fourths of 1942 and 1944 are the ones that have camped in my mind every holiday since. The latter reveals another typical American trait: curiosity trumps both fear and logic.

Sometime in late June, 1944, one of many rumors brought on by the terrors of war, had it that on the Fourth, German spies were going to blow up the Lake Cisco dam, thereby releasing tons and tons of raging water onto the celebrants throughout the park. Such a possibility, however remote, would certainly discourage attendance at that particular venue. You'd think.

Conversely, it may have been the largest crowd ever to gather there . . .

ALTHOUGH I was a few weeks shy of my eighth birthday, I still harbor a vivid picture of Jack, my next-oldest brother, standing at the top of that tower, almost fifty feet above the water level.

There remains the memory of my mom's gasp and her saying just beneath her breath, "Oh, God! He's going to jump off that thing!"

Dad looked up just in time to see Jack jump upward, do a complete flip, straighten out and enter headlong into the water, barely making a splash. Dad grinned, squeezed Mom's hand, and went back to reading his book.

The memory of that 1942 day was permanently etched by its significance. It would be the last time my entire family would ever celebrate The Fourth together. John L. and Jack would be leaving within the month to join a war from which Jack would not return. Consequently, it would be the last July 4th my mom would ever enjoy.

I was very proud of Jack that day. He already was my hero, and heroes just do heroic things . . .

A FEW YEARS ago, I drove down to that site just to walk around and reminisce. It was a mistake.

That area no longer was the playground of yore. The pools had all been drained dry, the former greensward with its tables, miniature golf, and skating rink were no more. An almost ghostly silence replaced the happy voices and splashing water and other noises of glee.

I listened carefully, hoping to retune my ear to the sounds of skates circling the hardwood floor and the ever-popular skating rink tune, "Oh jealous heart, oh jealous heart stop beating . . . "

Paradoxically, those sounds had been muffled by the prevailing silence . . .

As I sat in my car and took one last look back, the hollowness I saw and felt had rushed in to replace the aura of a time long departed.

Sadly, the Fourth of July upcoming will be observed not celebrated, and the playground area of Lake Cisco will stand silent, its proud times available only in memory. Much like the holiday itself.

God bless you, Lake Cisco. And all the wonderful memories you both spawned and nurtured . . .

## LANDMARKS

MORAN—On the occasions when I do come back home, what bothers me most are all those delightful things that I know I will never see again.

That's not to say I don't miss the people, all the old friends who were so much a part of my life, who shared my youthful dreams and schemes and who were very much a part of all I once did, honorable and otherwise. In rural Texas, friendship carried a special bond, a warmth born of knowing all that was to be known about each other without yielding to either pity or envy or, most of all, a sprouting judgment.

Sure, when I come home again I wish they were all here, just as they were back then, carefree, naïve, and guided by adventurous dreams and propelled by the belief that yon rainbow does have a reachable end. I miss them, one and all. But, because I always knew that, at some point in life, we all would have to venture elsewhere to pursue our futures. Small towns, then as now, have no way to retain what they have spawned and nurtured and, in some cases, tolerated.

Sadly, we remove ourselves from those friends but are consoled that, should fate take such a turn, home itself would be here forever, welcoming and unchanged, awaiting our return . . .

AND, DURING THE fairly frequent visits I made while my parents were still alive, that environment of comfort and warmth remained fairly constant.

During those visits, I would often stroll downtown or up by the school, or take a drive past some of the old swimming holes and, eventually, out to some of the old "parking places" where courtship served its apprenticeship. After dinner, Dad and I would sit in the porch swing, recalling old times. We would visit with passersby going for a walk and wave to old friends driving down our street.

Moran City Lake Dam

Dad would ceremoniously fill his pipe for his last smoke of the day. It's funny that when I would watch him pack in the tobacco, slowly and thoughtfully, then smell the aroma of his favorite blend, I'd get an urge to buy a pipe of my own and enjoy the same satisfaction that it obviously brought to him.

But, alas. Pipe smokers, I am totally convinced, are born, not made. My own efforts were futile. The tobacco, when I did keep the dern thing lit, burned my tongue. The smoke from the bowl curled back, straight into my eyes. When I would, frustrated by the effort, knock out the spent ashes and put the pipe in my pocket, I walked around smelling like a stale pool room . . .

MOM WENT FIRST, then when Dad died a few years later, my brother and I went down and closed up the house that had been my home through some very wonderful years.

Attesting to the difference of times, when we tried to lock the house we discovered there was no key. During all its life, that house had never been locked, not even when we would leave town. For several years, one of the keys had hung inside a closet door. It no longer was there, or anywhere else to be found.

We had to buy new deadbolts for all three doors. Neither of us felt right about having locked it before we left for that last time . . .

It didn't help that two of our longtime neighbors watched from their respective yards as we turned the key. Earlier, they had been over to chat, to visit, to offer condolences. But it seemed that when we locked the house, their demeanor changed. I felt them sadly believing that when we left Moran for good that we had taken our trust right along with us.

I had a sudden urge to go back and unlock the door. Instead, I did what I thought was the next best thing: I handed each of them a key . . .

Once, years ago, a bitter cold spell blew in when we were on a rare trip out of town. On the day we were to return, it was one of those very neighbors who had gone over, lit our fires and turned on the oven. No wonder he had suddenly felt that his own welcome had suddenly been locked out in the cold . . .

IT WAS YEARS later when I drove into town that I began to discover what all was missing and, in the process, was coldly reminded that structures, like people, weather and wear and eventually collapse to the very earth from which they sprang. Or they are removed physically, leaving an emptiness where once they stood.

First, it was the depot and the accompanying platform where we had played and often hid away from the prying and snooping eyes of adults who were committed to keeping us out of mischief . . .

I stood in that barren spot, listening quietly for the bleating sound of the old "Doodlebug" making either its 12:45 or 4:23 stop . . . or of one of the several freights whose lonesome whistle late at night added a melancholy touch to my boyhood dreams.

I thought of Brit, a boyhood friend whose father had died, leaving only him and his mom and few finances. Brit, an excellent student and a gifted athlete, quit school at the end of our eighth grade year. He took a job at this very M-K-T depot, where the caring agent taught him telegraphy. Despite his lack of education, Brit parlayed that skill into a long and rewarding skill before succumbing to a heart attack at a premature age.

Only in that town at that time could a school dropout have fared so well.

The depot, to me, was another monument to those times and those days and the people who made them what they were.

ON SUBSEQUENT trips, I was confronted with a plethora of things that, while they were once a constant part of my environment they were taken for granted, and now were suddenly a lonesome void. The old picture show, the Publix Cafe, John McCollum's pool hall, Doc Martin's "Drugs and Sundries," Garland Shelton's Barber Shop—all were gone.

Sure, I miss all my old friends whom I no longer see when I return. But we all pretty much left together, all leaving the anchorage almost as a unit. What we didn't realize that what we were leaving behind would not wait around for our return. It couldn't. With generation after generation growing up and moving on, there soon is nothing to sustain it.

Those things are gone now because, effectively, we all took them with us, leaving only locked doors to mark our passing . . .

## LUBBOCK'S ADVANTAGES

FOR MOST all of us fortunate enough to grow up in rural Texas, going to "Grandma's House" was always a special treat, often enhanced by such exciting offerings as haystacks with loose straw, barns with lofts, cows wearing bells, and "settin' hens" with eggs to protect and exactly the right attitude for the job. I thought back about those times and those occasions the other day when the wife (a.k.a. Nana) and I were preparing to host two beautiful granddaughters, Kendall (a.k.a. The Princess) and her lively and effervescent little sister, Hayden.

Now, Grandma's house of yore was a playground unto itself—hey, who could develop an agenda for climbing trees, skipping rocks, tunneling into haystacks, and tormenting guineas? And even if our expectations had been framed around the amenities that were our home surroundings . . . well, kids from Moran were not spoiled by an everyday stroll through a setting developed for Disney.

Given all that, one might have expected Lubbock to be sort of ho-hum for a pair of little livelies from a metropolitan area whose offerings include Fiesta Texas, the Riverwalk, Brackenridge Zoo, and all sorts of things that either clang or whistle or zoom.

NOW AT EITHER of their respective ages of twelve and seven, I would have been overwhelmed by the excitement of Lubbock. That's because I'd be coming here from a town whose population exceeded 1,000 only on days when everybody was at home. Back then, I thought Abilene, which may have had twenty or thirty thousand at the time, just might be the biggest city in the world. Wow. They had more traffic lights than we had street lights, and you could even watch Coca Cola get bottled there.

One advantage of growing up in a town the size of Moran is that the rest of your life would be filled with things you'd never seen before.

Despite all that, neither Nana nor I had any concerns about boredom spoiling their visit. Both had been here before—especially Kendall, the elder, who has made the annual trek since both she and the late Schnopper were pups. Hayden, meanwhile, was making her third visit, one solo and now two with her big sis.

Kendall's favorite stop each year has always been the Science Spectrum and the Omnimax movie that traditionally precedes our tour of the exhibits, hands-on devices, and other fascinating features. That would be the lead item on this year's agenda. Next would be the Joyland amusement park.

And, frankly, I was a little concerned about both.

ON OUR LAST visit to the Science Spectrum, I had been a bit disappointed. Some of the hands-on devices were either not working at all or were in a state of poor repair. And, for the only time ever, the movie we saw was boring. I don't remember its title, only that it featured an uninspiring huge school of fish that simply swam one way then another for about thirty minutes without causing or receiving apprehension or delight. And the Joyland I remembered from back when my own boys were small had about two rides, neither posing any threat to Six Flags or even a traveling carnival.

My concerns about either venue not only vanished, but were literally swept away by fun and/or excitement.

For openers, the Science Spectrum was the best it has ever been. Although it didn't mean a lot to my granddaughters, the exhibit of the old Margaret's store was terrific. The video commentary by Margaret herself really brought it to life. Lots of new "toys" had been added for their grasping and knob-turning pleasure, and the movie about Dinosaurs was fantastic.

The last night here, we made it to Mackenzie Park, and I was really impressed not only by the acres of rides that thrill, frighten and disorient, but by the staff of clean-cut, friendly youngsters that operate them. My only disappointment about Joyland is the continued absence of the large rollercoaster that was purchased from Astro World when that Houston theme park closed.

The official word is that there is much work to be done at the Mackenzie site to develop the sort of base required to erect and sustain it. One employee intimated to me that it's a bit more complicated than that:

"The problem is they don't have the money it would take to get it going."

I doubt that the two theories are mutually exclusive. But I digress.

ANYWAY, THE park without it worked well enough that we spent all three of its operating hours—which were 7:00 p.m. to 10:00 p.m.—either riding the rides or moving from one thriller to the next.

Hayden, bless her short soul, missed the four-foot standard three out of the four times she was measured to qualify for boarding. Strangely, the one where her head did touch the mark was at arguably the scariest ride of them all. Perhaps she made it because we had just got there and her coif hadn't yet settled against her scalp.

There is a concession stand available, but the girls never found a good time to pause for nourishment. They had a couple of sips of liquids between rides but never considered a burger break an option. So, it was shortly after 10:30 p.m. when we settled in at the I-Hop nearest our house for dinner. Or, being as we all chose pancakes or waffles, it was more like breakfast.

"Wow," exclaimed Hayden. "We never, ever get to eat supper after bedtime has passed!"

"That's because we're already in bed before then," Kendall explained.

THAT BRINGS US around to how those of us who live in Lubbock can compete with the excitement of places like San Antonio or maybe even Orlando itself.

It's something called Grandparent Rights (GPR) which involves, among other things, cookie baking, which happened on the second evening. Although some of them were a bit tough to chew, the peanut butter cookies were delightful—even the ones with the slick backs ("I forgot to do the fork thing on those," Kendall apologized, unnecessarily).

Another aspect of GPR is the suspension of all rules that do not address personal safety. As grandparents, we discover that our sons and daughters are prone to inflict requirements that are not supported by logic or reason . . .

never mind that they are often the same rules and regs that governed them when they were kids.

During Kendall's very first visit here I failed to communicate that our house rules were no longer in effect once she left here. Shortly after she got back home, she announced to my daughter-in-law that she no longer has to take an afternoon nap. "Granddad said so," she responded.

In denying guilt, my explanation was simple. Right after lunch on her first day here, she crawled up in my lap, gave me a hug, and asked if she had to take a nap.

"Are you sleepy?"

"No."

"Then I don't see any reason to take a nap."

Looking back, I suppose for a three-year-old, jurisdictional exceptions can seem complicated . . .

But maybe not. A week before their visit, Hayden explained the plans to a friend.

"We are going to *Camp Yes.*"

Wherever its location, "Grandma's House" is always the very same place . . .

# BOYHOOD FUN

Ray Anderson and Burle, c. 1943

### A Closet Poet, or Scalawag—Why Not Be Both?

MY BUDDIES and I adhered to an unwritten standard of misbehavior which was linked to the way things were in that place and time, which were, respectively, Moran, Texas, and the 1940s and '50s.

Due to limitations of space and, mainly, a badly worn memory, those canons won't be totally spelled out in this etching. Only those pertinent to the thesis will be exposed.

But to offset any suggestions that we were anything but good kids, I offer the following statement: Deep down, we were very good boys. Problem was, that surface was difficult to scratch through, especially if you happened to teach school, operate a business where we liked to hang out, or had a son our age whom you wish had a broader pool of friends to select from.

I brought up that last part because Don's mom was a lady of culture whose misfortune was to be trapped in an environment where the venues of entertainment were limited to the Capital Theater and the pool hall.

She would love to have had Don stay totally away from us, which would have suited us fine except he happened to own the only regulation sized football not locked up in the school gym. For Don, that football was his admission ticket to the rest of the kids in town and their activities, which included but were not limited to shooting snooker, swimming nude in one of the many swimming holes surrounding town, and helping ourselves to watermelons left unattended in the field where they grew.

By the same token, we were the same guys who never allowed a woman or elderly man to change her/his own tire, volunteered to help dig graves when somebody died, and did other applaud-worthy things I've since forgotten.

The big thing, though, is we were all members of the Moran High School football team, which was pretty dern good. Don didn't even try out for the team but did gain attachment through his role as student manager.

But I digress.

THE CULTURE at dear ol' MHS was typical of the times in small towns all across West Texas and maybe elsewhere. Although the enrollment was small the teachers and administrators were able and dedicated people. Discipline was enforced according to the severity of the transgression. Each teacher had his or her own paddle and blanket authority to apply it. Mainly, though, corporal punishment was under the purview of the principal. Although expulsion was an option, I have no recollection of it ever having been applied.

Our ag teacher was an okay guy, his only problem other than being an Aggie was he owned the biggest and most formidable paddle on campus, and he used it often. For some reason, we all liked him because he was the biggest Bulldog football fan among the entire faculty. He and his wife and small son saw every game, either at home or on the road.

While our football team was always of championship caliber, our basketball credentials were just the opposite. We were lousy. For one thing, at the end of football season Moran and Baird were both moved into districts with

schools that didn't play football. One of the most disastrous events came my senior year when we opened against
Eula, which was already 20-0 when we caught them.

Our lack of basketball prowess didn't bother our fans,
who during football season would spend all day Saturday
talking about last night's game and the rest of the week
looking forward to Friday. At our home basketball games
only our parents showed up, and they usually brought
along something to read.

DURING ENGLISH class my buddies and I sat at the
very back of the room, a space reserved for the football
players. Miss Haggard was our teacher, and she was a very
good one. I was embarrassed by the disinterest my buddies
showed her, and even more so by my pretending to do the
same.

Her lectures and readings were so powerful that she
almost drew me out of the closet. The next-to-last thing
I needed was for them to find out that I read for pleasure
books that weren't even written by Mickey Spillane or Ers-
kine Caldwell but by some stuffy author we were studying.

But the *last* thing I needed for my buddies to find out
is that not only did I love to read poetry, I was—gulp—a
closet poet . . .

I was so protective of my hidden life that when one
of my friends would be coming over to spend the night,
I'd rush home and move all the books and handwritten
"pomes" out of my room. Wow! Having one of them find
one of my poems would be worse than showing up at the
pool hall wearing a frilly apron.

MOST POPULAR BOY      BURLE PETTIT

Most Popular Boy, MHS 1952

So I can imagine the delighted look I got from Miss Haggard when I showed up at her door fairly late one evening and asked to borrow her book about famous poets and their works. My surprise was that she didn't look surprised.

I also left with her that night—at considerable risk—a composition book filled with poems and essays I had written. That did surprise her, but she agreed to protect my secret. My pals accepted that I made good grades in all subjects, especially English, but my literary addiction would be a bit more difficult to sell.

Miss Haggard not only stuck to her promise, she "made me" stay after class—supposedly for misbehavior—for several weeks, during which time she both tutored and encouraged. Today, I remain affected by what I learned from Miss Haggard and what I experienced with those old pals of yesterday.

I think of both "lives" every time I read the hauntingly melodic words of "To a Waterfowl" or get the urge to swipe a watermelon or flip over a privy.

I'm proud to be a product of those times and those people, closet and all . . .

## JUBILANCE, MAYHEM MARKED HALLOWEENS OF YORE

AS CLEAR AS an actual snapshot of yore, I can still see Moran's main street in what then was still a vibrant downtown area, all roped off as the staging point for the mixture of merriment and mayhem that marked the occasion.

That was a time when beliefs and traditions had not yet been chipped away by a new order of thinking that looked into a depth of the day and, in so doing, weighted down a lighthearted occasion with complexities far beyond its practical purposes of fun and games and creative costuming.

Inside those ropes, the younger kids scurried about, their faces hidden behind cellophane masks sold all over town for a dime apiece. Meanwhile, the older boys preferred to operate outside the ropes, where mischief for one became nuisance for another . . .

Halloween in Moran, Texas, had something for everyone. Everyone, that is, except those who termed it as a sacrilegious endeavor, a time to honor Satan himself.

Fortunately, that philosophy had not crept into the fiber of that town in those days where simple pleasures reigned supreme . . .

IT WAS THE annual Halloween Carnival staged and sponsored by the school itself as a fund-raiser for the twelve participating classes. Games of all sorts, most of which I have since forgotten, used up all the space in the block.

The most popular was the cake walk and, accordingly, was the top money-maker. The final walk filled up rapidly because it featured a five-layer cake contributed each year by the town's best baker, Mrs. Ray Blackstock. Her son, Rabbit, was one of my best friends and a member of a cast of us who, from the age of twelve on up, spent far too much time outside the ropes of accepted behavior, Halloween or not . . .

Until war's end and a few years beyond, the majority of houses in the city limits were still served by outdoor facilities. And each Halloween night, they may as well have had a target drawn where the crescent is usually depicted in drawings but never seen in real life.

When we got to town for the Carnival, my sister and I had already donned our masks and were getting ready to hook up with our respective classmates to do all that could be done within the ropes. Meanwhile, I watched with envy when my older brother, a high-schooler, met up with his buddies and, after getting a quick hotdog, they all dashed out into the darkness . . .

WHEN THE SUN came up on the following morning, backyards all over town were strewn by toppled toilets. It was almost as if a mysterious tornado had come through, targeting only outhouses.

Nowadays, in this litigious climate, lawsuits would have flooded the Shackelford County Courthouse. At the least, arrests would be made and sentences handed out. Finding the culprits would have been fairly easy for Emory and Henry, Moran's two-man police force. If they just checked out the houses where the privies were still upright, well, persons of interest would be obvious . . .

There was an exception.

The man whose name I won't use—hey, these ARE litigious times—looked exactly like a madman in one of the earliest horror movies named The Creeper.

Hence, he was known among all Moran boyhood as "Creeper." The guy also had some of the same characteristics. He was the meanest man in town and, appropriately, owned its meanest dog, a pit bull whose name was Bulger.

For several years, the biggest Halloween challenge was to turn over Creeper's _____ (think alliteration).

I ALMOST wrote that getting to the Creeper's, uh, outhouse would be akin to walking through the gates at Fort Knox. Bad analogy. The way Congress spends money, I doubt if they even bother to close them.

For starters, Creeper's backyard was encircled by a four-foot cyclone fence with a couple of strands of barbed wire across the top. On Halloween night, the Creeper would sit until bedtime on his back steps, a shotgun cradled across his legs. Then, he would turn on a spotlight, chain ol' Bulger to a post beside it, and enjoy a good night's sleep, comfortable that his early morning, er, ritual would not be delayed.

Even the brightest minds among Moran's scalawaggery never penetrated that security. For years after houses all over town—including his—had added indoor facilities, the Creeper's outhouse stood as a monument to man's determination to protect things of such critical need.

Eventually, my buddies and I became old enough to sneak out of the Carnival area and began our primary training for bigger challenges to come. Mainly, that was limited to hiding Mrs. Meredith's front gate, ringing Lynn Williams' doorbell, and taking Mr. Montgomery's rocking chair off his front porch and putting it in the school's fishpond.

Simple things, those.

SADLY, BY THE time we reached our teenage years, Moran had run plumb out of outhouses. Indoor plumbing had begun the demise of Halloween; wrong-headed thinking is now trying to finish it off.

But, alas. My pals and I did get into more than a little trouble when we donned paint cans and brushes and did our own brand of early-graffiti on the school sidewalks and selected teachers' doorsteps.

Then two bad choices were made: Jackie got the idea that if we put our own initials beside our work, the teachers would believe it to be a frame job. Bad move, for two reasons. One, given our existing "street creds," we weren't likely to be framed. Two, for that very reason, we would be among the first questioned, even without the signatures.

Incidentally, that paint was a lot more difficult and a lot less fun to remove than it had been to apply.

Rabbit, who had a penchant for taking all things to the next level, wrote the only off-color word of the night, and it was a doozy. Ironically, it was the only paint we didn't have to remove. When I ran my milk route the next morning, it already had been painted over.

We figured the reason it wasn't mentioned was because she would've had to say the word out loud. In those days, women teachers just didn't talk that way.

And Halloween, as intended, was enjoyed by all. Especially the Creeper . . .

## DELIGHT OF FRIGHT ALWAYS POPULAR VENUE FOR KIDS

IF THE SHRINKS have it right that the adversities that keep cropping up in our collective psyche are a direct result of the fears we have harbored through the years . . . well, it's a wonder we do as well as we do. One common thread that binds all generations is that, for whatever reasons, American kids have always delighted in getting the yell scared right out of them.

Of course, technological advances being what they are, the youth of today are able to shriek at ogres that are as real as any mammalian that crawls, flies, or slithers on the earth as we know it. Hey, those creatures from *Jurassic Park* are more believable than, say a wart hog, and armadillo, or maybe even some guy who sits just a few pews over from you at church. Even the good guys who have entertained my own grandkids give me the heebie-jeebies. How would you like to turn the corner and meet face up with a ninja turtle?

I CAN EASILY recall the first tyrannosaurus ever to grace the screen of Moran's Capitol Theatre. I thought for years that "Rex" was his given name.) I wasn't bothered that his movements were so totally mechanical that the strings making him work may actually have come into view now and then. What stuck with me through all these years were those live and kicking people he was picking up with those tiny arms and shoving into his mouth. His teeth looked like so many sabers!

Then there was King Kong, probably played by the same mechanical carcass as ol' Rex had worn, plucking airplanes out of the sky with the hand he wasn't using to hold on to the Empire State Building. And one real lulu that attested to the limitless imagination of youth yearning to be scared silly was one that involved the hideous exploits of a human hand, which—as best I recall—had set out to avenge whatever it was that killed the rest of it (him?). You talk about letting your fingers do the walking . . . well, how's about also doing your choking?

THEN THERE was The Creeper, who looked very much like a Moran citizen whose outdoor facility was the biggest local challenge any Halloween night ever had to offer. The two of them were also equally congenial.

Beginning on about October 28 and running through November 1, that old guy would spotlight his toilet from all sides and, with the approach of darkness, he would tether to a long chain the meanest pit bull ever to reside in Shackelford County. It was generally believed that for weeks prior to staking him out, Mr. Creeper would put his dog on a meatless diet, all the while exposing it to a school yearbook which pictured every boy in town.

It was the ultimate challenge of all of Moran boyhood to become the one who finally toppled over Creeper's Cr---er—uh, guess I'd better say "outhouse," and leave it to the brighter among you to figure out the alliteration. Being scared, you see, has more than one application.

BUT I DIGRESS. My generation, which is from an era where a windup toy was high tech, was introduced to intentionally induced fear through the telling of ghost stories while huddled closely before a campfire. Later, we would accept a dare to walk all the way through the Moran Cemetery—west to east and then back—only to pass some older guys draped in sheets and making sounds of the macabre.

In those days, every small town had some old vacant house—always a two-story job—out in the country where some kid susceptible to jitters or, in some cases, some guy's date would be taken and exposed to rattling chains, candles that seemed to ignite themselves, fluttering sheets . . . the whole works.

A favorite parking place for Moran lovers was "The Haunted Tank," which was in Buster Cottle's pasture. Legend had it that a man died there one cold wintery night while making out with his girlfriend with the engine running. How she managed to survive depends on who's telling the story. But, anyway, she did and, once he had taken his last breath, she crawled into the car with another guy and sped off into the darkness to faraway places from which she would never choose to return. The guy, then, patrolled the place every night from then on, hoping to find the person who had stolen his love. I never wondered why he wasn't also miffed about getting killed in the process . . .

All of which goes to prove nothing further than the original point of what a lasting role being frightened has always played. And, clearly, it has left its mark on several of us . . .

NOW, BACK TO the long-standing challenge of the case of The Creeper Who Stole Halloween, and a full generation of boys who plotted to topple the taunting toilet.

The years came and went, but it never happened. And, when Mrs. Creeper finally got her long-awaited indoor facility, Mr. Creeper personally tore the storied old outhouse down. To this very day, I believe he should have left it as a monument to, among other things, man's commitment to not allow a bunch of scalawags to interrupt his morning routine.

That would have been appropriate not only because of Moran's lack of having a Historical Marker, but mainly to pay tribute to what I believe to be the only man in Moran ever to resemble a movie star.

## BOYS AND TROUBLE

MORAN—One problem with being a kid is that trouble appears to be ubiquitous. It seems to lurk around every corner, just waiting to spring at a time when it is needed least.

And if you happen to be one of those guys who has a subnormal resistance to temptation, it's really bad, given that temptation is the most common propellant for trouble.

That thought seems to manifest every other year when I come here for homecoming and spend a couple of days wandering around some old haunts, kicking up memories—good and bad—from those carefree days of yore. Those were the days when the world was black and white, and solutions came easy for everybody except parents and most other grownups.

My buddies and I often spoke among ourselves about that last part. How could our moms and dads have made it this far through life without any inkling about how things really work?

But I digress.

EVEN THOUGH Bill and I were no strangers to mischief, we arrived on the school grounds with plans to do nothing we wouldn't have done with our parents standing right there watching.

Our houses—Bill lived exactly across the street from me—were little more than a block from the school. It was a favorite haunt of ours, partially because it had swings and slides and see-saws, the only playground equipment available. Moran had a city park which, actually, was a city park in name only. It was an area northeast of downtown that covered an acre or so of ground, but was used only for the annual July 4th barbecue. If it hadn't been on the way to one of our favorite swimming holes we never would have seen it at all.

It was a warm summer morning, and as I walked the beautiful, long native stone fence that surrounds the campus, I paused to marvel at how different a school looks when it is "out" for the summer. All three of the buildings visible from there looked almost lonesome . . . the gym, the grade school, and high school buildings . . . didn't even have each other for comfort. Without kids streaming constantly from one to the other, they were without their normal fusion.

Then with a sudden thought of how fast summer vacation seems to fly, my mounting sympathy turned to dread . . .

WE PLAYED for awhile on the swings, then climbed the fire escape that was the dominating feature of the east end of the grade school building. It was the only two-story building on the campus and had one of only two fire escapes in the entire town.

The other was on the west end of the First Christian Church building, and it was a lot neater. Instead of the iron steps like this one, it was an actual slide. That was where my friend Ray went to church, and he and I used to imagine what it would be like if it caught fire. We could just see those ladies, all dolled up in their Sunday dresses, zipping down that slide, hoping to land with their modesty intact.

They no longer hold church in that building, which has since been converted to a museum that is astonishingly awesome, given the size of the town and the resources available. Sadly, though, the old fire escape no longer exists . . .

Bill had followed me up the school fire escape and when he reached the top he tried the door that led from it into the study hall. It was locked, so we headed back down toward the see-saw. Being as neither of us trusted the other not to bail off and leave the other to crash butt-hard onto the ground, we walked on past and headed toward the backside of the three buildings.

BILL AND I had much in common; but, thinking back on it, so did I and most of the other Moran boys of that era. We all were equipped with an ornery streak that never totally defined us because, when it counted most, we all were capable of doing "the right thing."

Most all of us did a little smoking, had an occasional chaw of Brown's Mule, cussed when we were off to ourselves and, using words that had begun to inhabit our respective vocabularies, would speak of topics inspired by young hormones just beginning to boil.

What caused that day to take a bad turn for Bill and me was when we reached the back of the high school building and found the door leading into the boys' restroom not locked. Understand that this was a time in history when outhouses, even in rural communities, were in greater abundance than indoor facilities. Our house, being relatively new at the time, was among the minority. Bill's house had an outdoor toilet.

I am continuing this story based on an assumption that the statute of limitations expired long ago. To say I'm not proud of what ensued does not mitigate my guilt.

It all started with Bill's being intrigued by the workings of a flushing commode. I walked up just as he had lifted the lid from the tank and was watching all the gushing activity that resulted from the flick of the handle. In order to impress him with my superior knowledge of such mysterious equipment, I was in the process of showing him that by lifting the rod that had the big ball on the end of it, I could totally stop the flow of water into the tank.

Problem was, I pulled up too hard.

The next thing I knew, I was standing there with the rod and ball in my hand, watching the water spew out of control. The bleeping thing had broken off, and here we stood, staring at each other. After but a few seconds of voiceless communications, we did what we always did when things went awry: We got the yell out of there.

LATER THAT day, Bill and I were in the pool hall shooting a game of 8-ball when somebody walked in looking for Emory, the deputy sheriff who, along with Henry, the constable, maintained Moran's law and order.

"He ain't here," the proprietor answered. "He and Henry and the sheriff out of Albany are at the schoolhouse investigating a rash of vandalism. Some thugs broke into the high school and tore up a bunch of commodes in one of the restrooms."

Maybe a part of me wanted to blurt out that, dammit, nobody "broke in" and it was only one commode and it wasn't vandalism it was an accident. And there dern sure weren't any "thugs" involved.

For reasons that should be obvious, I kept quiet. So did Bill.

Only now, all these years later, do I wonder about our lack of contrition. We did consider turning ourselves in but dismissed it quickly. Confession may be good for the soul but, at my house, it could be tough on the butt. That's because it was often a reminder of some past transgressions.

Like I said, trouble just seemed to follow my buddies and me around . . .

I wonder if it helps any that, standing here only a few feet from the scene of that crime, my contrition has finally been served . . .

## ME 'N CUZ

I THINK IT was my Uncle Floyd who said it first, although I have heard it many times since. He had me and Cuz helping him tear down some feed shocks and doing a few other things around the place. At the end of the day, somebody asked him how it went.

"Well, one boy is half a man. Two boys are half a boy . . . " Had he ended it right there, it wouldn't have been original. But he went ahead and added, "but these two particular boys add up to one single pain in the (anatomical part deleted)!"

Anybody who remembers my Uncle Floyd will realize that he rarely put three words together that two of them were not what they refer to nowadays as "expletives." I think that term became popular in the post-Watergate days when family newspapers were publishing what they could of the Nixon tapes.

But I digress.

Cuz and I were close as lots of first cousins got back in the more pedestrian life that was rural America during the days of WWII and several years to follow.

I thought of him today, being as I am writing this on the anniversary of the bombing of Hiroshima. He was at our house when the news came on the radio, and we knew from what all we were hearing that our big brothers would soon be coming home.

If it also happened that we didn't go on and get into trouble that day, it was even a more historical date than most of the world will ever realize.

ALL OF OUR KIN was fond of both of us, separately. But even our kindly grandmother would wrinkle her brow and swallow deeply when she saw us together. As tots, Cuz and I were not good for each other. That didn't improve noticeably as we moved on up the grades to graduation and a year or so beyond.

Cuz was the quieter of the two, although he learned to cuss before I did. I think that's because of the difference in the words our respective fathers chose to use when something went awry. On our very first day of school, Cuz got a busting for something he called Kenneth Clinton. He got another one the next day for what they nowadays call "retaliation." Even though Kenneth did not rat on him, he still blamed him for the paddling.

Cuz was exactly six months my senior, yet he almost always willingly went along with whatever action plan I devised. There were times when I would wish later that he had balked, but it never happened.

One instance that comes to mind is the time when we needed a couple of 1 × 12s to build something and the two boards I selected were on the backside of our aunt's outhouse. We wisely took them off the back because that part of the privy was out of sight of the house. She didn't discover the new opening as quickly as she might have, being as the next time she went in there it had turned dark outside. But because the winter breeze was from that direction, she hadn't been seated long before she knew something was terribly wrong . . .

Even though she'd had several nieces and nephews over there that Sunday, she immediately accused Cuz and me, and our dads responded accordingly. I don't remember them even giving us a chance to deny the charges.

MOST OF WHAT Cuz and I did was harmless, unless you count the time our younger and snobbish cousin got pushed out of a tree house . . . and maybe the time we put him in this boat we had built and didn't want to wait until warm weather to learn whether it would float. Or the time Cuz gave him crackers with what he thought was peanut butter spread between them. He shouldn't have accepted anything Cuz offered him . . . especially when he was in the henhouse at the time.

That kid was three to four years younger than we and he always wanted to follow us around. That wouldn't have been so bad, except that he was whom our moms kept urging us to be more like. He never got his school clothes dirty, he voluntarily did his lessons before going out to play, and he said yes ma'am and thank you and please in a sing-song voice that made us gag.

Also, we didn't like his mom. She always bragged about him to our mothers and glared at us like Tom's Aunt Polly used to look at his pal Huck. The only thing we agreed with her about was that he shouldn't hang around us.

PERSONALLY, I thought we had worked pretty hard that day tearing down the feed shocks and stacking hay. Cuz's dad didn't realize that we were exerting a lot of effort chasing down the mice and snakes and things to put in the jars we'd brought along for that very purpose.

If you've ever torn down feed shocks you know what all you can find camped out beneath them. The mice and spiders were good for scaring girls, and snakes work on purt near anybody.

And, sure. We clowned around a lot that day. It's too bad that it would be several decades before management would recognize the benefits of providing recreation in the workplace. That Cuz and I were that far ahead of our time went totally unrecognized.

UNFORTUNATELY, boyhood is a fleeting stage of life. Neither Cuz nor I really grasped it at the time, but the farewell party he helped host for me the night before I left for the army would be the last carefree occasion we would ever spend together.

I came back from the army, went off to college, got married and started a family. I was the luckier of the two.

Cuz later did an army hitch, returned, and was having considerable success as a cabinet maker. He never married and, for reasons I never understood, began drinking excessively. He lost his business and, in a few short years, died both broke and lonely.

Once, when he was still at the top of his game, Cuz visited us here in Lubbock. My boys were small at the time, and they bonded with Cuz just like their dad had done all those many years ago.

One morning I walked into the room where my three sons were sitting in a circle, laughing aloud at whatever Cuz was saying. I grew very nervous. Sensing how uneasy I was about my boys hearing some of the stories he might be telling, I got Cuz aside and told him I sure hoped he wouldn't bring up anything that they might try to emulate. He assured me that he didn't tell them about any of our deeds of mischief, only about some funny relatives we'd had.

I felt pretty good until a few days later when Kyle chuckled aloud and said:

"Did you guys really put Norman in that boat . . . ?"

## MESQUITE BOWL

EACH TIME I see a football player escorted to the sidelines because his helmet came off on the preceding play, two things come to mind: Rabbit and the Mesquite Bowl.

Now, Moran was a football town, attested by the fact that on Friday nights both the pool hall and Capital Theater were practically vacant. That's on the weeks when the Bulldogs were playing at home. But, come to think of it, it wasn't much different when the game was out of town.

Moran people really followed those 'Dogs, mainly because, year in and year out, they were fun to watch. And, besides that, what if we beat Baird in Baird and you happened to be the only one at the barber shop Saturday morning who hadn't seen the game?

I'm sure that in some countries a feller could get executed for less.

Football was such a major part of the community structure that you could hardly pass a vacant lot without seeing boys from every age group engaged in a pickup game. And if you happened to see a softball amidst the game, it was there because nobody owned a football. So it was subbed in to be passed and handed off and fumbled just like it was the real thing. The only adjustment that was made was when it was time to punt or kickoff, the ball was thrown. Hey, it's hard to get much foot into a softball . . .

But I digress.

THE MESQUITE Bowl was started right in the middle of the regular season, and had Coach Allen been aware that about a dozen members of his team were out in the pasture behind Cuz's house engaged in a grudge game of tackle . . . well, coaches tend to get nervous about such things, especially when that represents half of the entire roster.

It was Cuz himself who gave the field its name. But, come to think of it, it wasn't a major strain on his imagination. That's because it was a large clearing in a mesquite thicket that was about half the length and width of a regulation field.

But the dern thing looked real. We even marked off the yard lines, right down to those diagonal stripes in each end zone. I always figured that if you were looking down on it from high up in the air, you might well think it was the real thing. Except you might wonder about the goals posts, of which there were none. No problem. After each touchdown we went for one (the two point conversion was still several years down the road).

Adding to the color, Don—our student manager—broadcast the game from his makeshift press box, using a corncob he'd blackened with shoe polish for a microphone. He was also the time-keeper, using a stopwatch that was among the equipment over which he was the sole steward.

We had no refs, which would have prevented some vocal exchanges that sometimes got physical.

SO EACH Saturday afternoon, we'd hop on our bikes and pedal the couple of miles out to the field. I don't remember how we divided up the two teams, except we tried to have an equal number of linemen and backs on each team.

That is, except for Rabbit. Not only was he the biggest player on our Bulldog team, he was an all-district tackle who moved quite well for his 200 or so pounds.

It was my misfortune to be on the other team, which had nobody even close to Rabbit's size. What made matters worse was that Rabbit—as his team's captain—got to assign positions. Given that authority, he no longer was a tackle; he was the starting fullback.

Now, our uniforms were sweatshirts, jeans and tennis shoes (pronounced tenny shoes), which made ramming a shoulder into one of Rabbit's massive thighs not a painless experience—especially if you were still sore from last night's game.

Getting tired of slipping on that native buffalo grass, I showed up one Saturday with my football shoes. I ignored the complaints and wore them anyway. It not only gave me a noticeable advantage, it caused some resentment that carried over into our regular team practice every day the following week.

I got the idea after Monday's workout when Bill slipped his shoe back on and, as soon as I walked out of the shower, he tried to step on my bare foot. Fortunately, he missed and I caught him with a towel pop right where it hurt the most. The shoe he threw at me sailed over me and narrowly missed Coach, who had stuck his head out of his office door to see what was going on.

THE NEXT Saturday, everybody showed up in his game shoes, except for Rabbit.

He arrived wearing his full uniform, game jersey and all. Those oversized shoulder pads he liked made him look like the beanstalk giant with an Iago attitude. His eyes were staring hard from beneath the new plastic headgear we had just got before the season opener.

That was the beginning of the end of the Mesquite Bowl.

Coach Allen suddenly emerged through the mesquite barrier just as we lined up for the kickoff. Don, who saw Rabbit sneaking out with his uniform, felt obligated to warn the coach about the impending danger. Also, as the only available Mesquite Bowl sub, he may have feared he'd wind up on the field.

"Okay guys," the coach was saying, "if you want to practice, I have just the place for it." He picked up our game ball, Don's stopwatch and, for a moment, seemed to consider peeling Rabbit's uniform right off his body.

We never played there again.

A few years ago during a visit back home, I wondered out in that pasture and finally located the old Mesquite Bowl. It was fully overtaken by trees and bushes, and the rains and winds of time had completely erased the yard lines.

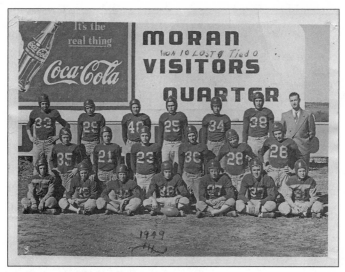

Moran High team, 1949

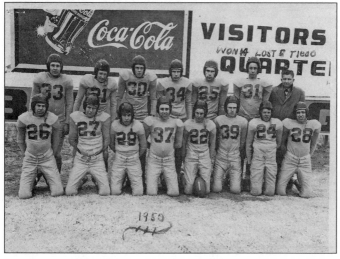

Moran High team, 1950

Only the image of Rabbit in that big No. 33 jersey remained vivid . . .

## THE FIGHT

THE GOOD NEWS is that kids of today don't fistfight much anymore. The bad news is that nowadays they just shoot each other.

During my boyhood back in Moran, fights—although not an everyday occurrence—weren't all that unusual, either. Sometimes they started out as a friendly scuffle (do boys still scuffle?), then somebody would get mad. Maybe somebody flirted with somebody's girlfriend or, even worse, took her out in public. Then there were the designated fighting words, the biggie of which compared somebody's mama to a female dog. Hey, any retort that began with "sunva" had better end with "gun."

Usually the scraps that erupted from a scuffle gone awry didn't last long, shortened frequently by the appearance of a teacher, coach, or some other adult. The ones that attracted the greatest interest were those that resulted from a mounting grudge, the girlfriend thing or when two guys everybody always wanted to see match up finally got crosswise.

That last instance was of great interest because, in the boyhood culture of my day, who could "whup" whom was a popular topic, especially when it involved two of the toughest guys on campus.

Anyway, you could always tell when a significant fight was about to happen. There would be two guys walking briskly and brusquely, being followed by a long line of boys. Girls, for some reason, never liked to watch boys fight. Yet, I always believed that most any girl liked to know, down deep, that some boy thought she was worth risking a couple of teeth for.

But I digress.

In most cases, that parade began at the schoolhouse after the last bell, made it all the way through town, picking up along the way spectators who recognized what was up, and ended down at The Bushes.

"THE BUSHES" was a mesquite thicket just across the tracks from the Katy depot where hobos of another era had camped en route to wherever their shambled lives might take them.

Hobos had mainly disappeared, although on rare occasions we would run up on one when we wandered into that hideout to roll a smoke (tobacco—that *was* a long time ago) or to stare at one of those vest pocket books featuring real comic characters doing things we'd only heard about, or to just hang out.

In the depths of that thicket was a clearing where the two contestants would square off, ringed by the onlookers. Sometimes one of them would dare the other to throw the first punch; other times it would just erupt. Worst of all was when they would start to debate the issue. That generally meant we'd walked all this way for nothing, that both were more eager to talk than fight, which would lead to somebody's remarking, "One of 'em is scared and the other'n is glad of it."

Strangely, of all the fights I watched at The Bushes, not a one of them earned a remarkable spot in my memory.

Two other fights did, and neither happened in The Bushes nor started in the outlined manner. One of them became a Moran legend. It was of marathon length.

The other, I was involved in. It was very short.

The former occurred a generation too soon for me to witness, but it was still talked about throughout my life. Now, I knew both of those men as the prominent ranchers and as the leading citizens that they became. From all accounts, they fought for two solid hours, and my dad—who did see it—reckoned by the way they looked at the end that both of them had lost.

The one I was involved in was not only short, but almost had a tragic ending.

RABBIT WAS a heckuva man even before he left school to join the Marines. He was over 200 pounds and was the best down lineman in our district. On the night in mention, he had just finished boot camp, was home on leave, and was in the sort of shape Coach always wished he'd achieve during football season.

He, Cuz (aka Kamber), and I were riding around over country roads in Cuz's '48 Ford, sort of hanging out and listening to Rabbit's stories about Drill Instructors and such. It was late at night, so we were surprised to meet a car on this narrow road crossing Buster Cottle's pasture. The guy driving it didn't pull over to let us pass. He clearly was a stranger.

Cuz leaned out the window and told him to move over. The guy shouted back two words I can't print but, for the grammatically astute among you, one was a verb, the other a pronoun.

Cuz got out, and so did the other guy. When Rabbit saw his size—about 6′2″ and over 200—he figured he'd better take over. Cuz weighed 140 on a wet day. Rabbit walked up to the guy and swung a right hook that caught the guy square on the chin. I swear, it would have dropped a Hereford bull. But not this guy.

He took a slight step backward, shook his head, and lunged forward, wrapping both arms around Rabbit's neck and putting on the squeeze. Cuz and I looked at each other and, realizing that Rabbit's final breath was near at hand, we jumped in.

The bout was soon over. The guy, we later would learn, was from an area town. But that night we were just glad to leave him on the ground, not seriously hurt but yielding to the odds. We jumped into Cuz's car, drove around his, and headed home.

SOON AFTERWARD, I received my own draft notice and headed off to the Army. During the next few years, I never thought much of that night except to shudder occasionally at how close ol' Rabbit had come to death.

When I completed my Army hitch and returned to Moran, the talk all across the area was about a guy who was on trial in Abilene for murder. Rabbit quickly told me that it was the same person we had met that night in ol' Buster's pasture.

During the time I was gone, John McCollum sold the pool hall to a Mister Greer, who happened to come from the same town as the guy on trial. Not only did Mister

Greer know him personally, he was sort of defending his having murdered somebody by explaining what a tough life the fella had growing up, that his home life was deplorable and, all things considered, he wasn't all that bad a guy.

Rabbit blew up, going into a rampage about how he hoped the (expletive) got the chair, that he was a sorry sack of (expletive), and on and on.

"I'll tell you one thing, Rabbit," the pool hall man began, "that guy is the toughest man probably in this entire part of the country, maybe the whole state . . . "

"Whatta ya mean, tough?" Rabbit demanded. "Hell, one night me and ol' Burle and Kamber took him out in nothing flat." For years I had never questioned how we had brought that ordeal to a necessary ending. But the way Rabbit put it blustered the heroics.

No, kids don't fight with their fists much anymore. And they do shoot to kill. I doubt they feel more shame after having taken a life than I suddenly was struggling with over having helped save one.

What I am glad of is that the guy we met that night wasn't armed.

## WASTED YOUTH

THERE WERE ALREADY at least three, maybe four, reasons why I decided long ago never to run for President. Then another came up recently when reporters probed Gov. Romney's boyhood background and, as a result of their findings, found sufficient ammunition to fire off a volley of shots at his character.

Personally, I know only one or two people I grew up with whose past could survive such retrospective surveillance, and neither of those guys would be interesting enough to check on anyway. That their teachers would still recommend them today is all the explanation that last sentence needs.

But I can see my own interview having a terrible outcome. It probably would go something like this:

1. **Reporter:** Is it true that you once belonged to a gang?

   Me: Yes, but . . .

2. **Reporter:** Was that gang involved in underground activities that were performed covertly?

   Me: Here's what the deal was . . .

3. **Reporter:** Stick to either "yes" or "no" answers, dammit!

   Me: I'll try.

4. **Reporter:** Is it true that you were guilty of theft of agricultural products?

   Me: Well, uh, yes.

5. **Reporter:** Is it true that you were guilty of vandalism?

   Me: Well, uh, yes.

6. **Reporter:** Is it true that you once ran out on an accomplice when law offers surprised you in the act of thievery?

   Me: Well, uh, yes.

7.  **Reporter:** Is it true that you once were a member of an organization that was openly committed to gender discrimination?
    Me: Well, uh, yes.
8.  **Reporter:** Is it true that you once introduced a dangerous animal into a high school when classes were in session?
    Me: Well, uh, yes.
9.  **Reporter:** Is it true that you were a part of a group that was frequently involved in nudist activities?
    Me: Well, uh, yes.
10. **Reporter:** Is it true that you once took money that belonged to your church?
    Me: Well, uh, yes.

SO THAT INTERVIEW ends and all the reporters present dash off to their respective outlets to write, broadcast, twitter or whatever those revelations to a public dying to know what makes me tick.

That fantasized scene would have found me standing alone at the dais, wishing at least somebody other than Fox News had stayed around to hear me explain fully each point addressed above—which I will now do, just in case I someday change my mind about entering politics:

One: It's true I did belong to a gang. It was called Our Club and it consisted of me, Brit, Ray, and Cuz. Our respective ages were 9, 10, 8, and 9. Our club house was a chicken coop that had been vacant since the one remaining rooster flogged my dad.

Two: We did have occasional underground activities, and some of them were indeed secret. Some of our meetings were held in a T-shaped culvert tall enough for us to sit upright while performing our secret activities. Those included learning to roll a Bull Durham cigarette, passing around a corncob pipe filled with coffee grounds, and biting off chunks from a plug of Brown Mule. Then there was this magazine that Cuz swiped from under his big brother's mattress . . .

Three: I don't think that was really a question, was it?

Four: When we were a bit older we did occasionally sneak into various watermelon patches from which we did leave with what I suppose were indeed agricultural products. I believe you would concede we paid for our crimes if you knew what it was like to pick pellets of rock salt out of your, er, lower set of cheeks.

Five: Vandalism, you say? It was Halloween night and some of us did a little shoe polish artistry on certain buildings and car windows. We might have gotten away with it except that a guy named Rabbit decided if we put our own initials on the work, it would appear to the authorities (superintendent, principal, constable, etc.) that we were being framed. Problem is, nobody else was even questioned. Rabbit, incidentally, was never listened to again.

Six: Several of us guys liked to hang out at the ice house/Magnolia filling station at night. Its owner, John Gardner, did not want to roll his soda pop box in every night while locking up. So, he had this metal bar placed across the top with a padlock at either end. Boxes in those days were exactly that—boxes with Coke or Dr Pepper logos on the side. They were nonelectrical, just iced down drinks.

We learned that by prying up the corner of the hinged lid, Danny, who had real skinny arms, could reach in and pull out a bottle of pop. We had been doing this long enough that it had become both an art and a science.

The abandoning part came one night when the constabulary drove up just as Danny was reaching around in the icy water for a bottle. As soon as I saw the lawman turn the corner, I dropped my grip on the lid and joined my buddies in getting the yell out of there. Danny literally was caught with his hand in the cookie jar.

To our defense, we did all came back to face the heat. But Danny somehow never got around to remembering that we did return and admit to being complicit. He griped for weeks about his sore wrist . . .

Seven: Yes. Our Club was expressively discriminatory toward females. In fact, the sign on the door said No Girls Allowed! Remember our ages (see Item 1 above) at the time. A few years later we made up for it by openly encouraging them to enter whatever door we happened to be behind . . .

Eight: Well, sort of. Cuz and I caught a large rattlesnake, which—with the superintendent's permission—we brought into the school building to be viewed by students who had never seen one. But he gave his permission only after assuring himself that there was no way for the snake to escape its screened enclosure.

(That smart alecky interviewer should have pursued that question further: Something happened later that wouldn't have been so easy to explain away. But I digress . . . ).

Nine: Yes. Moran had no public swimming pool, just a large number of swimming holes in all the surrounding creeks. Nobody I knew owned a bathing suit, so we all swam in the nude. General knowledge of that fact—plus the remote locations of all the swimming holes but one— gave us all the privacy we wanted.

Ten: Yes, only it was probably more than once. When I was a kid, each Sunday my mom would give me a dime to put into the collection plate at Sunday School. If she gave me a dime coin, I put the whole thing in. But, if she gave me two nickels, there were occasions when only one of them wound up in the dish.

The scary part is, if this had been an actual interview, I doubt that the reporter would have limited his questions to those easy ones above. Like I said at the start, there are several reasons I will never run for president.

Somewhere, somebody would have leaked the cherry bombs, a certain school trip, and the rest of that rattlesnake story. I just hope Danny's wrist got well . . .

# INFLUENTIAL PEOPLE . . . AND CHARACTERS

Frances holding a rattlesnake

## BOYS WILL BE BOYS, BUT NOT WHILE UNDER AUNT FLORENCE'S COMMAND

IT WASN'T that Cuz and I were bad kids; in fact, we were actually what you'd describe as pretty good boys . . . but only in the singular. Problem was that we sort of brought out the worst in each other. That didn't change much—it may even have worsened—as we moved on into our late teens, and perhaps a year or so beyond.

But the chain of events of which I am about to speak took place when Cuz was ten and I was six months younger. We got ourselves into one mess after another, and the fact that we were victims of a whole series of unintended results did not mitigate the situation or the severity of the resulting punishment.

Now, we did not wind up in reform school, but for a few days and nights we probably wished we had.

Our transgressions had to do with, in no particular order, a bothersome young cousin who was four years our junior, a cigar stub somebody left in a smokestand, a haystack that was more flammable than we could have expected, and the crowning blow that began with a couple of 1 × 12s we needed for a boat we were about to build. We pulled them off the back wall of a functioning outhouse.

AUNT FLORENCE was our great aunt, the sister of our maternal grandmother, but believe me, she was spawned in a different corner of the gene pool. While Grandma was sweet and kind and, of greatest import, tolerant, Aunt Florence was, well, selectively congenial.

She had no children which, given her attitude toward kids, was a good thing. It was her contention that all kids should be seen and not heard and, if they were boys, they should be neither.

I hated going to her house, even with my mom. While it was filled with things that begged to be felt, thumped or shaken, I was forbidden to touch any of it. So, mainly I would stand close to my mom's chair, urging her to say goodbye and to get the yell out of there. Aunt Florence's immediate scowl told me at once that the softness of my whisper needed more work.

I swear that woman could hear a fly tiptoeing across a powder puff . . .

IT WAS WHEN Cuz and I decided to let that little tattletale of a cousin play with us that resulted in our respective moms throwing up their collective hands. We had just finished building our little boat and had dragged it over to a pond for its maiden voyage.

I won't use the actual name of this little cousin because I'm not sure that childhood tattletelling isn't the developing stages of a litigious personality. Anyway, he wandered out just as we were preparing to test our new craft's seaworthiness.

It turned out that among the things we did not know about the shipbuilding business is that when you nail the tin bottom onto the 1 × 12 sides, you'd better use a good layer of tar and a lot more nails than we had access to.

When we asked this little cousin did he want to play, he jumped at the opportunity. I couldn't imagine anybody being so gullible . . . not after Cuz once made him what he thought was a peanut butter and cracker sandwich. I won't say what had replaced the peanut butter but will point out that Cuz was standing in the henhouse at the time.

We had barely placed him aboard when he, boat and all, began to sink. Two of our older brothers heard him crying at the top of his voice. While those two were pulling him out of the pond, Cuz's dad grabbed the napes of our respective necks and headed for the woodshed. Literally.

Hey, where we put the boat into the water wasn't two feet deep. It wasn't like we had cast him into the bleeping Bermuda Triangle . . .

OUR FIRST NIGHT at Aunt Florence's house began early. That's because we were dropped off there just after supper and, after a stern orientation lecture, she showed us to our bed and told us to get in it.

I lay there for hours, staring toward a ceiling I could no longer see because of the darkness. Cuz was asleep, or so I figured. Early on, we were speaking in low voices when she burst into the room and told us to get quiet and go to sleep. "No more talking!" is how she put it.

My thoughts reeled back to the events that had brought us to this point and led to this incarceration.

Our little cousin had the most doting mom in history. And the boat deal really set her off. She began bringing up such incidents as her clumsy little angel falling out of a tree house and blaming Cuz, and the time I latched the shop door not knowing he was still inside . . .

Anyway, that had our two moms wringing their hands and not considering the source of the complaint.

They were pondering a course of action when Aunt Florence spoke up:

"Let me have them for a week," she said, then glared at the two of us for a full minute before adding, "I'll straighten them out."

IT WAS STILL pitch dark outside when she pounded on the door and told us to get ready for breakfast. When we sat down, we were served something that looked very yucky.

"Calf brains and eggs," she explained. "You better eat fast; there's work to be done."

Even in the dim glow of the kerosene lamp the dish looked terrible. I couldn't eat it.

"If you don't eat it now, I will put it in the icebox and it will be your lunch."

That's how our week started and it didn't get better. We spent the day hoeing the garden and gathering blackberries. Cuz plucked one from his pail and popped it into his mouth. She went ballistic.

"You are not to eat the berries! I hope you enjoyed that because it will replace your dessert tonight."

That was tough. The only tolerable part of this stay was her fantastic cobbler.

Lunch that day was a nightmare. While Cuz chewed on a drumstick and slopped cream gravy onto a big, fluffy biscuit, I was trying to get down the cold eggs and calf brains from breakfast.

Our work days began in darkness and ended in darkness. Milking, gathering eggs, hoeing, chopping wood, slopping hogs, cleaning chicken pens—then it was supper and off to bed.

Horseplay was out of the question. Now, it's one thing for a ten-year-old to be told not to run in the house, but she forbade us to run outside.

WHEN SATURDAY finally came our "visit" was up. Our moms would be there soon to pick us up, so we were excused from all chores.

When they arrived, they sat down with Aunt Florence in the kitchen, where she poured coffee. We sneaked up to the door, just out of sight, to hear her report. What we heard caught us both off guard . . . especially her opening remark.

"They are good boys, and you can be proud of them. All they need is structure, and this week I gave them structure."

In the car, on the way home, Cuz said, "If that's structure, I don't like structure. Do you?"

I said I liked it better than calf brains and eggs.

Aunt Florence did prove one thing: We could spend time together without getting into trouble . . .

## Jamie

OF ALL THE kids I knew growing up, only one of them had a Father. I didn't like him and, come to think of it, I didn't care much for the kid either.

Jamie moved to Moran from California, which was nearly all he could talk about. He compared everything we had in Moran to what he was used to back there, and our offerings always came up short.

"Our movies—we had several of them—had ushers," he once said. "They led you to your seat with a light, and Father would hand them a coin for their trouble."

In Moran, our "pitcher show" had no ushers, we needed no dern light to find our seat and, of greater import, our "fathers" were called Dad or Daddy or Pop or, in reference among us guys, "my ol' man."

Jamie was an only child and, the way I figure it, the only thing his "Father" did right was deciding to quit right there.

THERE WAS about the Moran of that day a simplicity that we all enjoyed but didn't particularly like having explained to us. I didn't get "dropped off" at the show, ask to be excused from the presence of my folks, or wear short britches with long socks.

I walked to town, said bye if I remembered to, and wore a pair of jeans that reached all the way down to my bare feet. And so did Ray and Rabbit and Cuz and Danny and several other guys that—for reasons I don't understand even today—I prevented from cleaning Jamie's clock every time he opened his mouth.

I wasn't all that interested in protecting Jamie, but I was pragmatic in some instances. For example, if one of us beat up on him, all of us would wind up in trouble. His "Father" already had called Emory once when Cuz spat tobacco juice on Jamie's white shoe. Emory, a deputy sheriff charged with keeping Moran safe and peaceful, explained that it probably was an accident, that Jamie should have moved his foot.

Actually, Jamie had. But Cuz—the only tobacco-chewer in our group—was a precision spitter. Hitting a white shoe on the move was no challenge for ol' Cuz.

Anyway, even though it was Cuz who hit the mark, all of us heard about it.

MY AUNT MERLE, who was a neighborly sort, took kindly to Jamie's folks when they moved in next door to her. Now this aunt, who was my Mom's youngest sister, was a very special person in the eyes of Cuz and me.

She was kind, patient and, mainly, tolerated short-comings in kids. Mom thought it was because she had none of her own. I believe it was because Cuz and I were pretty good nephews, besides having a charm above what you'd expect from a couple of sixth graders.

Aunt Merle convinced me that we should include Jamie in our activities, and that once he got used to the things we liked to do, he likely would become easier to tol-erate. So, swallowing hard and taking in a deep breath, I invited him to go swimming with us out at Wash Hole, one of our favorite swimming holes. It was the one closest to town, maybe a mile's walk from the pool hall. It was on Deep Creek, just below the bridge on the Albany highway.

The best place was Round Hole, which was on Battle Creek, but it was about a three-mile walk.

Jamie surprised me when he accepted. But my plea-sure dissipated when he said for us to go on, that "Father" would drop him off. I told him how to get there and left.

ONE OF THE challenges at Wash Hole was to climb up the steep creek bank on the south side while protecting your modesty, however meager, without losing your footing. Nobody in my crowd ever saw a bathing suit, let alone owned one, and that bank was in clear view of the highway bridge.

Diving off Top Bank at Wash Hole was one of the rites of passage for Moran boys. Another was climbing the water tower, but that was an advanced course generally postponed until the seventh or eighth grade year.

Anyway, we all were in the water, choosing sides for a game of Alligator Gar, when we heard footsteps coming down the brushy trail. It was Jamie and Father. I couldn't keep from snickering when Father said he would pick Jamie up at "precisely 3:30."

Father left and Jamie, fully clothed, disappeared behind a thick willow bush. Shortly, his re-appearance put us all aghast.

Here stood Jamie wearing more clothes than the rest of us had taken off. He had on what looked like bottoms from a pair of striped long-handles, a top that resembled an undershirt, and a pair of webbed things on his feet. All that, and a pair of goggles that made his eyes look both funny and concerned. Surely he had seen naked boys before . . .

That Jamie did not get drowned that day can be credited only to my respect for Aunt Merle . . . and the fact 3:30 got there just in time. I kept my buddies at bay, except for that one time he got tossed off of Top Bank.

He sputtered and coughed a little, but he was alive and unbroken.

THE SUMMER passed swiftly, as Moran summers always seemed to do. And, by late August, Jamie had started to adjust to what his Father once told my ol' man was "a total absence of couth."

We heard less and less about California and more and more about how much he had enjoyed sneaking into the traveling carnival peek show, swiping a watermelon off that parked truck, and learning how to make a straight-in pool shot without scratching. He had begun to wear the pair of Cuz's jeans that Aunt Merle sneaked to him, and— something none of the rest of us ever did—bit a chunk off Cuz's plug of Brown's Mule.

On our last trip of the summer to Wash Hole, Jamie walked along with the rest of us, barefooted and without a shirt. To top it all off, when we got there he produced a cigar, lit it, and passed it around.

When we asked him where he got it, he smiled broadly and said, "I swiped it from my ol' man's humidor . . . "

His using the term "my ol' man" bought him a free pass for the word "humidor."

Jamie left the next week, moving back to California. There's no way I will ever know for sure, but I'm betting that he was soon telling his buddies that things out there are just not as good as what he was used to back in Moran . . .

It was years later when Aunt Merle would reveal something to Cuz and me that Jamie's mom had quietly told her on the day she left. She had liked the change she saw in her son at summer's end. She had been afraid he was going to grow up to be just like his Father.

That's what can happen if you don't have an ol' man . . .

## AUDREY

THE PASSING of Audrey Brooks went mainly unnoticed by a world whose mind has been on other things. But to a small community in West Central Texas—and many who gravitated from there in body but whose spirits were left lagging behind to dwell among the memories—it was a significant marking.

Audrey was at once Moran's untitled historian, community activist, volunteer nonpareil and, perhaps of greatest import, its very conscience. For years she also wrote a column in the county's weekly newspaper to which—mainly because of her—I have been a constant subscriber.

Her column frequently told me things I either did not know or simply had forgotten. But it almost always clutched my interest and held on to it, even though her writing style was neither spell-binding nor dramatic. That it informed me was in conflict with how she once described its intent.

But that's getting ahead of the story.

AUDREY PARKER BROOKS was born in or near San Saba and came to Moran in the early 1930s after marrying Lucion Brooks, whose family was among that community's pioneers.

Her column was titled "Barbed Wire and Memories," and that was no misnomer. Her favored topics had to do with the ranch where she still lived at the time of her death, and the givings and misgivings of repairing fences, and dealing with everything from renegade bulls to rattlesnakes, including the time one of the latter struck Lucion in the leg.

She wrote often of the old days in Moran, when it bustled with life and activity and even minor spurts of growth. And, up until the very week of her sudden death, the lucidity of her written message masked her age. At 94, she still managed to pluck just the right word from her remarkable vocabulary.

While her column was what marked her, it did so superficially. Her essence ran much deeper and, in some instances, completely away from what one normally expects from a columnist. Moran has a museum that belies both its size and resources, and Audrey Brooks was the driving force behind its inception and, later, its continued growth and significance.

It started when Rockwell Bros. Lumber Company became one of the several businesses to fall victim to the requiem that has befallen Small Town Texas. Audrey got the company to donate its building to the community for a museum.

"Audrey didn't provide all the money," a longtime Moran friend told me recently, "but she certainly was the propellant behind the project."

Response was such that the museum soon outgrew the old lumber company building. It was then that Audrey set her sights on the old First Christian Church. It had been vacant for several years due to a diminishing congregation.

A beautiful structure now as then—it was constructed at a time when building architecture was a true art form—a process of upgrading, touch-ups, and replacing the stained glass made it perfect for its new purpose.

I ALWAYS TRIED to visit with Audrey when I would return home, often only by phone, to "catch up" on what was happening in this town, the field of my very roots.

Once, when I came in to speak at the semiannual homecoming event, she wrote a column that was, generally, quite complimentary of how I looked ("he's put on weight, but it looks good on him"), how I dressed ("his suit looked expensive and it fit him perfectly"), and my message ("his talk was humorous and not too long").

But then she zinged me: I left the building as soon as my speech ended, almost sprinting to my car. Tech was playing the Aggies here that evening, and I barely had time to make the kickoff.

"He spoke and ran," she wrote, "clearly eager to see Moran appearing in his rearview mirror . . . "

I never tried to explain my reason for haste. That I later returned to speak again made my point . . . to me, at least.

ONCE WHEN I was home, I learned that some issue had grown out of control, having divided the town down the middle. Lifelong friends no longer were on speaking terms, and whatever it was had spilled over into one of the churches and even the school system itself.

When I got back here, I called Audrey to find out what was happening. She gave me the Readers Digest version, except she condensed it even further. I half-teasingly chided her for not writing about it in her column.

"Look," she said, "unlike you, I am not a journalist. I am a regular citizen who happens to write a column that I hope readers will find entertaining. Besides that, everybody here knows all there is to know about the issue. Why should I be trying to tell people what they already know?

"The beauty of this community is that we've always been a family. This is a 'family' spat, and family spats always work themselves out—unless outside influences set them in stone."

I ONCE MENTIONED to Audrey that I have often toyed with writing a book about Moran, about its characters and their ways. She encouraged me, saying that I had the background and—as she put it—"a sense of the ridiculous" necessary to spin it into a readable yarn.

That idea has never totally left me. It is a town of characters, of history and of the fabric that made rural Texas unique in its thoughts, its lore, and its unique behavior.

But in telling the story, I would be compelled to bring out that latest issue and some earlier ones that divided—things like the wet-dry election in the mid-'40s—and, further, some of the scandalous love affairs that the remaining old-timers still discuss today. It would be the type of book that Audrey Brooks would never write. I'd hope it would be one that she would have gladly read.

It's the review she might have written that I would surely have dreaded . . .

## BOB TERRY

ROBY—Sometimes Bob Terry tells the truth but, when he does, it doesn't do a lot of damage to his stories. That's partially because some of the things he's actually done are more remarkable than the ones that bubble over from his ever-boiling imagination.

Bob holds court here each morning, sitting at a round table where he's surrounded by friends and relatives and an occasional visitor to the storied old Silver Star Café, nee Silver Spur, where customers can see aged license plates from twenty or thirty states, a clock that runs backward, and a sundry of memorabilia from days long past.

Along with the license tags—some are sixty or seventy years old—the walls of the Silver Star are decorated by news clippings, a rattlesnake skin and, for purposes unknown, a long slab of wood sliced from a giant mesquite tree. It is one of two popular coffee spots in this city, the capital of Fisher County. About a half-mile to the east is Nubbins, which is the morning hangout for a different set of regulars.

My longtime friend Freddie was once a part of the Nubbins bunch, but for "no particular reason" he began breakfasting at the Silver Star.

As a relative outsider, I see little difference between the two groups, who share common interests, needs, and favorite topics. It may come down to colorful characters— Nubbins has Tubby, Silver Spur has Bob. If Bob is the more interesting of the two it may be because he's more unpredictable. Nobody knows what Bob Terry may say next.

Maybe not even Bob Terry . . .

ON THIS DAY, Bob was especially wound up. A neighbor's rooster has been waking him at an ungodly hour. He started the morning out trying to convince Freddie to go buy the rooster and use it to bait his coyote trap.

Somebody suggested that perhaps Bob was overreacting; that, as a country boy, he should be accustomed to such normal rural sounds.

"This rooster is different," Bob said. "He ain't like a regular rooster. And it's not just that he crows but how he does it. The damn thing crows in Spanish and I can't understand him. That's what keeps me awake."

Bob grew up in Roby, graduated from the local high school, and during the years since has been involved in a number of endeavors, some of them quite successfully. There was the flying business and, later, a bulldozer operation. Somewhere along the way, he took tours up to Longhorn Canyon, a picturesque area of gorges and bluffs in the northwestern reaches of the county.

Yet, rural life being anchored to the legends it produces, Bob's legacy will be marked not by those normal activities but by the things that set him apart from the crowd he daily addresses.

"Quite often ol' Bob will spend a couple of hours quoting the Bible," one of his friends explained. "Maybe it will be a particular Book from the Old or New Testament . . . even Revelation."

One morning somebody suggested that maybe he shouldn't be quoting scriptures while wearing a Budweiser hat. Bob paused a minute, took the hat off, looked at the

Bud sign on its front, put it back on and went right back to his message.

MOST OF WHAT Bob has done has been harmless fun. But he has had his brushes with the law. Two stories of such encounters smack of color and improbability. But, as stated earlier, where Bob Terry is concerned, truth may be fiction's next of kin.

The other day he was telling about a time when he got pulled over just outside the Hawley community by a local gendarme.

"I was about six miles outside of town running pretty fast when he stopped me," Bob related. "He walked up and asked me for my driver's license. I said I don't have one.

"Then he asked me for my proof of insurance. I said I don't have any insurance.

"He asked if I had been drinking. I said, yes, I been drinking since early that morning.

"That sort of set him back. He told me to sit still, that he was calling for a backup. He called a state trooper, who showed up very soon.

"The trooper asked for my driver's license. I showed it to him.

"He asked for my insurance card. I showed it to him.

"He asked me to blow into this machine. I did and it registered zero.

"The DPS guy turned to the local cop and said he has a license, he has insurance and he hasn't been drinking . . .

"I leaned out the window and said, yeah, and the next thing you know that SOB will say I was speedin'!"

MANY YEARS BEFORE, back when Bob had his own airplane, one of his escapades would become a part of the rich Roby lore.

It was about midday when people around the courthouse square heard an airplane overhead. They looked up to see this single engine aircraft circling the town. It was acting a bit erratic, climbing, banking, dipping and making wide circles around the city. Some thought it was just a pilot cruising around, enjoying a relaxing ride on a beautiful day.

Suddenly, with no warning, the airplane went into a dive and, a few feet above the pavement, pulled up, flew under the only traffic light in town and proceeded at full speed just a few feet above U.S. 180, which serves as Roby's main thoroughfare.

That the local citizens were both amused and entertained by Bob's barnstorming maneuver did not impress either the FAA or the DPS, whose involvements were both immediate and stern.

THOSE ARE but two of the many Bob Terry stories that have been re-circulating for the past few weeks. The one about the cop in Hawley was one I heard first-hand from Bob himself. The one about flying under the traffic light in downtown Roby had been floating around for years.

By now, being prepared to believe anything I heard about this phenomenal individual, I wondered if both those stories were true.

"The one about the cop in Hawley wasn't. I just made that up."

He then pulled off the straw hat he was wearing that day, examined the brim, and swatted Freddie across the back and remarked:

"You better go get that rooster. If you don't I'm gonna have to learn to speak Spanish."

Bob Terry is as likeable as he is colorful, and his stories get everybody's day off to a cheerful start. All that considered, that rooster might do well to stop and think about who he's talking to—whatever his language.

But Bob made it clear the other morning that he isn't fond of everybody that lives in his home town. He walked in and announced that he was writing a thesis. Somebody asked about his topic.

"It's called The Jerks of Roby. And it'll be pretty long."

"Jerks" is my word, not his. Bob's title was anatomically definitive . . . but unprintable.

Truth of the matter, Bob loves his hometown. But "Good Guys of Roby" just wouldn't fit his style, which is to grab your attention.

Actually, Bob Terry is known locally for two personal traits—loyalty and verbosity. In a single sentence, his friend Leon paid tribute to both characteristics:

"If I got stranded some place far away, even if it was Timbuktu or Kalamazoo, I could call ol' Bob and he'd come straight after me. But, man, I sure would dread that long ride home . . . "

## Bill Banowsky

THAT A LUBBOCK Church of Christ preacher buzzed off to Chicago to spend a couple of nights in the Playboy

Mansion is intriguing, but it's not the main part of this story.

Nor, for that matter, is the fact that this preacher was young and handsome and charming and very, very married . . . and did I mention that he also was charismatic, back when that word described a personality trait, not a secular genre? Or that he went there at the personal invitation of Hugh Hefner himself?

The story actually is about a handful of preachers who, in my own subjective view, were the most interesting I have known during my near half-century in Lubbock. Elsewhere in these pages, the A-J is focusing on the past century. Those writers, bless their hearts, are harnessed to the facts of history.

My bases are things I saw, know for sure, or . . . well, just have my own mind made up about. That's how all columnists work, no matter what they tell you.

THIS CITY HAS been blessed with more than its share of preachers of significance. But to me, four stick out above the others—some for what they did, at least one for what he both did and didn't do, and a couple for . . . well, just who they were.

In no particular order, I would name Dudley Strain of First Christian, Hardy Clemmons of Second Baptist, and Morris Sheats of Trinity Church. The fourth, I'll get around to later.

Dudley and Hardy both were exceptional, both in the pulpit and as pastors of their flock. Sheats was a dynamic individual who took a church that was nondenominational—albeit heavily anchored to its Assembly of God roots—and made it the largest congregation in a town long dominated by Baptists, Methodists, Churches of Christ, Presbyterians— all the more conventional flavors.

Then, alas. Sheats suffered from the rigors of a political campaign that not only failed, but left his image marred in the process. He had run against Kent Hance in the Democratic Primary as both were hoping to fill the Congressional seat being vacated by the retiring icon, George Mahon.

Hance won, then went on to beat a guy named George W. Bush in the general election. Incidentally, to this day, the only political race Bush would ever lose was that one to Hance.

I CAUGHT UP with Bill Banowsky in Puerta Vallarta, where he has a home. I got his number from his life-long bride who was at the couple's other house in Dallas. He loves it down there; she said she prefers being in Dallas, near their kids and grandchildren.

Much has happened to Banowsky that far overshadows the topic I had called about. He left his post as senior minister at Broadway Church of Christ to become president of Pepperdine College at the ripe old age of 31. From there, he went on to become president of Oklahoma University. He left OU to become CEO of the sprawling Gaylord corporation.

Now retired, he spends most of his time there on the western coast of Mexico, writing and reading and relaxing.

He took me through the long and remarkable trail that brought him there from Lubbock, where he spent five years at the Broadway church. Despite all his accomplishments during all the days since, the events of one January morning in 1968 are still at the front of his mind.

*PLAYBOY MAGAZINE,* under Hefner's direction, had launched a campaign that it said would identify the lifestyle of a changing culture in America. He called it The New Morality.

In Lubbock, Texas, Banowsky—a young fundamentalist preacher—called it hedonism, the philosophy that pleasure is the most important pursuit. Although not an admitted reader of the magazine, he was offended by the very premise.

"TWO GUYS ON my staff—Rex Vermillion and Jim Bevis—wanted me to debate Heffner on that topic. I at first was simply amused by their suggestion, then it became obvious that they weren't kidding."

Banowsky contacted Hefner and, to both his delight and surprise, he went for the idea. He invited Bill up to Chicago to discuss the matter face to face and, almost before he knew it, he was off to the Mansion. His wife agreed, but with one caveat:

"She insisted that I take this guy on my staff along with me," he chuckled.

Now Mrs. B trusted her husband . . . but given his age and . . . well, like Ronald Reagan used to say, "Trust everybody in the game, but always cut the cards."

HEFNER, ADMITTING that he was no debater, assigned the late Anson Mount, who had the two oxymoronic titles of Sports Editor/Religion Editor, to represent the magazine. The debate was held at 9:00 a.m. one

Sunday morning in Lubbock Municipal Auditorium on the Tech campus.

Under ground rules established earlier during the meeting in Chicago, Banowsky's only advantage seemed to be the home court. And, face it: With a crowd consisting of more than a few college students . . . well, *Playboy* did have its following.

In later years, Banowsy told me the other day, he would have two debates on two very significant topics and win them both. Measured for gravity, they both were much heavier than the debate in Lubbock which—at Hefner's insistence—would be titled, "It's a Playboy World."

AMONG MOUNT'S mistakes was to do something that every sports editor, even those employed by duller publications than his, knows is fatal: He not only underestimated his opponent, he also guessed wrong at what would be Banowsky's game plan.

Mount got the advantage of speaking last, both on his affirmation and the rebuttal. If he had expected to be facing a ranting and raving and scripture shouting preacher, Mount was in for a shock.

Instead, he heard Banowsky connect eroding morality's influence on everything from the economy to public confidence and, further, to a nation's own self-image. He backed up his remarks with statistical data gathered from several countries, especially those in Scandinavia.

The scriptures he used were mainly to punctuate a point. It didn't hurt that Banowsky's superior oratory skills, his personal charm, and his calm and witty demeanor left his opponent in a pontifical lurch.

The debate started at the time Sunday School was happening at Banowsky's church about a half-mile away. When it ended, he dashed back to preach his regular weekly sermon.

Lubbock has had, during my years here, some exceptional preachers. But, in my opinion, Bill Banowsky was in a league of his own.

He probably still is.

## ANN GUTHRIE

DUE, AT LEAST in part, to a book written by Tom Brokaw and through the physical and fiscal contributions of Tom Hanks, our fighting men of World War II have finally been recognized for their courage and gallantry and, of greatest import, for preserving a way of life even the founding fathers could not have foreseen.

Today, just before I sat down to begin my bi-weekly writing exercise, I was scanning the obit page when a swallow of coffee was almost blocked by a sudden gulp in my throat. Time and years had claimed another member of the Greatest Generation. And this time it was a person whose friendship I had cherished for many years.

In fact, it was almost exactly a half-century ago that Ann and O. C. Guthrie moved into a house just across the street from us. I thought it fitting that both were pictured above the obituary that caught my eye. After all, theirs was a story that presented all the elements needed for a dramatic love story—including a happy ending that had bounded precariously on the seas of a war that seemed to rage forever.

IN VISUALIZING the members of that Greatest Generation, the thought normally focuses on the soldiers, sailors, and marines that fought the Axis on all fronts and, despite tremendous losses, won the war through a determination bred by hard times and fueled by a resolve linked to an unwavering belief in what they were protecting.

But the females of the era were made of the same fabric which was seasoned by the hardships of the Great Depression and were directed by a moral compass that made "doing the right thing" the only acceptable path.

When Orbie proposed, he didn't give Ann much time to think about it. After all, he was on leave and time was short. She accepted and thus began a saga of love and separation, of drama and suspense, and, eventually, of happiness and peace.

Shortly after Ann became pregnant with the first of their four children, Orbie headed into the teeth of the war in the Pacific, flying torpedo bombers off such carriers as the *Enterprise*, the *Intrepid* and the *Midway*. As an iconic member of the famed Torpedo Squadron Ten, he became one of the nation's most decorated heroes.

Back home, Ann was removed from harm's way, but only physically. Knowing the nature of Orbie's missions— all seemingly pitting him against the odds—her every breath began with a prayer and ended with a thankful sigh. That she actually believed in her heart that he would make it safely home sustained her.

"I had to believe he'd make it," she once told me. "The only other choice was simply not acceptable . . . "

Lt. Guthrie, meanwhile, was not so sure. In fact, years later in writing about his tour, he admitted to having conceded that his return would be unlikely. Torpedo planes had to come in low, literally sweeping the waves, lay down their payload, then pull up fast and hopefully speed away to the safety of an open sky. Needless to say, casualties were heavy.

"The first time I became a little optimistic was once late in the war when thirteen planes flew off the deck and all thirteen came back. It was the first time I actually believed that I just might make it after all . . . "

THE WAR ENDED and Orbie did indeed arrive safely back home. But if Ann held any hope of his looking for a calm and safe job at a desk in some office somewhere, she would dismiss it in a hurry.

Instead, Orbie joined the highway patrol. And even though that was considerably less risky than buzzing the deck of an enemy battleship, it was no job for the meek or the timid. Guthrie and his fellow patrolmen were equipped with brand-new 1946 Fords, a sidearm, and maybe a shotgun. Radar was unheard of, and radios were available only to those stationed in urban areas, which Orbie was not.

By the time I met Guthrie, he already had progressed to the rank of sergeant and was responsible for overseeing all the patrolmen in the Lubbock region. I sensed that he found the administrative gig a bit tame.

Once when I went with him to make his rounds, he talked about the youngsters under his watch and all the

great equipment they had—radios, radar units especially—
and how much easier it made their work. He recalled his
first years on the job and the challenges they brought.

"If a speeder went by, it was you and him," he said,
almost wishfully. "There was no way to call ahead; you
chased him down and dealt with whatever caused him to
run."

ANN GUTHRIE'S war, then, was fought not on the
global battlefields, but, in its own way, shared the intensity.

She and thousands like her—the female members
of the Greatest Generation—maintained not only their
homes and the very home front the Japanese had put at
risk on Dec. 7, 1941, but also served physically in aircraft
factories, ferried airplanes to various bases, conducted war
bond drives, and took shifts at spotting and identifying
aircraft. All that in addition to taking a job to sustain her
and her baby daughter while dreaming of the day when
the war would end and her husband would return and the
aura of normalcy would shine on their lives.

It finally happened, and the couple settled into a life
that produced four offspring, an eventual retirement, and
a long and happy journey together.

Ann was buried Thursday, placed beside her husband who—perhaps to his surprise—made it to 87 before
his death just over two years ago. She was 86 years old.

Just as Ann and Orbie shared their lives, they now
share a legacy . . .

## REQUIEM FOR A TIME WHEN JULY 4 WAS GIVEN ITS DUE

I WATCHED with boyish pride as my dad made his way to the make-shift stage to join the Baptist preacher and Mayor Sam Sherman, who were already in position. At opposite ends of the flatbed trailer, which was decorated with a skirting of red, white and blue crepe paper, stood the American Legion flag and Old Glory itself.

The preacher, whose name has since escaped me, was there to give the invocation. Mayor Sherman would later read from a prepared speech. My dad's job, as post commander, was to welcome all in attendance to the barbecue, sponsored by Post 343, which was named for his brother who had been killed in France during World War I.

I don't remember any of Dad's words, except I'm sure his mind was on the war that was raging across the globe, and on his two sons who were fighting somewhere in the Pacific and a third who would soon be approaching draft age.

Mom was among the women preparing to serve barbecue beef and cabrito with all the usual trimmings—potato salad, beans, onions, etc. The food line had already begun to form.

THAT WAS ON July 4, 1944, exactly 72 years ago tomorrow. I remember telling a young pal standing beside me, "That's my dad," an unnecessary explanation, given that everybody in Moran knew everybody else, both by sight and by name.

Trite as it sounds, for America it was the worst of times; it was the best of times.

It had dispatched an entire generation to all corners of the earth to defend not only its homeland but every free country in the world against the tyranny of Nazi Germany and the cruel aggression of the Empire of Japan.

Times could get no worse than that.

But, domestically, the entire nation had closed ranks. Patriotism had never been higher, with the most likely exception being the activities for which this holiday commemorated.

The celebration that day in Moran was an annual event, sponsored by Ernest F. Pettit, Post 343, and served to further kindle the patriotic catalyst that spurred all the war efforts on the home front.

That patriotism involved all ages. War Bond drives, scrap iron collections, and elementary school classes competing against each other in the race to see which would sell the most U.S. Savings Stamps. They went for a dime apiece, and a book of them could be turned in at the Post Office for an $18.75 War Bond which, upon maturity, would be worth $25.

The meal was free. A rancher donated a calf, a farmer provided the goat, and families each brought a covered dish. The meat was cooked overnight atop a bed of mesquite coals. It then was covered with burlap bags and a layer of soil.

DAD, WHO HAD been wounded in France just a few weeks before his brother was killed, was among those who believed we were late getting into the war. He thought we should have jumped in when Germany invaded Poland in 1939.

He was a typical Texas Democrat, conservative in his beliefs but leery of all Republicans, for whom he and all other Dems blamed the Depression. Conversely, Dad had no use for labor unions, and when John L. Lewis called a nationwide coalminers strike, he believed he should be arrested and charged with treason. That strike was detrimental to the war effort and, according to Dad's logic, was called to retaliate against FDR's decision to go to war. Lewis was an avowed isolationist.

Dad's views on labor unions never changed nor did his political affiliation. Twenty years later when his party moved too far to the left for his tastes, he never left the party. At that juncture when the party left him, he simply stopped voting. Becoming a Republican was never a consideration.

FAST FORWARD to the present where a different form of war with different type enemy has taken the world in its grasp. Instead of battalions of enemies wearing identifiable uniforms exchanging gunfire, cannons roaring and aircraft strafing, the enemy now are terrorists relying on sneak attacks, suicide bombings, and random shootings. They are identifiable only after the fact.

Even the nation itself lacks the very unity from which the patriotism of all those years ago glued us together in a single purpose: Win the war, preserve our freedom. Today's leadership—all three branches—is driven only by its partisan political callings. And both parties are equally culpable, yielding to their extreme factions. All decisions are considered not by logic but how it fits the party's narrative; consequently, a deadlocked Congress is mutually impotent.

As a result, an electorate disgusted by the legislative constipation had its own revolt, flocking to three candidates, not one of which, in my opinion, is worthy of holding the world's most important position. The two remaining candidates, both of whom have negative numbers in the critical area of public trust, will compete for the office. One, God help us, will celebrate the next July 4th as President of the United States.

WHEN THE MEAL ended in the Moran city park that day, Dad and a dozen or so veterans, all proudly wearing their Legionnaire caps, began folding up chairs and clearing the debris.

After the "housekeeping" work was done, they—all WWI veterans—stood around chatting and sipping on ice tea they had rescued before the large container was emptied. The entire conversation was about the war effort. I don't recall a single mention of the 1944 Presidential race, where Franklin Delano Roosevelt would be challenged by New York Governor Thomas E. Dewey.

Nobody was talking, or maybe even thinking, about politics. There was a war being fought, many of our boys were dying, and a common Axis enemy had drawn the country together. Little did I know at the time that more than seven decades later I would be looking back on that very day—and that very mood—with wistful nostalgia . . .

I still miss you, Dad. And all you stood for . . .

## FATHER'S DAY

IT WAS A Father's Day that had routine written all over it . . . early church, Sunday school, lunch and, later, the U.S. Open followed by dinner with another couple. My plans included mainly an unruffled day with only my wife and pup and a Sunday paper to affect my time.

Then the phone began to ring. First it was Kevin, my oldest son who lives just outside Waco. A few minutes later, it was Scott, my youngest, calling from San Antonio. Shortly after those calls, Kyle—the middle son who lives here in town—dropped by with Gary, my oldest grandson.

Each wished me a happy Father's Day and, in their respective styles, said nice things about me and thanked me for what I had meant to them. Without exception, each closed out the conversation with the same phrase: "I love you, Dad." Kyle punctuated his sentence with a hug just before heading out the door.

The afterglow of those expressions of warmth was not savored for long. My feelings of euphoric appreciation for three thoughtful sons turned immediately into guilt.

It was that damned book . . . a book I had never even read, but whose pages were at the top of the news and in the forefront of a mind rueful of words I had left unspoken all those many years ago . . .

THE PASSING OF Tim Russert practically on the eve of Father's Day emphasized the impact of a book he had written about his father, in which, among other things, he said to his dad many things that he never could have comfortably expressed to him face to face.

That has left me, and likely many others on this very day, to ponder something that we all have left undone.

We are the ones from a generation born to fathers that provided a legacy whose material worth was as vague as its value was clear. Big Russ, whom Tim wrote the book about, was considerably younger than my own Dad. But his life and the lessons he provided were powerfully similar. Unlike my father, the elder Russert is still alive.

The Depression years stranded my father with few assets, a wife, seven kids, and no way to earn a living that did not involve sweat, strength and exertion . . . days that began before daylight and ended after nightfall. And that was only during the times when work was available at all. My three oldest siblings—a sister and two brothers—also took work where they could find it, contributing all they earned to the family coffers.

Times were almost untenable. Yet, as the youngest member of the clan, what I mainly recall about those days is that I got a lot of attention, and much of it came from my Dad. I can remember him coming home and, in total exhaustion, collapsing on the floor.

I would run over and jump right on top of him, not realizing how tired he must have been. Instead of scolding me, he would grab me, tussle my hair, tickle my ribs, and then give me a playful slap on the butt and tell me to go find my brothers.

Dad expressed no affection verbally. It just wasn't his nature. But the warmth of his character enveloped us all.

LOOKING BACK on it all these many years later, I realize that my father, like Big Russ, was a great teacher.

Dad's own education had been limited. He attended classes in a one-room schoolhouse in the Deep Creek community just northeast of Moran. I don't know how much formal education he received, but he had seen a lot of the world during service in WWI.

He was not eloquently articulate, yet I suspect that even if his vocabulary had been extremely elaborate, he still would have chosen the same words he always used. Being clear, concise, and understood were his only objectives.

Still, there was much profundity in what he spoke.

An example I recall happened one time when I was telling him how a buddy and I had been watching this man, who we knew to be illiterate, working on a house he was building. The man could neither read nor write—he signed his name by drawing a simple "B," which someone had taught him in order for him to execute necessary documents. My friend and I had been amazed at how ol' B cut and measured and was moving right along with his project.

"B's a great carpenter," my Dad said. "There's not a better one in the country."

I was amazed. "But, Dad, how can anybody who can't read or write do anything that requires thought and figuring?" I asked.

"Something you never want to do," my Dad declared, quite forcefully, "is to confuse intelligence with education."

It was many years later while I was serving on the board of regents of one of the state's top universities that I came to appreciate the full validity of that statement. On more than one occasion during that time I was able to keep my cool by silently reminding myself, "Don't confuse intelligence with ..."

MY FATHER'S DAY ended on a different note than it had started. But mainly, I wound up feeling guilty over having spent much of the day hearing my three sons saying to me things I never got around to telling my own father. That he had been so much more deserving than I only added to the guilt.

My dad was of a different bent, not only when it came to expressing his feelings but, even more so, in accepting praise from others. In fact, when he knew that such remarks might be forthcoming, his evasive action was both immediate and effective.

My oldest brother, John L., my lifelong hero, was of that very same nature. There was much I always wanted to say to him but never could. Then Tom Brokaw wrote the fantastic book, *The Greatest Generation*, that was a perfect description of that brother. So I got a copy, wrote on the inside cover exactly how I appreciated all he had meant to me, and sent it to him.

Predictably, he did not respond. At his funeral just over a year later, his widow told me how touched John L. had been by what I had written. She said he smiled, wiped his eyes and put the book carefully aside.

Tim Russert's book would have been the perfect conduit had he written it thirty-something years ago. I believe my dad's reaction might have been similar to my brother's.

Sadly, I will never know.

Yet I close the day with one pleasing assurance: My sons will never have to regret the words they never spoke.

Thanks guys. I love you . . .

## An Unwise Decision Became a Lifetime of Ecstasy

GOD KNOWS, she could have done much better; I only could have done worse.

She had beauty, charm, grace and intellect . . . and a well-planned future. I had the rather shattered background of a college dropout, an oilfield roughneck, a soldier, and was now earning a living as an equipment operator in highway construction. My only long-range plan was to hold destiny at arm's length until something fell out of the sky and landed at my feet.

And, come to think of it, that's exactly what happened . . .

FRANCES HILL was just completing her third semester at North Texas State in December 1956. I completed my hitch in the U.S. Army and returned home just as she arrived for the Christmas holidays.

We had met back in September. I was home on leave, and her family had moved to Moran a year earlier. We did not date during my three weeks back home, but it wasn't because of my having failed to ask. I was disappointed that she was not smitten by my charm and wit, but was encouraged at how politely she parried my best moves. Her reply of "no" was uttered through a beautiful smile.

She did eventually provide me with a lock of red hair that I had to bring back to collect a wager. Actually, it had been more of a dare than a bet, the background of which was more complicated than interesting.

Suffice it to say that when I arrived at Fort Lewis, Washington, after duty in the Arctic, a Moran buddy stationed there greeted me with a report on this beautiful red-haired girl he met and dated while home on leave. He described her as not only being drop-dead pretty, but also a very nice person. Among his advantages was that she and he belonged to the same church.

Thus my wager on the lock of hair.

Only by threatening that if she didn't provide the real thing, I just might cut one off a Hereford calf—and claim it was hers—did she acquiesce. To say that did not go well back at Fort Lewis would be an understatement.

Enough about that.

WHEN I ARRIVED back home, my inroads had paid off. Shortly after I got back to Fort Lewis, I wrote her. She responded. So, for the next three months our letters gained in frequency if not in intensity. They read like correspondence between two friends. That's because you couldn't hear my heart shift gears each time I opened one of her letters.

Anyway, to my delight, when I asked her for a date that night she readily agreed.

For reasons I still can't fully understand, Dan Cupid involved himself in a hurry. We were together every night until she had to return to school. And we then were involved in a flurry of letters, phone calls and, when possible, I would head for Denton.

Incidentally, North Texas at the time had a very sexist rule: Female students had to be in the dorm by 10:50 p.m. on weeknights, 11:50 p.m. on Fridays and Saturdays. There were no regulations placed on male students.

So it amounted to long drives and short visits.

MARRIAGES, AT least the successful ones, contain certain inalienable elements: Love, commitment, dedication leading to a carefully planned wedding. Our conversations, now moving in that direction, had two other requirements: I would agree to join the Church of Christ, and I would finish college.

The first would be easy; the second, not so much. Because I eschewed a full scholarship a week before classes started, I had not a single hour of college credit.

What had been casual conversations about marriage were spurred by a sudden sense of urgency.

A. J. Hill was a great man. He was a former star athlete in college, an educator, a rancher and already a leader in the Moran community. Now his concerns were about this guy his daughter was seeing too much of—nothing personal, just that he had in mind for her someone with, uh, better credentials.

Hey, did it not matter that I played football on an MHS championship team, that I had been voted Most Popular Boy my senior year, that I had been a dern good derrick man, was once Soldier of the Month, and was now was able to operate every piece of heavy equipment the Highway Department owned?

Apparently not.

ABOUT THREE weeks before her semester finals, Frances learned that her dad had decided that she would spend the summer in Texas City with her uncle and aunt. Evidently, he believed if he could keep me away from her for that long, she might forget all about me. Or, maybe I'd find somebody else; or, if he were really lucky, I'd wind up in a jailhouse several counties away.

What followed was at once the dumbest and wisest decision of which I would ever be a part. She suggested that we elope. And, suffice it to say, her Christian upbringing and Victorian standards played a role in my eagerness to agree.

On May 29, 1957, we were wed in Ranger by a Church of Christ preacher—we waited in our car outside until he had finished his Wednesday night service—spent our wedding night in a motel in Eastland, from where she rode the very bus her dad already was to meet in Cisco.

That wait for "something to fall from the sky and land at my feet" had come to pass. Despite the odds, everything wound up in storybook fashion. I enrolled at North Texas, my father-in-law and I became very close friends, and she and I were handed our degrees on the same afternoon.

I now had fulfilled her every requirement. She rewarded me with three wonderful sons and six decades of love and friendship and unfettered devotion.

Our love story ended on June 8, 2017, sixty years and ten days after a foolish decision had become an enchanted path to happiness.

God bless you, Frances Hill Pettit. Although you are gone, a lifetime of memories will keep you forever at my side . . .

Frances, c. 1970

# FOOD

A pot of beans

### Family Memories Wrapped Up in an Ice Box

EACH TIME I look at the old ice box that occupies a special place in our house in rural Fisher County, my thoughts go back to a hot Sunday afternoon in the summer of 1942 and the times and the circumstances surrounding my family and others like it.

Mom's day always began facing the heat produced by a wood-burning cook stove, which she and Dad acquired the day after their wedding twenty-odd years before. Ah, but those had been the days. The "Roaring Twenties" had served them well as they started a family, bought a new car and, even as the family grew, their life was directed by neither luxury nor need.

The Depression had changed all that and, even worse, the nation was now embroiled in a World War that was certain to involve at least two of her four sons. While much of the country had begun to recover from the economic crash, rural areas had seen little change. The REA had not discovered that part of the country, and—along with heating and cooking with wood-fired stoves and fireplaces—our home was lighted by kerosene lamps.

Money was still scarce and the three oldest siblings contributed to the income. Dad was recovering from pneumonia which almost took his life and, to make matters worse, drought and crop prices kept Shackelford County farmers in a state of financial despair. Through it all, we as a family never considered ourselves as being poor. Mom saw to that. She reminded us frequently of how much better off we were than a lot of "other folks."

I never met any of those "other folks" but, looking back on it from this vantage, they must have really been destitute.

Motivated by Mom's cheerful nature, we were a happy clan.

MOM WAS NOT partial to Jack, but she did consider him to be "special." That never bothered the rest of us because, come to think of it, we felt the same way about him. He was the second oldest son—the third oldest of the six kids—and he was born with a personality that set him apart.

His smile was quick and his dark eyes beamed with the joy and mischief that defined him. Jack was an outstanding athlete, tall and rangy, and his job delivering ice door to door developed arm strength that belied his size.

At least in my mind, he was the best football player on the Moran Bulldog team. And, in a small way, I contributed to his training. For training, he would sometimes eschew the bus ride and jog the several miles to school. When I was in the first grade, he would put me on his shoulders to enhance the challenge. I loved it.

TODAY, WHEN everything from a loaf of bread to a bottle of germ killing soap carries an expiration date, I think back to times when we gathered eggs straight from the nest and put them on a shelf alongside the mustard, mayonnaise, syrup, jelly and such. We preserved the meat from a hog-killing with a sugar cure product.

Some items such as milk, cream, butter, etc., did require refrigeration. Jack would bring home a block of ice, which Mom wrapped in an old quilt along with the other perishable items. Mom often wished aloud that she had room to "keep" more stuff.

Ice was available in blocks weighing 12½, 25, 50, 75 and 100 pounds. Along with the $5 per week salary, Mr. Sherman allowed Jack to bring home a 75-pound block every Saturday. Not only was it used for refrigeration, but Mom also would chip off enough for iced tea or lemonade.

Besides having no gas or electricity, we also had no running water. A cistern just off the back supplied water for our every need. An outhouse down the path from the backdoor completes the picture that illustrates the times . . .

THAT SUNDAY morning, now seventy years ago, Jack got up early and walked into town. It was surprising to see him coming up the lane driving the ice truck. He was never allowed to bring it home. After delivering the Saturday ice, he would return it to the ice house and walk back.

When Jack backed the truck up to the front porch, Mom opened the door to see what was up and her eyes almost popped out. In the bed of the truck was a big, beautiful oak ice box. It looked brand-new. In the years to come, Mom would eventually own refrigerators that were top of the line. But, never, ever would any among them match this.

A wealthy woman on Jack's route had got an Electrolux. Jack asked what she would take for the old ice box. She said $7. Jack offered $5 but said he couldn't get it until payday. She agreed.

I HAVE NO idea how old the old icebox was at that time. But it was in perfect condition, which was a good thing. It had much more work to do.

Our circumstances improved with the times, and in early 1945 we bought a new home in downtown Moran. But due to wartime shortages, appliances were not available. Dad managed to get a new gas range but, not only did Taylor Furniture not have any refrigerators, there was a long list of people awaiting their arrival.

So, that icebox was moved into the space built for a refrigerator where it served us for another year until the new one arrived. Even then, Mom would never let it go. Neither will I.

Jack went into the Army a few months after buying the ice box, and on Dec. 29, 1944, he was killed in the battle of Peleliu.

A friend knowledgeable in antiques recently visited our place in the country. The old icebox naturally caught his eye. He looked it over closely, made a whistling sound and said, "Do you have any idea how much that thing is worth?"

"Yes," I said, through a wistful smile. "I really do . . . "

## Veggies

MANY YEARS AGO, as a boy with lots of time and no transportation, I developed a special touch—better make that "knack," being as it was more of a thump than a touch—that would determine without fail anything you wanted to know about a watermelon.

It wasn't just a matter of being able to tell whether it was ripe enough to steal . . . uh, pull. I could also tell you whether its insides were red or yellow, and even whether it had yet weathered a frost.

Science has recently debunked the thumping method of determining a melon's ripeness. That might have carried more weight with me had Science not been the same folks that said that Sam Killough and Bill Brewster couldn't remove warts simply by rubbing on them.

Now I have great respect for Science—as long as it knows its place and stays there, goosing mice that are stalled in the maze, peeking knowingly at beakers held just above eye level, or looking into microscopes while saying such things as hmmm and Eureka. Because what scientists know about watermelons and wart removal will bring them neither fame nor grants nor tenure, their knowledge of both is based more on spontaneous assumption than extensive research.

But I digress.

I STARTED this piece off with the purpose of telling what all I don't know about certain fruits and veggies, but got sidetracked into boasting about something I do quite well.

First, I must admit right about here that, unlike many of my gender and marital situation, I love grocery stores. Maybe that has to do with getting to spend all that time surrounded by food and fixings.

Also, there is apt to be something humorous to occur right where you would least expect it. A good example happened a few days back in the dairy area, where I watched a lady sneak a single egg out of a carton and drop it into her purse. I knew immediately that she was not an experienced shoplifter by the look on her face when the snapping of her purse was followed by a squishing noise. I had hoped to be near the cash register when she started wiping the runny yuck off her checkbook. But I was distracted by an offer to try a sample of peach cobbler and forgot to follow her.

Incidentally, my youngest son works for a large grocery company in San Antonio where part of his job involves going to store openings. Once when I was down there, I went with him and pointed out a few things I thought might be helpful. One involved how they stock the shelves.

I pointed out the great distance that separates the pinto beans from the cornbread mix. Same thing with the catsup and potatoes. Earlier, I had made the same suggestion to a young man who used to run my favorite Lubbock store. He gave me the same strange look I later would get from my son, only without the mutter. That he soon afterward got promoted into management indicates that he had strengths in enough other areas to offset the lack of synergy in his stocking scheme.

MEAT, BEANS, and potatoes have always dominated my food choices. Most fruits don't flutter my taste buds. Bananas are always too ripe or too green, apples are hard to bite, pears are too mealy, and grapes leave your mouth full of seeds and nowhere to spit.

Prunes keep me dashing off without time to even grab up the sports section, plums look sweet but inevitably taste sour, and raisins are just grapes with a bad history.

Melons in most all forms are fine, but a cantaloupe that didn't grow up in Pecos will probably disappoint you.

Avocadoes usually wind up in guacamole, which I never eat. That's because once at an outdoor festival I dropped a scoop of it on the ground. A nearby cat approached it, took one look, then covered it up. My attitude about guacamole is purt near the same as that cat's.

And, in my personal opinion, more good food has been ruined by coconut than by burners left unattended. I hate biting into a delicious looking cookie only to find it laced with coconut. That ranks right along with having already taken a mouthful of milk when you notice the expiration date was a week ago Thursday . . .

And lately, as if polluting sweets weren't bad enough, they've even started adding coconut to shrimp. Can beer be far behind . . . ?

MY TWO VERY favorite fruits are the exact same ones that I know absolutely nothing about selecting. Oranges and peaches both are very adept at promising more than they deliver.

For example, I have seldom seen an orange that didn't look attractive and that didn't emit an aroma that prompts salivation. I couldn't count the times that I have been lured into picking up a few of them, squeezing them gently and bringing them, one at a time, up to my nostrils for a final check. Same thing with peaches. They always look delicious, feel just right, and smell like you can imagine them tasting.

I often think back to a bunch of oranges I once bought in Brownsville that were so sweet and juicy that I almost wanted to go back and eat the peel. And few things can compare to July peaches in Fredericksburg—even though the absolutely best peach I've ever eaten was one I got from a fruit stand in Ruidoso.

The mark of a good peach is that it's so juicy you'll need a shower as soon as you've finished eating it. One reason I remember that one in Ruidoso so well is because my favorite shirt still carries its stain. I'm looking at it right now . . .

AS I MENTIONED, I have no problem getting home with a watermelon that's everything I had expected it to be. And, finally, I developed a way of knowing whether the oranges and peaches that I bought will be as sweet and juicy and tasty as I had hoped: If I buy just two or three of either, I'll get home to find them flat dab delicious. However, if I go ahead and get a sack full, each one will taste like a wad of cardboard that's been in the sun all summer.

Several weeks ago, coming back from San Antonio after the July peach season had passed, we stopped in Mason at a roadside stand. The lady said her peaches came from Colorado, which has a later grow-off. She even gave me one to sample, and it was very good. I bought a whole bushel.

To give you an idea of how that went, I am sitting here right now on the patio, lobbing them set-shot style toward a garbage can. Deuce ran and grabbed one of my misses. He immediately put it down and went back to chewing on his tennis ball.

If you happen to look for me in the store, I'll be easy to spot. I'll either be standing by one of the sampling tables, thumping a watermelon, or scowling at the peaches.

Actually, I'm pretty good at all three . . .

## EVERYTHING YOU NEED TO KNOW ABOUT RED BEANS

THIS DAY GOT off to some start. I not only caught my wife money-laundering, but I went and spilled the beans.

Even though that's *exactly* what happened, it's not what *really* happened (despite how it sounds, that sentence did not get accidentally imported from one of the Leach v. Everybody stories).

The truth is my wife did not money-laundry. She laundered money. What she did was toss into the washer a pair of britches that had four one-dollar bills still in the pocket. And I didn't squeal on her. What I did was spill purt near a whole pot of beans—literally. They went all over the place, the counter top, the cabinet door, and in and on and around both of my house shoes, which already were housing my two bare feet.

That the two mishaps occurred on the same day prompted me to tailor them into a single sentence in quest of dramatic impact. When, actually, what this piece is really up to is to establish, among other things, that I may not know about some things but I do know about beans.

In fact, beans—red beans—are probably why I am alive today. But that's only part of the story.

TO BE THE simple staple that I grew up believing them to be, red beans became an item whose description

I would later find myself defending among people who didn't know beans about red beans.

When I was in the army, it took me to places where nobody spoke fluent Shackelford County. You can imagine my horror the time in Virginia when I ordered a side of red beans and what I got was kidney beans. Maybe the two are related, but I don't believe the Moran pintos would have claimed kin.

And, speaking of pintos, my friend Adams—a country boy who should know better—tried to convince me that pintos and red beans are *not* one and the same. Shame on you, Bill, for reading Yankee publications.

What's even worse than that, a kid moved to Moran from somewhere else and called them *brown* beans. Granted, they cook into a color that's more brown than red; but, then, how many redheads actually have red hair? Unless dye has been applied, it's really more of an orangey brown. I married a personal example.

I realize that by now there will be those among you who can hardly wait to take pen, aka keyboard, in hand to question my expertise on this very important topic. Don't waste your time.

Although I don't recall having ever read a word about red beans, or even pintos, and I know for sure I've never done a search on them via Google or anybody else, I already know everything there is to know about them.

That's because I have spent a lifetime researching the product itself. And those who have different views of what red beans really are, I suspect, are the very same people who sugar their cornbread.

THE DAY I spilled that batch of beans all over an otherwise spotless kitchen, I already was feeling depressed by the chore at hand. I could sense my late parents cringing from above at the exact sort of waste they had oft warned me about.

This big pot of beans would have fed their large family—two parents and six kids—at least two meals. And, except for Sunday when fried chicken would be added to the menu, beans would represent both the entrée and all the sides except cornbread (sans sugar, of course). My family not only survived on red beans, we thrived on them.

My wife loves to cook beans for a couple of good reasons. One, she knows how much I love them. And, two, she can just add a pan of cornbread to complete my meal. Being from a background that was, let's say, a little less pedestrian than my own, she finds it amusing to watch me crumble up my cornbread and cover it with bean juice before adding a sprinkle or two of pepper sauce.

That I sometimes gnaw on a large onion that I hold like an apple while eating my beans and cornbread does not amuse her. Sometimes her advanced degrees in foods and nutrition seem to cripple her sense of humor . . .

And neither she nor my three sons ever learned to fix their beans the same way. They certainly didn't understand my stashing a piece of cornbread to later be crumbled into a glass and soaked with milk for a bedtime snack.

But I digress.

THE POT OF beans that I was disposing of was a casualty of our lifestyle, not my appetite.

My wife will fix a big pot of beans, figuring that I'll gladly be feasting on them for several meals. Then, for whatever reason, we'll find ourselves either eating out or dashing off somewhere for a few days, leaving the beans to grow stale in the fridge.

That's where this story was heading originally.

Because of our trend toward impetuous mobility, I had to learn the hard way how to get rid of beans whose use-by time has expired. As a kid, if we happened to have any leftovers, Mom poured them out for a delighted Tuffy, our dog who otherwise would be chasing down a rabbit for supper. That wouldn't work with Deuce, for many reasons.

Anyway, after learning that a garbage disposal can handle only so many beans in one gulp without an assist from a plumber, I devised a better method.

At the grocery store, I always answer "plastic" before the sacker even finishes the question. That's partially because those bags are multipurpose; but, mainly, I figure it's a good way to get back at Al Gore, whom I'm still ticked at for inventing the Internet.

So when I get ready to empty the leftover pot of beans, I simply pull the plastic bag over the open top of the pot, sort of like putting a toboggan cap over your head. Then I turn the entire thing upside down until all the beans have emptied into the bag. I tie a knot in the top of the sack and carry it to the trash can.

What I learned the day of that spillage is that before you turn the pot upside down, make sure (1) that there's not a hole in the plastic bag, and (2) that you don't have it only halfway over the sink.

Everything else about red beans I obviously already knew.

My wife, though, is still researching what all to do with money . . .

## NEW YEAR'S COMMUNION

IF YOU THINK there's not magical powers packed into one tiny little legume, you should have seen how it had me hopping around exactly one week ago today.

That, of course, was New Year's Day, the day that often follows a night of raucous revelry. But it was neither the raucous nor the revelry that sent my feet floorward at an hour when even most chickens were still in the sack.

We had spent a delightful evening, uneventful but age-appropriate, with a few close friends who were gathered with Morris and Janice in their beautiful new home to watch 2011 come to an end. Good riddance, we all agreed, glasses held high and lips poised to pucker.

It was only after the midnight toasts, the usual round of goodbyes and the fairly short drive back home that panic struck. In fact, I was already in my pajamas, had set the coffee pot for a later than normal perk time and was about to join my wife, who already was snoring away, when panic struck.

I dashed into the kitchen, swung open the pantry door and began a can-by-can inventory of every shelf. Finally, my fears were realized:

There was not one single black eyed pea in the house. By then, it was after 1:00 a.m. and, not only would nothing be open at that time of day, I wasn't sure about how it would be later on, after sunup and beyond.

New Year's Day is a holiday for many operations . . . perhaps even my favorite grocery store. Now, Chris is a very accommodating store manager, but even if I knew his cell number, I don't think he'd like opening a back door to sell a single can of goods.

And, even if it is already open, who knows whether there will be any left . . .

SPEAKING OF black eyed peas, I am trying vainly to remember the first time I was exposed to this tradition that's as Texan as my very drawl. I do know two things—it was a long time ago and, in this state, it's as ritualistic as communion itself.

Even though it has no religious connections that I'm aware of, there is that similar urge to comply with something that's at once both abstract and compelling.

Now both my parents, as pragmatic as the times that spawned them, pooh-poohed at everything they identified as superstition. Neither ever really believed that breaking a mirror brought seven years of bad luck, that opening an umbrella in the house would jinx something, that you never moved on Friday, and that you always left the broom behind when you did move. I could go on and on about things they didn't believe in but always avoided.

But when it came to black eyed peas, they didn't even pretend disbelief. Hey, times were tough in those days and they didn't want to contribute to their getting any tougher.

Anyway, for as long as I can remember, we always had black eyed peas every January One. That's the one day they replaced red beans as the dinner and supper staple.

Of course, we had black eyed peas at other times, too. Mom would spend hours snapping those things until she had a "mess" of 'em big enough to feed her large brood. She cooked them shell and all, along with all the ham and fats that were such an important part of our diet before doctors invented cholesterol.

Just the memory of those peas, served alongside onions and cornbread, makes me want to run right out and start a garden.

But I digress.

I SAT THERE last Sunday, sipping coffee and reading my favorite newspaper and watching the pendulum on the clock swing to and fro. I figured that if the store did happen to be open, it wouldn't be this early.

I thought back to our early years in Lubbock when the only store in town that opened on Sunday was way out there at that five points intersection. Neither Furr's nor Piggly Wiggly nor Safeway would open. And, in later years when they did, only selected items could be sold. Blue Law, it was called.

When I decided it was time to make my move, to set out on a modern day hunt, my prey a can—any brand, any flavor—of black eyed peas, I jumped into the shower where I normally do my best thinking and wondered what my dad would think of my fretting, which was still intensifying.

Now my dad did not believe in worrying. He considered it to be an absolutely needless drain on both your time and your psyche. He contended if there's a problem looming out there, determine what you can do to head it off, then do it. But once you determine there is nothing you can do about it, move on to something else. Worrying sure won't change anything but your own comfort and attitude.

He also once told me that there's a very good chance that the crisis you see coming down the road will wind up in the ditch before it ever makes it to you.

SOON, I WAS parked in the lot, heading for the door at a pace hastened by a burst of delight that the store was obviously open for business. Now I had only to be concerned that the seasonal run on that particular merchandise had not exhausted the supply.

You can only imagine my excitement when I found the shelf stocked with a variety of my quarry. There not only was plenty of them, but I also had choices. So I grabbed a store brand complete with snaps and dashed to the front, where I had my choice of checkers, all sleepy but friendly. Back home I now could relax, sip coffee, and finish reading the paper.

I caught myself pondering the problems of the world. If my ol' man was right, many of them will slide off into the ditch before they ever arrive.

One of them already did . . .

### Of Beans, Sweet Milk, and Evolving Language

MY BUDDY Morris and I were sitting in one of the restaurants here at the OFH getting ready for lunch. Neither of us paid much attention to the menu because, in that particular eatery, we pretty much knew it by heart.

So when the waitress came to take our order, Morris asked for chili. I ordered a bowl of red beans with cornbread.

"I'm sorry, sir," she replied, very politely, "we don't have red beans."

"But you ALWAYS have red beans," I protested.

"No, sir," she said. "The only beans we have are pinto beans . . . "

A few weeks later, same campus, different restaurant, different young waitress, same result: "I'm sorry, sir. We don't have red beans on the menu today, only pinto beans."

Leads me and all other members of Texas heritage and rural upbringings to ask a couple of common questions:

"What were these kids raised on?"

Why do they think God invented cornbread? And chow-chow?

THOSE TWO incidents led me to remember a trip to San Antonio several years ago. We were going to visit the kids and my late mother-in-law, then a ninety-year-old with the same mental and physical dexterity that had spurred her through a life of many facets.

Roberta had been, among other things, a school teacher, a rancher, and an accountant. She had also been a bridge player whose focus on the game and her relentless competitive spirit took the word "game" out of any game she played.

But I digress.

Along about Coleman, it occurred to me that we would be arriving in Fredericksburg right at lunchtime. That wasn't exactly accidental, being as it is one of my favorite eating spots, and I have a habit of planning all driving trips using taste buds as my compass.

"Roberta," I said, "how do you like German food?"

"Don't know," she replied. "I've never tried it."

That surprised me somewhat because, as much as she had traveled, I figured she'd been in Germany. I knew she had been across Europe, even Moscow, where she was six weeks after having hip replacement surgery. She was in her eighties at the time.

Anyway, once we arrived I led them to my favorite restaurant. I asked Roberta what she wanted. She said for me to just order whatever I was eating. I did.

When asked for our drink orders, my wife and I asked for tea. Then they asked Roberta, and that's when things started going downhill.

"BRING ME A glass of sweet milk," Roberta replied.

"I'm sorry, ma'am, but we don't have SWEET milk . . . "

"You don't have sweet milk?" Roberta responded in a voice more demanding than asking. "Then just bring me water . . . if you have any of that!"

Turned out that the water was the only thing she liked about the meal.

Soon the waiter returned with a loaf of black bread, one of my favorite items. I sliced each of us a piece and while I was buttering mine, I saw Roberta staring at hers.

"What's wrong with this bread?" she asked. "It looks like they burned it."

I tried to explain that's how it was supposed to look. She wasn't buying.

When the meal came, Roberta nibbled a bit but mainly just moved things around with her fork. I felt terrible. I knew she had been hungry when we stopped to eat, and one thing Roberta never did was miss a meal. The cabbage she did eat wouldn't have been all that filling.

As we were driving away, I apologized to Roberta, saying how sorry I was that she didn't enjoy her meal.

"Well," she declared, "it only stands to reason that a place that doesn't have sweet milk wouldn't know how to make bread . . . "

On the way home, I promised myself, we'll hit the McDonalds in Brady . . .

GENERATIONAL changes affect not only the diet but the language itself. Not only have pinto—nee red—beans lost their position as the main staple of the Texas supper table, it also has been a while since family members had a choice of buttermilk or sweet milk to wash down their cornbread and, uh, red beans.

And our generation can't get too smug when questioning the culinary vocabulary of millennia. Or, for that matter, their very language, which has been affected by devices that many of us can't even turn on.

A couple of years ago, a friend of mine was on a train trip with her hubby when she received a text message from her daughter. She didn't know how to answer it, so she enlisted the help of a young lady walking up the aisle.

Sure, said the girl, I'll be glad to answer the text. My friend gave her the message, she typed it in, hit the Send arrow, and headed on to her seat at the other end of the car.

To appreciate the impact of what happened next, you need to know that my friend is a woman not only pure of heart but equally pure of language.

This lady—to protect her identity, I'll just call her "Nan"—got a startled reply from her daughter, who was well aware of her Mom's inability to text. She demanded to know, "Who are you and what have you done with my Mother?"

"Nan" chuckled about the message but didn't understand the first three letters that opened the response. So, she called out to the girl several rows ahead and in a loud voice, asked:

"What does WTF mean?"

The entire car responded with a hushed silence, then a few chuckles and, finally, unbridled laughter.

Somebody quietly explained it meant "what's goin' on."

Close enough for the time at hand . . .

By now, WTF has worked its way into the everyday language, however electronically. It and SNAFU, an acronym with a military origin, have now joined the vocabulary, typed or spoken, of many who're unaware they just dropped the F-Bomb.

In fact, even though it's not the way she would have put it, WTF is exactly what Roberta was thinking when she first saw that black bread.

Neither language nor food is exempt from bad taste . . .

## Housekeeping Filled with Pitfalls for the Amateur

HAVING USED the exact same recipe is no guarantee that the meatloaf you cooked will come out tasting just like the one that Mama used to make. "Reasonably close" was both my hope and my expectation.

Despite my following carefully the exact directions— still in her very handwriting—what came out tasted not like Mom's or my wife's but, rather, more like something you'd expect at a restaurant: all right, but not like Mama's or, for that matter, what my wife always fixed using that same recipe.

For the past three years, I have been chief cook and housekeeper, due to my wife's lengthy illness. Fortunately, here at the OFH we have four exceptional restaurants and a lady who regularly comes in and cleans up my place. Still, I hate for the cook stove and other appliances to just stand around with nothing to do.

Actually, all those duties started six or seven months before we moved over here.

I had help from a professional caregiver who also was to prepare the noon and evening meals. And she was a great cook—of Mexican food. Nobody could do that better. She even made her tortillas from scratch, and I'm here to tell you, not even Abuelos or Garcias and any of the other exceptional Tex-Mex restaurants, of which Lubbock has plenty, could come close to hers.

Problem was, as much as I love Tex-Mex, I don't want it at every meal. Unfortunately, her skills at my everyday favorites were, uh, not so great.

IT WAS ABOUT that time that my friend Linda suggested that I get a Crockpot. After she explained to me what they looked like, I dashed out and bought one. Following the instruction booklet and Linda's directions, I soon had a rump roast en route to my table.

And it came out great! Thanks to her having advised me to get one of those plastic liners, my cleanup came off without a snag. Then, guess what? I put my brand-new Crockpot in the pantry, on a shelf alongside two others just like it . . .

Sometime before that, my friend Janice had taught me how to cook baked potatoes in the microwave. Sounds simple. But I would never have thought about rubbing olive oil over them, then punching several holes with a fork.

Next, Linda taught me how to use that same cooker to make a big pot of red beans (pintos, to all you foreigners from up north). And Gladiola already had instructed me on cornbread. One yellow packet, a couple of eggs and a cup or two of milk is all that took.

Between my newly found culinary skills and the abundance of restaurants right here on campus, I promptly progressed from a couple of excessive pounds to several excessive pounds. And inches. By the way, if you ever need some britches let out, I found a great alteration shop . . .

But I digress . . .

BEING THE HEAD homemaker is smitten with challenges much greater than cooking. I have found some things that only the female of the species can do. Primary among them is dealing with Saran wrap.

Its first challenge has to do with pulling out the exact amount you need. Then, according to directions on the box, it should tear off as easily and accurately as, say aluminum foil or waxed paper, both of which are incarcerated in the same type container.

Not! As soon as I got my free arm unwrapped from what I had unreeled—do you suppose Saran makes that stuff from the skin of a boa constrictor?—I tried to tear it off using the little teeth attached to the lid. It immediately crumpled and the entire roll came flying out of the box.

So now I'm on the kitchen floor trying to press it out flat while holding it with my knees in order to make the desired cut with scissors. Next thing I know, my arm, the scissors and my very psyche were in the clutches of this demonic fabric. I looked over my shoulder just in time to see the rest of it roll under the dishwasher.

HERE AT THE OFH, they will gladly make your bed if you'll have the sheets laundered, folded, and placed neatly and accessibly.

Now, running the washer should have been easy. I stuffed the sheets in on top of some smaller items, such as dirty socks, underwear, washcloths—the like.

I then tossed in a lid full of detergent, closed the lid and hit the start button. I stood there and listened to the water gushing in. When it filled and started to swish the load back and forth, I went on to other callings.

After a bit, I heard the most gawd-awful racket coming from the utility room. I walked in to hear the washer giving out a loud "Whomp! Whomp! Whomp!" I started to retreat only to see the dern machine following me to the door!

Despite it angrily bouncing back and forth, I got my finger on its Off switch and shut it down. I raised the lid and found both sheets on one side of the machine and all the smaller stuff on the other.

By simply reloading the wet sheets I corrected the washer's bad behavior and pushed it back into its assigned nook.

After successfully drying the clothes, I found something even more challenging than the bleeping Saran wrap: The ever-popular fitted sheet.

I tried everything from the Internet on down, only to discover that the single human being who can fold a fitted sheet is the guy who puts them in the package at the factory. It's certainly not the Internet instructor, who starts out by saying, "Put the four corners together . . . "

Fitted sheets don't have corners, dammit! Just pockets. Corners, you can fold; pockets you can't. The only credible instruction would be simple: Wad the bleeping thing up and stuff it into the drawer.

Not a great day. But I did learn something in the process:

Some aspects of this housekeeping gig prove that making a meatloaf may be the easiest thing you do all day . . .

A pan of cornbread

# THE OLD DAYS

Burle's brother's '48 Chevy

## SECRETS OF A BYGONE ERA BARED BY BOYISH HUNTER

THIS IS A story that should not be told without preamble. It occurred during a different era, an era that was both governed and measured by the work ethic; it was a different area, an area where rural boyhood thrived without the sophistication of city life; it was a different set of rules and standards, both of which were sustained more by internal cognizance than by external laws . . .

It was a time when the word "allowance" had a plethora of meanings, none having to do with money doled to those who merely stood and waited. It was a time, an area, an era where getting something for doing nothing might have been everybody's fantasy but nobody's fact.

What we actually are revisiting is a culture, the very way of life for those whose needs and wants and expectations had not been seasoned or skewed by an enlightened world that lay sprawled out somewhere beyond their realm. At school, the curriculum focused on honing academic skills and blending them with behavioral morality. The Three Rs seemed to be more comprehensive, if not downright meaningful, when supplemented by the painful consequences of misbehavior . . . misbehavior that required neither definition nor interpretation beyond that of the applicator.

The setting, then, is rural Texas at a time of innocence, at a time of people being at peace with themselves. It was a time whose naiveté should not be confused with ignorance, which did not abound.

THE BOYS WERE walking against the briskness of a north breeze across turf not yet warmed by a hesitant November sun, laughing and talking and horse-playing their way across a field of winter wheat. They had walked the county road until it passed Clyde Bynum's house, then they climbed through the barbed wire fence and headed across the field toward Pennell Bluff, a rocky cliff that dropped off almost without warning onto a plateau of grazing land below.

The field we crossed belonged to the Bynums but none of us had the foggiest who owned the pasture with the magnificent boulders and crevices and caves and every form of wildlife known to the region. On the way out to the field, we stopped to remove a length of barbed wire form the fence, taking it from the overwrap at the corner post. That allowed us to get what we needed without affecting integrity of the fence itself.

Jackie, John, Cuz, Tuffy, and I were very familiar with this entire section of land, having made this trip many times despite our youthful years. Sometimes, it was just for fun. But most often it was to go "skunk huntin'," which we did in the combined interest of fellowship and revenue. Jackie would fashion the wire into a skunk retriever; Cuz was the knife man, a guy who could skin a skunk with uncanny speed without damaging the pelt and, consequently, its value; John owned the hide stretchers, wooden devices used to pull the pelts taught for scraping and seasoning.

Tuffy had the hardest job of all, beginning with sniffing out potential dens and letting us know when we had bounty. Then, once the skunk was pulled into the open, he applied his own form of euthanasia. My part was . . . well, Tuffy was my dog and he was a critical part of the hunt.

Besides that, he went where I went, and ol' Tuffy knew no fear. He is the only dog I ever knew of that fought a raccoon in the water and won, and he also was a great snake dog. He had been rattlesnake bitten so many times that the venom no longer had significant effect.

He also liked to take on the skunks, knowing how sick he would get in the process. In our gang somebody had to do it, so that was ol' Tuffy.

ALL OF WHICH takes us back to the culture and its influence. Boys grew up with fathers and brothers who worked hard and who, for sport, mainly hunted and fished. Their hard work paid little. Cash flow came from selling butter and eggs to downtown grocers and an occasional fryer to individuals for their Sunday dinners.

As kids, we had some sort of job or no cash. I was working at a dairy out on the Albany highway, going there early in the morning and returning after school each day. There were also miscellaneous means, such as mowing an occasional lawn and collecting pop bottles for their two-cent deposit.

Skunk hunting was more about income than it was about sport or fun. Pelts, which we sold to either Rufus Andrews or Mister Patterson or Dan Anderson would bring from fifty cents to a dollar, the average being about six bits. In perspective, a show ticket at the Capitol Theatre in Moran was nine cents, a milkshake at Doc Martin's drugstore was fifteen cents, and comic books would run you a dime apiece. None of us were yet into girls who, come to think of it, might not want to get all that close to a skunk hunter anyway.

How we selected our buyer had much to do with their own cash situation. The time we got twenty one day— fifteen from under one rock—we had to scatter the sales out among all three, being as not any one of them happened to have that much money on him that day.

REMOVING THE SKUNKS was quite easy. Jackie would separate the two strands of the barbed wire, forming a v-shape at the end. He would probe it into the den until it hit its target, then he would carefully crank the wire until it had a grip on the skunk's pelt, hopefully its tail. Once the skunk was attached it was simply a matter of dragging it out, jumping into the clear, and leaving ol' Tufffy to complete the project.

Cuz and Tuffy

Obviously, we didn't always avoid the spray. At home, our respective moms would fumigate us to the best of their ability, lecturing us appropriately, and hoping that our shoes would elude the teacher's olfactory sensors the next day. Of course, none among us had a spare pair of shoes.

Years passed, turning boys into men and exposing old cultures to new ideas and new thoughts and, often regrettably, bringing new ways of measuring old values. Boys grow into men, and men go off in quest of other worlds, other cultures, other challenges. In their new lives, their skunk hunting pasts remain hidden from new associates who would never understand, leaving false assumptions room to fester.

It was indeed a different time, now tucked away in history. But much of what those boys learned has lingered through the years.

Only the aroma was left behind . . .

## GERMLESS MORAN

MORAN—I was parked here the other day, sitting between the two rows of buildings that once vibrated with the murmurs of life, when a guy on the radio began talking about the Swine Flu and how it could be quickly conveyed between one person and the next. He said schools, where kids lived closely and behaved like, well, kids, would be something akin to a human germ culture.

I had docked here against the curb in front of Garland Shelton's old barber shop, just across the street from where

Jinks Raymond's store used to be, and was sitting there absorbing the youth-filled memories that still flow freely up and down the sidewalks and alleyways that were so much a part of whatever we all would eventually become.

The Moran kids were much a part of the rural culture that spawned and shaped them, typical in most every way of a generation that would fortunately see America at its best. Although it is tempting to refer to that era as the "time of innocence," it would have been difficult to find a pure form of innocence amid the mischief that seemed to be boyhood's chief propellant.

That having been said, it proved to be a Moran generation that turned out all right. Its kids went on to run banks, teach school, work in the media, craft cabinetry and defend the country. One or two even went into the ministry.

I shuddered at the thought of how the Swine Flu would have wrecked all that. It was a generation that did take certain things seriously, but fretting about the possible presence of germs was not among them.

I SMILED SILENTLY at the thought of words that were so much a part of the Moran vocabulary of those days . . . "Bite-ums" and "No bite-ums," "gimmee a puff," or "dubs on first swallow." None has a place in the culture of today, and that has to be good.

In health class back in grade school, we learned about bacteria, and those weird looking microbes later would be viewed up close through the one microscope available in high school biology class. But, to us, all that was vaguely interesting but totally irrelevant.

We were taught, both at school and at home, to wash our hands, brush our teeth and change socks fairly regularly. But that was done more in the interest of society than public health. My Mom used to say, "If you can smell yourself, that means others have been smelling you for three days!" That impressed me to the point that each morning I would catch myself sniffing each sock before I put it back on.

But I digress.

THOSE RULES OF propriety over a personal snack or goody applied only if it was proclaimed immediately. Sitting here, I could almost hear Rabbit coming out of Doc Martin's drugstore yelling "No Bite-ums!" and wielding a double-dip chocolate cone over which Danny would argue that he'd already claimed "Bite-ums."

Had Danny been right, Rabbit would have been honor-bound to hold the cone over for his buddy to have a lick. Usually, it was clear who had spoken first but, again according to the code, all ties went to the one who owned the cone (or candy bar, sandwich, etc.). Why it was so important to get the protected phrase spoken first was that the guy who beat you would not be the only one entitled to partake of your bounty. One kid's "Biteums" worked for the whole gang.

I recall one especially horrible incident when I walked out of the house with a big, red apple. I had no idea that four of my buddies were outside. One of them shouted "Bite-ums" before I even knew they were there.

Adding injury to the insult, I not only didn't get a single bite of my apple, I got hit with the core.

Remember the old game of *"Apple-Core-Baltimore, who's your friend?"* The unfortunate person who was named got pelted with the core . . .

Some rituals left behind go un-revived for good reason . . .

SO IT IS NOW obvious to me that whatever germs one of us had were shared by the whole gang and, along with it, a goodly portion of the entire school.

Much of that had often been brought to mind before I ever got down here or had heard the guy on the radio telling me how to avoid Swine Flu, which he called "H1N1." Political correctness should consider the feelings of hogs, I suppose. But, being neither a PC guy nor one who likes to use alternating letters and numbers, I'll stick with the term Swine Flu, thank you.

Watching football on television, where close-up shots frequently show the players getting a drink from a squeeze bottle through a straw-like thing that they very carefully avoid touching with their lips, always reminds me of how it was back here, all those years ago.

The student manager of the Moran Bulldogs brought water onto the field in a carrier that held a half-dozen quart milk bottles (remember when milk came in quart bottles, complete with cream lines?). Each one of us would take a couple of swallows and pass the bottle on to the next guy.

It only occurred to me recently that the Moran Bulldogs football squad was made up of a couple of dozen kids who practiced varying degrees of oral hygiene. In fact, I remember asking one of the guys if he ever brushed his teeth.

"Nah," he said. "It makes my mouth bleed. And, besides that, my sister keeps hiding the tooth brush."

BEAR IN MIND that ours was a generation of country kids who were brought up drinking cistern water out of an oaken bucket, taking each sip from a long-handled dipper that was shared by friend and family alike. Drinks at mealtime were served in individual cups or glasses (i.e., Mason jars), but when you just needed a periodic quenching of thirst, you dipped it from the bucket.

Our cistern was right next to the back porch and water was drawn by a hand-operated crank that lowered and raised the bucket. The supply—which served for drinking, cooking and personal hygiene—was dependent upon rainfall. I remember watching my dad connecting the gutter that ran the length of the eaves to a tin pipe whose other end was placed into the opening of the cistern. He always waited a few minutes for the roof to wash off before catching any of the water. During times of drought, Dad hauled water in from town or anywhere he could find it.

So with such intimate oral exchanges of food and water or puffs from the same hand-rolled and licked cigarettes, the kids who trotted up and down these very streets would have been likely victims of today's Swine Flu. But maybe not.

We never seemed to catch anything else . . .

## MEMORY BRINGS MELODY TO THE SOUNDS OF SILENCE

IT WAS A time of historical transition and the noise of change played in the background—not ignored, mind you, simply unheard, buried perhaps by the seemingly more relevant thoughts of the day . . .

Sitting on the front porch of our house, which faced the busiest residential street in town, I watched—in an order since forgotten—Sam Diller ease past in his brand-new Packard, Will Plummer plug on by in his Model T coupe, Dan Anderson clop past in a wagon pulled by a team of mules and, of special significance, Pete Morris galloping along, astride his dun-colored gelding.

That was Moran, Texas, circa 1949, a time when cultural changes were coming rapidly but not with such speed as to leave history buried in the wake of its process.

Dan Anderson still made his living plowing and cultivating local gardens with his team of mules; Will Plummer retained and drove daily the two Model Ts he'd bought new almost forty years before; and Pete Morris used his horse to run his twice-daily paper route. Sam Diller's having the latest Packard was nothing new. Except for the war years when car manufacturing was halted, he bought one every time the new model hit the floor. He continued that practice through 1956, the year when the once prestigious automobile ceased to exist.

EVEN THOUGH I tend to remember Moran as a quiet town, it really wasn't. Only in the late hours of night and the wee hours of morn did silence prevail. As a kid who, along with a buddy worked at a dairy just outside the city limits, I can remember riding through the downtown area and hearing only the sounds made by the tires of our two bikes rolling against the pavement.

We both were still too sleepy to be conversant except to occasionally point and chuckle at the night watchman dozing in his pickup. Henry's main responsibility was to make the rounds of all businesses, checking and re-checking whether all doors were locked and there was no activity within. It was not yet 5:00 a.m., and between then and when we arrived back in town two hours later, people would begin to stir. Even then, the sounds of activity did not overwhelm . . .

Moran had its mixture of early risers and late sleepers and, because we delivered milk by the quart to most residents, Bill and I knew who fit into both categories. Those were days when all houses were left unlocked and, when requested, we went through the front door and straight to the refrigerator (or ice box) to make sure the special order of whipping cream was not exposed to the morning heat.

In that process, we also learned who in town snored loudest . . .

CITY ORDINANCES in Moran were few and often ignored. Those that were observed did not address live-stock; thus, among the regular sounds were mooing of a cow staked on a vacant lot to graze, the braying of Dan Anderson's mules and, just before daybreak, the crowing of roosters from any number of yards.

The majority of people owned a dog, and all were kept outdoors. Strangely, few wandered off their property unless thusly lured by a female canine in the mood for love. Our dog, Tuffy, almost never barked. If a strange dog strayed, or even threatened to stray onto our property,

Tuffy's menacing growl, backed by his considerable heft, inspired a sudden change of direction.

The neighbor's chow, named Snuffy, was one of the few house dogs in town. When he did go outside to "do his business," Snuffy sometimes threatened people walking down the sidewalk, but even he carefully avoided Tuffy's turf.

Rattles and cars were frequent companions in those days when pre-war automobiles were still in the majority. Loose or missing bolts and screws and absent or leaking mufflers were either ignored or tolerated. Hey, the old car runs good and that's what counts!

SITTING THERE on that front porch, I might hear anything from the steel tires on that mule-drawn wagon, the un-muffled engine of the Ford tractor Jake Burton used for both farming and general transportation, or the melodic whistling of some person trying to dislodge a haunting tune from his mind.

That's without mentioning conversing pedestrians and playful kids and the bike of some boy who'd rigged a playing card to flutter against the spokes, hopefully emulating the sound of a motorcycle.

Then there were the "functional" sounds of the time: A fire whistle mounted high off the ground not only served its obvious purpose but, at 12 noon six days a week, it sounded a single bleat. That told workers and others for more than a mile away it was time to break for lunch.

Then there were the bells, one in the grade school building and another at one of the churches (I believe it was the Church of Christ), that beckoned the citizenry.

THAT DAY, as the time of the automobile was stretching into its third decade as the dominant mode of transportation, I had no way of appreciating what I had just witnessed. Only now do I realize that what a teenager observes as boredom will someday be recognized as history.

How often I think of the people and things that I allowed to merely slip through my life only to appear later as a trove of treasured memories.

But I digress.

Although car production was back in full swing, the throwback to days preceding the dominance of the "horseless carriage" was disappearing before my very eyes.

Dan Anderson's mules, which were still a significant part of the village landscape, would be the last of the draft animals that constructed this very town site late in a previous century. The paperboy's pony would likewise close the door to the only mode of transportation either of my parents ever knew when they were my own age.

So, was Moran actually a quiet little town? Perhaps so . . . but its memories grew louder with the passing of time.

I heard them plainly today . . .

## SMALL CLASS HAD ITS ADVANTAGES . . . ALSO ITS DRAWBACKS

A FEW YEARS ago I got this call from an old friend who runs the school houses for a neighboring town. Graduation was just around the corner, and he wanted me to give the commencement address. I considered it to be at once a rare opportunity and a nice way to goose my ego. You see, those of us who exercise mainly on written verbiage do so for a good reason:

Most words of more than a couple of syllables are much easier to spell than they are to say ("sacroiliac" comes immediately to mind) and, of greater import, my Shackelford County drawl doesn't generally muddle up in my typing.

The churning my ego got from the invitation lasted until I got home and heard my wife asking casually what others already had turned them down . . .

Commencement addresses usually are given by people who combine diction with scholarship or by people who are left over after the diction and scholarship folks are already taken. She did not say that, in so many words, but I know how she thinks.

ANYWAY, WHEN the guy called me, he did not mention who else had been contacted and, frankly, it never occurred to me to ask. Hey, the ceremony was still three or four days away, and that's the sort of question that might have come to mind had he called on the morning of the event. What he did say, sort of apologetically, did get my attention.

"We're a small school," he said, humbly adding that "we only have a hundred graduating."

*Only* a hundred? You call that a small class, I thought, my mind rolling backward to my own graduation night. There were six of us.

Granted, we were an extra small class, even by Moran High standards. We had a large class in front of us and an

Moran High FFA class (1951)

even larger one behind us. All told, ol' Moran High was about the size of that school's graduating class.

I found myself wondering how much noise we could have made in home room had there been a hundred of us. After all, our class motto was—no kidding—"Little But Loud."

WHAT HAPPENED to my class was the result of the state's decision to adopt the 12-grade system. I was in the first grade at the time. Most everybody in my class skipped the second and went straight on to the third. Several moms, my own included, did not want their little darlin' moving ahead that fast. They figured we'd be graduating too young, or whatever.

Anyway, we started out small—probably about a dozen that first year—and sort of underwent numerical atrophy after thereafter.

On a side note, one of the students we lost along the way recently surfaced right here in Lubbock. Cora Beth Whatley joined us in the 10th grade but moved on after just one year. Since her arrival in Lubbock, we've talked several times. I was mildly crushed that, in trying to remember what I looked like, she had to find my picture in an old yearbook.

Not I. As soon as I heard her name, a clear vision of her (circa 1950) came abruptly into view. Cute girls obviously are easier to remember than, er, reasonably dashing boys . . .

But I digress.

WHERE I WAS heading with this had not to do with speaking vs. writing, or me confessing to having remembered the names and faces of all the girls who moved away (if we ever lost a boy it probably was considered good riddance, competition for the remaining girls being what it was).

The point is that such a small class had advantages and disadvantages so distinct that you tended to remember both. In other words, there was good news and there was bad news, and both of them had to do with Individual Attention.

Those who needed extra help with algebra got it. Those of us who needed to get by with something got caught.

Six kids are easy to watch, even by a yawning teacher. A teacher writing on the blackboard knew who was talking because she recognized all our voices, even when we whispered.

I swear, I hear "Turn around, Burle!" in my sleep . . .

SOMETIMES THE traditional class projects that were no sweat for a class that had a couple or three dozen kids became a heavy load for the six of us. One had to do with my own introduction to journalism.

The mascot for dear ol' MHS was a Bulldog. Accordingly, our yearbook was called "The Kennel" and our school paper was—get this—The Bow Wow. And it gets worse: I wrote a gossip column titled "The Sniffing Puppy."

Anyway, it took a lot of work for us to publish either, let alone both. And only now do I stop and pity Miss Haggard, the teacher in charge.

As juniors, our class was responsible for the concession stand at football games. Being as all four boys played and the two girls were cheerleaders, our moms did the cooking, the selling, and the cleaning.

The money made by the junior class—we also put on a three-act play and charged admission—was used for another small town ritual known as The Senior Trip. We may have been the first class in MHS history to make that week-long trip without spending a dime of our parents' money. On a per capita basis, we were loaded.

Perhaps the best thing about being from a small town, a small school, a small class are the relationships that develop. The six of us literally grew up together, harboring no pretenses, assuming no airs. It's hard to be phony around people who already know where the warts are. They not only know the name of your dog, they know when and where you got him.

Generally speaking, being from a class of six students has served me well through all the years to come. On every resume that I would eventually compose, I made mention that I was among the top ten graduates in my class. Come to think of it, I think I wrote that down for the guy who introduced me at the graduation speech.

I started to put down "in the top five." But with my luck, somebody would've bothered to check.

## HOG PENS OR CLASSROOMS, LIFE'S TOUGHEST LESSONS ENDURE

EVERYTHING I EVER needed to know, I learned in a hog pen.

That's not exactly true, but it was right there among nearly a score of registered Durocs that one of life's most lasting lessons anointed my psyche like so many buckets of slop splashing into a wooden trough.

The story all started with a field trip late in the school year when I was a senior matriculating in, among other things, vocational agriculture. Football season already had been spent and, with spring near at hand, Mister Hudgins lined up a number of field trips to neighboring farms and ranches. Mister Hudgins taught ag and personal character in whatever order he deemed appropriate, and the senior boys of Moran High provided him ample room to develop both.

Now, before the story unfolds, it will be helpful to remember that it happened at a time in rural America when smoking not only was acceptable but was purt near expected. Camels and Luckies were enjoying record sales and, instead of having a Surgeon General's warning down the side of its pack, Old Gold was boasting of having "not a cough in a carload." Probably 90 percent of the men folk smoked ready-rolls without offending anybody.

Mister Hudgins was a member of that majority, as were several scoundrels among his charges. And, with the passing of that final football season, they were even beginning to come out of the closet (more accurately, from out behind the bus barn).

ARRIVING OUT AT Oscar Wise's place to view some prize Herefords, Mister Hudgins, as was his nature, lit up. It was then that Jack, one of the bolder smokers in our group (he even carried a pack in his shirt pocket) posed what proved to be a very telling question:

"Mister Hudgins, if you can smoke on a field trip, why can't we?"

Being both a forthright and thoughtful man, he pondered the question a moment, then responded:

"Okay, that seems fair. But there's one condition. If you smoke around your parents, you can smoke when I smoke . . . which is never on the bus or any school property." Being also charged with our discipline, he added a stinger: "But I warn you right now before you light up, if I am ever around any of you when your dad is present, I am going to offer you a smoke, and you'd better take it."

My first reaction was, Gulp! But then I weighed the odds of him coming around when both my dad and I were at home and felt relieved enough to drag off a deep puff and send a smoke ring swirling across the landscape. I figured my demonstrated skill would imply that I was one of them who smoked in the pool hall without cupping his hand around the cigarette and not taking frequent peeks out the door to see who might be coming.

SOMETIMES, A kid can't buy any luck. Mister Hudgins showed up one day just as I was adding maize to a self-feeder, and was commenting on how great this last litter was looking when my prideful look turned to sheer panic. I looked up just as my dad opened the gate and was greeting Mister Hudgins. My mind flashed back to the time several years earlier when my father caught me and my cousin with a sack of Bull Durham. The resulting sting began to echo on my flinching backside.

Clearly, I would be subjected to a form of discipline that was more sophisticated but equally effective . . .

As the two walked toward me, I saw Mister Hudgins reach for his shirt pocket. I immediately found a reason to dash off to the opposite side of the pen, where I adjusted an insulator on the fence. This sort of exercise went on for what seemed to be hours. I swear, that guy became a chain smoker. And each time he reached for a cigarette, Zoom! I was off to another part of the lot.

My fortune then turned. Mom beckoned Dad to the phone, Mister Hudgins bade him goodbye and thoughtfully drove away.

MISTER HUDGINS was at once our best friend and our worst nightmare. An Aggie by education and probably even religion, his barked out order to "grab yo ankles" preceded activity that, in reality, hurt you a lot worse than it did him. Corporal punishment was a way of life in

those unenlightened school days and, through his application of that paddle emblazoned with the AMC logo,
Mister Hudgins moved that all the way up to Sergeant
punishment.

When I arrived at the ag building the next day that
paddle came immediately to mind, and I wasn't sure why.
After all, he did not get around to offering me a cigarette
. . . nah, forget it; he knew.

So it was no surprise whatever when he looked at me
all during class and reminded us that he would be drop-
ping in now and then to check our projects as he was preparing semester grades. Glaring straight at me, he reiter-
ated the promise he had made to "you smokers" out at
Mr. Wise's farm.

"Be advised," he said, dismissing the entire class
except for me, whom he wanted a word with.

Gulp, I thought.

"THAT WAS AN interesting visit to your place yesterday," he said, raising his palm to let me know he wasn't
ready to hear me speak. "Your hogs are in great shape, and
Red Cloud is ready to show anywhere, anytime. Your project deserves an A."

I sputtered, and his hand came up again.

"I'm not through, you know that. While I found your
work to be great, I discovered some flaws in your character. I had you sweating bullets out there, didn't I?"

"Yessir."

"Let's talk about those flaws. I want you to name
them."

One by one, I mentioned honesty, integrity, truthfulness, each drawing a nod of his head.

"You cannot have a successful life without those basic ingredients," he said, watching my fear mate with guilt. "But," he added, raising my spirits, "I think those were lapses, not actual flaws. I am counting on you to address them at once. And, while you're at it, there's one more you failed to name."

He called it, "Poise under pressure."

I learned a lot in the hog pen that day. But, then, I had a great teacher . . .

## FROM AUTRY TO ZHIVAGO, MOVIES CHART PHASES

THERE ARE two topics that, because I'm exposed to them at varying intervals, I write about only on fitting occasions. Even then I begin with the following disclaimer:

When discussing movies I am no Wm. D. Kerns; when science is my topic I am a regular Werner von Gomer.

Actually, I hate science for the same reason I detest math: Both disciplines are too dern exacting. Because of that, I focused my educational challenges on the study of words, any one of which is tolerant of interpretable dexterity. Also, English and journalism put less pressure on one's gray matter.

As far as I know, I have never had an IQ test—except in the Army, which keeps all such results as a military secret (that was possible back then because email and electronic devices had not yet been invented). Anyway, I always felt comfortable that my IQ would at least reach the level of my body temperature.

But I digress.

I started out to write about movies I have seen, some quite recently, and—unlike my friend Kerns—only once have I ever known who directed them. In his world, not knowing who the Director was would be like a sports writer covering a football game without knowing who the coaches were.

That's not a perfect analogy, being as I've never heard a movie audience boo the director. The point, though, is otherwise valid.

MY TASTE IN movies has evolved, at least somewhat, right along with my expectations. Years ago, when the Capital Theater in downtown Moran was my venue of choice, my measurement for a good movie was one that had a lot of shooting and no kissing.

The Saturday matinees were special. Not only did you get a lot of action throughout, but it led up to a dramatic ending. Either the main character would make a heroic stand or the posse would arrive just in time . . .

Still bothers me why the wheels on the stage coach always turned backwards.

But, again, I digress . . .

Looking back, I can tell exactly when that criterion began to change. One was when I started focusing on Elizabeth Taylor herself and not on her pretty horse with the funny name.

The other was when The Outlaw came to town. The gunfight scenes were great (remember when Billy the Kid clipped Pat Garrett's ear with a perfectly placed shot?). But then it occurred to me that I also liked the way Jane Russell looked in that blouse whose top six buttons were missing, and then figuring out what probably popped them off . . .

Not long after that, I began meeting this one girl at the show (after her parents had paid her way in). I still remember the first time I dared hold her hand while wishing mine would stop sweating.

The excitement started at school earlier that day. I passed her a note asking if I could sit by her at the show that night. She turned around, smiled and nodded. My life's priorities were about to make a sudden change. But that's another story for another time. Besides, I'm still smarting over the rejection slip it got me from *Cosmopolitan* . . .

MY TASTE IN movies has evolved considerably since those cherished days of yore. Actually, they haven't changed as much as they have broadened.

I still long for good Westerns ("oaters," as they are called by whoever makes up the crossword puzzle). Two of my all-time favorite movies were *High Noon* and *Shane*; in fact, *High Noon* may have been my very favorite until *Doctor Zhivago* came along . . .

Both those movies feature conflicts of Love v. Heroism and do so in dramatic fashion: Here's Gary Cooper risking both his life and his brand-new marriage to Grace Kelly to face Frank Miller, who has vowed to kill him. Then in *Shane*, here's Alan Ladd whom Jean Arthur falls in love with despite being married to Van Heflin and the mom of Brandon deWilde. So, right after shooting hired gunman Jack Palance, Alan Ladd rides away with Brandon deWilde chasing after him shouting over and over, "Come back, Shane . . . come back Shane . . . "

Meanwhile, Jean Arthur has to get re-accustomed to being married to a dirt farmer.

Incidentally, it was *High Noon* that introduced us to both Ms. Kelly and Lloyd Bridges, whose young butt Cooper had to kick just to prove he was still sheriff and Bridges was still just a deputy.

MY MOVIE GOING comes in spurts, one of which I've had in the past couple of weeks or so.

First off, there was this show based roughly on the professional life of Florence Foster Jones, a woman who gained fame while singing off-key. Meryl Streep was great in the title role; but, then, what has she not been great in?

Then I saw *Hell or High Water*, which was surprisingly terrific. Jeff Bridges did a great job as a Texas Ranger stationed in West Texas, so great in fact that it was easy to forgive him for saying "Ole-ny" for Olney and "Brah-zos" for Brazos.

The last one I saw was *Sully*, which basically was about a veteran pilot who crash landed in the Hudson River. All 155 passengers walked (floated?) away alive. The gist of the story featured Sully insisting on the one hand that he was not a hero while, at the same time, having to prove to investigators that he was.

I would rate those three movies from purty good to dern good. I don't know how that would translate into those little stars the real critics use. And I don't know who directed any of them, which is normal for me.

That one director I do remember? It was David Lean who directed *Dr. Zhivago*. And the reason I remember him is because I intended to write him a letter thanking him for all those scenes involving Julie Christie.

That's because they reminded me of why my hand got all sweaty that night in the Capital Theater in downtown Moran . . .

## SUITS

A FEW WEEKS ago, I was bundling up several large garbage bags with clothes that either no longer fit or that had spent months—a few even longer—in a guest room closet that had become my auxiliary repository for things unused, unwanted, unworn.

While folding and stuffing it all into containers for the trip to Goodwill, I began counting the suits—all still in great shape—that were included among the items bound for the needy. As I pondered about whose backs all these garments eventually might be covering, I wondered about the practical nature of donating suits, ties, and dress shirts. Would Goodwill make better use of jeans and khakis and such? Even an Oxxford, a Hart or a Burberry would give little protection against the cold.

Anyway, as I was searching the pockets of one of the suit jackets, a line from an old Tom T. Hall song suddenly sprang to mind . . . its tenure for dormancy far outdistancing even the oldest of these threads. Tom T's song was about a guy who had died, and he was expressing guilt about not attending the funeral, explaining that he couldn't go because "the problem is I don't even own a suit."

THAT BROUGHT back a bevy of memories, most having to do with how people were expected to dress for funerals and such during the era Hall had written about in that song, "The Ballad of Forty Bucks."

Now, I have always been a fan of his music, that particular number being my favorite. That's because I grew up with some people whom it brings immediately, and warmly, back from some cherished times of yore. It also reminds me of a time when, like Tom T. Hall, I didn't own a suit . . . well, I sort of co-owned one, but that's getting ahead of the story.

I grew up in an era—and an area—where most men's wardrobe consisted mainly of work clothes, a pair or two of dress pants (which oft times were khakis, neatly starched and ironed), and one suit.

The suit was worn on Sundays for church, at whatever intervals church attendance occurred, and funerals. Mainly they hung in the closet, down at the darkest end of the rod.

MY SENIOR YEAR in high school, we made a family trip to Abilene to pick out a suit for me to wear to graduation. Kids were not included among those expected to wear suits and ties for church; but, unlike today, they were expected to wear one under those gowns that were a part of the commencement exercises.

I also had to go to Cisco and have a studio picture made for *The Kennel*, which was the name of our yearbook. Hey, we were Bulldogs! I still have that copy of the annual, showing me looking distinguished in this double-breasted suit with a necktie this wide. You could tell by my expression that, way ahead of the commercial, I liked the way I looked.

Before we headed out to get the picture made, I had to run up to Aunt Merle's and get her to tie my tie. Dad could have done it, but he spent too much time explaining how unacceptable it was that I couldn't do it myself. Later on, I would find that the Army sergeants would feel the same way about it, but that's a different and unpleasant story unto itself.

I DON'T KNOW whatever happened to that suit. The last time I remember wearing it was when Jack and Shirley got married a couple of years later. But what I do remember is that when I got out of the Army, my older brother who still lived at home at the time had helped himself to my civilian wardrobe, including a pair of char-treuse boots I bought just before I got drafted. A wiseacre buddy told me that if the draft board had seen me wearing those boots, I might not have been called up.

But I digress.

The reason my brother helped himself to my clothes may have been because I had worn out all of his while he was gone. He finished his Army hitch just before I started mine.

ANYWAY, HE DID spring for himself a suit, a dark blue, single-breasted number with two inside pockets. He said I was welcome to use it anytime we weren't heading for the same funeral. Neither of us spent many Sundays in the Moran Methodist Church, a fact our Mom mentioned often.

As I have written hereabouts before, my wife and I eloped. Because we kept the secret from everybody, I had to think up a story before running by his place to pick up the suit. He had gotten married in it a year or so before.

THE NEXT SUIT that I owned all to myself is one my wife scrimped and saved up for while we were starving our way through college. It may not have been the best Penney's had to offer, but it sure looked pretty to me.

I wore it to work on my very first day at *The A-J*, only to learn everybody else in the sports department wore sports jackets and ties. No male would dare show up in our newsroom without a coat and tie, even sports writers and photographers. I still have a picture of my old sports staff, and we all were dressed funeral-ready, with one exception. We had a summer intern whom we cut a little slack in deference to his age and financial circumstance.

All of which brings us back to where all these suits came from. After a few years of writing sports, the corner offices decided I was having far too much fun. Being a sports writer is great, partially because the bosses not only don't know where you are, they don't even know where you're *supposed* to be. I have always thought my move into management had certain punitive implications . . .

Whatever the reason, that's where this accumulation of suits began. For the next thirty years, I wore a suit and tie to work every day. Toss in church attendance, funerals, and all the other ancillary functions a community expects from The Editor.

As a retiree, my daily attire has reentered the comfort zone. Sneakers, jeans, and just any old shirt fit my present lifestyle just fine. But not wanting to find myself in the same embarrassing situation that ol' Tom T. Hall got into, I did hang onto a few suits and ties.

I had to. I think my brother finally wore out that other one . . .

## PPR

THE MORE I read about the Police Panty Raid (PPR) that occurred over on Slide Road the more my mind gets tuned to thoughts of community standards—community standards being the litmus test that supposedly determines whether something's crudely vulgar or merely delightfully inspiring.

Being a person who has by now grown relatively long of tooth (the word *old* is no longer PC under the standards of *any* community), I have seen that criterion evolve drastically through the years. To those who just asked "How drastically, O Wrinkled One?" I offer a quick example:

Back in the house where I grew up, had I spoken the term that even kindergartners now use to say "ticked off," I'd have been slapped away from the dinner table so sharply that my mouthful of pintos would've pelted the back bedroom. The "F" bomb (and I'm not talking stomach gas) would have drawn capital punishment or purt near. Nowadays, in conversations involving all genders, it appears regularly, not only as a noun but as a verb, an adjective, and even an occasional gerund.

One of my little Baptist buddies once got his mouth washed out with soap because his mom misunderstood when she heard him talking about one of those spotty dogs that ride on fire trucks. Another had his *Nyoka* and *Wonder Woman* comic books trashed because the attire they wore did not meet household standards.

It was that strict, really.

AS OUR COMMUNITY standards here in River City have grown tauter and tauter of late, the trend in other places—college campusi come quickly to mind—have relaxed considerably since the days when I matriculated at one of our state's largest institutions.

When I started dating this particular co-ed, the rules at the girls' dorms were stifling. If they weren't in by 10:50 on weeknights (11:50 on Saturday night), they were locked out.

Boys, who went generally ungoverned, were then left idle right at the shank of the evening, leaving them vulnerable to the clutches of mayhem. Even in that precinct which was inconveniently dry at that time, beer and college guys had a way of finding each other. And, otherwise, there was always the college swimming pool to sneak into. It was surrounded by a Cyclone fence topped with several strands of barbed wire, on which little strands of denim and khaki attested to frequent breeches of its security.

Nowadays at that same institution, the precinct is wet, the campus police force has grown a hundredfold, and boys and girls live and maybe do whatever they please under the same dormitory roofs.

But I digress.

MORAL STANDARDS tend to bend and sway not with the times, nor with the officials who tend them, nor even with the mindset of the public itself. It seems to be strictly an individual thing, a matter of choice.

For instance, adult beverages provide an ambiguity of philosophy that crosses all lines—economic, ethnic, social and even religion. While many of my dearest and closest friends enjoy a glass of wine, a frothy beer or a salted margarita, I have another set of compadres whose attitude about anything alcoholic is clearly from the opposite spectrum. Neither education nor sophistication has moved them off the notion that there's demon in any rum, mayhem in all martinis, damnation in every daiquiri.

To those folks, anybody who has even a beer a month is a drinker and he who imbibes more frequently is a drunk. They believe a drinker is better than a drunk, but he still ought to be ashamed of himself. That conflicts greatly with the philosophy of a guy I've known for years who often enjoys a bedtime bolt and, even though he is the typical social drinker, he believes it is therapeutically advantageous to give at least a semi-annual embrace to the handiest porcelain.

WEEKS HAVE now passed since the storied PPR and, despite all the publicity and its resulting fallout, I still have a lot of questions about that raid. Like you, I hear a lot of things from a lot of folks, some of whose thoughts are energized politically.

Many just see it for its humor. A wiseacre buddy of mine asked if I knew how many cops it takes to raid a nightie shop: Four—one to bust the offending clerk and three to study the evidence closely enough to describe it in delightful detail to all their buddies back at the cop shop.

A former city employee believes that it—along with the arrest of the male dancers—is an ongoing attempt by city hall to dampen the public's high regard for the LPD, thereby making it easier to lessen its share of the fiscal appropriations that some bureaucrats would prefer to spend elsewhere.

City Hall insists that it sent the police there only in response to a complaint from the public. What really got me was when they added, "we always respond to a public complaint." To which I have but two words, the first being "bull" and the other I'll leave up to your individual standards.

You see, I have personal knowledge that it just ain't so.

FOR A COUPLE of years now, I have complained about Berl Huffman's name being misspelled on a sign on the north loop, giving directions to a complex dedicated to him and all he's meant to Tech, this community, and everybody who appreciates wit that's soaked in wisdom.

In fact, I took my complaint all the way to the top. I brought it up during a lunch I had with Hizzoner himself, saying it needed to be fixed.

"Consider it done," the Big Guy said, emphatically. Months later, at a town hall meeting in my neighborhood that was attended by Hizzoner himself, I mentioned it again. That's when one of the staffers on hand volunteered that it was his area of responsibility and that I could consider it done.

As of the day of this writing, it still reads "Burl" Huffman. Maybe if I went out there and hung on it a pair of . . .

Anyway, by now, just about everybody has had his say about the PPR, its motivation, and where it will eventually lead us—in addition than that special edition of *Texas Monthly*, which annually reserves a page for Lubbock.

But, through it all, one thing has been determined. Community standards ain't always determined by the community itself.

## AGING AND THE AGED

EVERY NOW and then something happens that makes me wonder if I may be older than I think I am. One such example cropped up this very week.

A group of us were sitting around at our regular Tuesday breakfast meeting, jawing about this and that when somebody brought up the topic of Army coffee. I wondered aloud if the "new Army" still serves it in the old aluminum canteen cups.

A fella across the table said he didn't know about the new Army, that he had been in the old Army, back in *1996*. He seemed somewhat puzzled by the way my eyebrows suddenly moved about a half-inch higher up my forehead. And I can understand why, even though 1996 was the year I bought the socks I was wearing at the time.

Hey, if I had told him I had already been out for forty years when he went in, he probably would have wondered if a government mule had been among my initial issue. It wasn't. But an M-1 rifle was, along with all sorts of other equipment—including the aluminum canteen w/cup that brought up this subject to begin with.

So, I dropped the Army topic and began another subject with my friend Morris, who is among more than a few in the group who are even older than I am.

Time is a funny thing, a relative thing. My dad once told me that nobody is ever pleased with his own age. "People spend the first half of their lives wishing they were older and the last half wishing they were younger." There were a few times I can remember wishing I were older, most of them having to do with a Breckenridge, Texas, establishment called Partner's Place.

But I digress.

SPEAKING OF age, last weekend I had the unusual experience of seeing it from two wide ranging chronological spectrums (spectra?). We were at our place in rural Fisher County where I spent considerable time with my mother-in-law and a group of her fellow residents at an assisted living center about twenty miles up the road.

Roberta is four months past her 100th birthday and her friends around her are mainly within eight or nine years of that. Some even closer. A day later, we were entertaining our grandson Christopher and four of his friends from Tech, where they all are in their junior years.

Somebody once told me that being around young people makes you feel younger yourself. I've heard the same thing about being around older people. I can loudly attest that neither experience worked for me even though they came back-to-back.

At Roberta's place, I watched a group of her peers playing "Train," a game I have only recently been introduced to but have yet to get the hang of. Here were these Super Seniors doing it with scientific aplomb, definite strategies at work, and they weren't having to hesitate and count the spots on the dominoes. Hey, a double-six was as big as I'd ever had to deal with, and having a rock with eight spots on one end and seven on the other . . . well, the color coding ain't all that clear, either.

THAT VERY EVENING, back at the ranch, literally, Christopher's long-time pal Greg was rigging up his awesome looking telescope, getting ready to examine Jupiter and the bevy of moons that surround it. Being as Lubbock is the smallest town any of the five had ever lived in, such access to an unfiltered sky and its nocturnal brilliance was a treat. From our back yard, the only lights in sight were those shining down from a jillion miles away.

Now, using a telescope to look at the constellations was not new to my generation. So watching him rig up his tripod, then mount the device atop it was pretty much old hat. In fact, I was feeling pretty good. Here was a group of kids that helped me download and operate some neat apps, showed me how to do a couple of things with my computer, and sported cell phones that did everything but cook, finally doing something I could identify with. Then alas . . .

Next thing I knew, Greg unfolded his laptop, punched a few keys, and voila! Here on the screen were all the coordinates he would need to zero in on Jupiter itself.

Back in my day, I would spend half the night looking through the lens trying to locate the moon, even at its fullest. It didn't make me feel any better when he explained that his equipment was pretty pedestrian, that the "real nice ones" allowed you to program the telescope with what you wanted to see, then let it capture it all by itself.

When he asked me if I wanted to come out and look, he probably was puzzled by my reply: "No, thanks. I'll wait for a full moon . . . "

Instead, I made my way through the darkness to the barn, where Ol' Red was parked. I climbed in and just sat there for a while, carefully thinking about absolutely nothing.

It felt good.

THIS WAS NOT unusual, my using Ol' Red's comfortable cab as a place to ponder most anything but, especially, life itself. That old truck and I bonded long ago and our mutual alliance has never waned.

I did think back to that morning at breakfast and about the Army canteens of yore. I hated the bleeping things. By the time the aluminum rim was cool enough to not sear your lips the coffee inside was too cold to drink.

I recently tried to count the number of vehicles I have bought and sold since the day I rolled that brand-new red pickup off the lot. That was only a year or two after my friend got out of the Army. Maybe that's why 1996 didn't seem to be very long ago.

After you reach a certain age, feeling young ain't all that easy to do . . .

## FONE BOOKS

NOT MANY YEARS ago, the demise of the telephone book is something I would have found mildly upsetting. Hey, here was a part of our very culture being swept away on the wheels of progress which, to my age group, is a four-letter word.

Not all progress, mind you: I like the fact that I can drive a car more than 100,000 miles before turning it over to the junk dealers; and not having to use that little key to open my can of Folgers is an improvement. If I thought hard enough and long enough, I might add two or three other conveniences to that list. But that's not my topic.

It has to do with the recent announcement that the telephone directory will be discontinued, relegated to that flourishing landfill where memory is the smoldering ash.

Right now, I'd like everybody who thinks life was better before the cell phone to hold up his—or, dammit, her—hand. Politically correcting the long accepted syntax is another peeve.

But I digress.

NOW I'M NOT ready to say that I liked it better when we had only one phone *company*, but I'm dead sure about one thing: I liked it a whole lot better when we had only one phone *book*.

In fact, my theory is that it was not the social impact of the cell phone and similar technology that sounded the death knell for the telephone book but, instead, was the influx of inferior products that were being published and distributed in droves.

Lost in the process was the old traditional phone book and the culture that embraced it. Shoot, I remember being excited each year when the new directory would come out. And the arrival of a new phone book wasn't just a big deal to me, personally. It was actually news. Down at the *A-J*, the phone company flak—Joe Riordan was a name that comes quickly to mind—would drop by with an advance copy so that we could do a story on it. We always did, too, because we weren't the only ones excited about it.

First off, there was the cover story. The book always featured some local event or landmark. From there, the reporter writing it up would zero in on what would be every reader's obvious questions (how many pages compared to last year's book?) to the creative (whose name is the first one listed and whose is the last?).

But people had to wait until their own copies arrived to check the important things . . . like whether their name was spelled right and how many people whom they've never met had their same surname. Heck, I used to call all the Pettits (none would ever claim kin) and, because there was no such thing as Caller ID back then, they'd usually answer the phone . . .

A COUPLE OF days after the advance copy came, somebody downstairs would bring a large stack and place them on the newsroom floor by the elevator. They must have counted them, because it worked out that there was only one for each desk.

And, perhaps because reporters are born believing that the world around them is prone to thievery, they all immediately put their names on the new book. The office's notorious germaphobe, who was on the dayside staff, locked his up at night because that's when sports writers roamed the newsroom. He could only imagine what all they'd handled on the way to work . . .

Then, during the past year or so, phone books began coming in by the dozen and from every direction, cluttering every door stoop in town. And, once they arrived, they were about as inconvenient as they were unattractive. For some reason, they all adopted a small, square shape and were printed in a type face that, by comparison, made the words in box scores look huge.

I'm sure it all had to do with the cell phone craze and the competition of trying to be the book that winds up in everybody's car seat. Heck, I even pitched one of those cut-down versions in my car in case I needed to call somebody whose number isn't already in my cell phone.

Then, while cruising on the Loop one day, I opened it to get a number. And the act of trying to read it made me as dangerous as a Texting Teenmonster, being as I had the opened book pressed against my nose in an effort just to read the name, let alone line it up with its number. If I hadn't been afraid somebody would report me to Willie, I would have tossed the dern thing out the window. The rage was there, but messin' with Texas wasn't something I wanted to get caught doing.

I SUPPOSE IT'S only a matter of time before somebody publishes a book of cell phone numbers. As it appears now, we have produced one entire generation and the better part of another that doesn't even have a regular home phone—or, "land line," as the current vernacular dictates.

While I'm at it, I've got to say that I am as frightened by this electronic era as I am miffed by the boxy little phone directories. What's scary is that I can't keep up.

Now I got into PCs early on, buying my first one before the hard drive was even available. And, in the meantime, I believe I have owned every generation of desktops, including the two new ones I'm using now.

Where it all got away from me was at the cell phone level. I am totally happy to have a cell phone that just makes and receives calls and, if pressed, I will accept one that takes pictures.

But the only ones I have been able to find lately do all sorts of things that I can get done with some other devices that are simpler to use. The one I am carrying now seems to believe that actually calling and talking to somebody is passé.

Given a normal sized keyboard, I am far above average as a typist—as well I should be, given the number of sentences I have banged out during a fifty-something year career of peddling words door to door. But I am so bad at texting that I do it only in the interest of communicating with my grandkids. When it comes to typing with my thumbs, I am, well, all thumbs.

BACK TO THE phone book of yore, I did manage to hang onto the last one that found its way to my door several years ago. I plan to keep it . . . perhaps in the lard can with my 78 RPM records, Parker 51 fountain pen, and beer can opener.

It will be out of place, though. It would be the only thing in that container that wasn't replaced by something better.

Ma Bell may not have done everything right, but she sure put out a heckuva good phone book. Had to be good. It was the only one in town . . .

## Changing Times

IT USED TO be that you could smoke purt near anywhere you wanted to but had to be very careful where you cussed. Nowadays you can cuss purt near anywhere you want to but have to be very careful where you smoke.

Early on in my life, when I would hear Tommy Duncan croon about how "Time Changes Everything," it never occurred to me that it was more than a pretty song; it was prophesy set to fiddle music.

Listening to young people talk or just reading what part of their blogs you can understand, you'll be hearing and reading words that would have had every generation from Bob Wills to Early Elvis spitting soap bubbles until dawn's early light. Or dern close to it.

A friend of mine who's a retired teacher was recently doing substitute work in a rural West Texas school, the sort of environment where prudence once ruled by acclimation. So you can imagine her surprise, not to mention her chagrin, when a junior high girl in the class raised her hand and, without even being recognized, said in a loud voice, "Hey, Teacher. I've got to go (pee)."

"Look, young lady," my friend said, after giving her startled psyche a few seconds to settle. "You will address me in the language you would use if I were your grandmother."

The student, with a puzzled look, replied: "Well, that's exactly how I would say it to my grandmother. What's the big deal, here?"

The teacher insisted that in the future the girl was to ask to go to the restroom without explaining what she was going to do once she got there. Too bad that soap bars now come with For External Use Only written on every wrapper, and rulers are available only for drawing straight lines and measuring stuff . . .

A FEW YEARS ago while serving on the board of regents for my alma mater, we were asked to approve construction of two new dormitories. No big deal. Only after the ayes had overwhelmingly prevailed did somebody mention that both facilities would be coeducational which, to those of us who had done our own matriculating on that very campus, could just as well have heard the word pronounced "cohabitational."

"It's the trend," the administrator explained, "and it is what the students want."

Hey, it was what many of the male students wanted when I was an undergrad, but it was not nearly what we got.

Conversely, the pretty little co-ed I was dating back then lived in a girls dorm which, by today's standards, would be considered more Victorian than protective. Boys were not allowed beyond the lobby, where they were closely watched until their date came down to meet them.

The girl had to be back in by 10:50 p.m. (the dorm doors were locked at 11:00 p.m.) on all nights except Saturday, which got an extra hour.

Girls, during those days of being recognized as "the weaker sex," were protected accordingly. Boys, whose roguish behavior was assumed to be an uncontrollable part of their makeup, were subjected to no curfews. Boys will be boys, you know . . .

If a co-ed did anything deemed to be "un-lady-like," she had little hope of successfully explaining—let alone defending—her case. A good example was a girl who lived just down the hall from my future bride. She came back from a date with two problems. One, she had beer on her breath. Two, her pedal pushers were on wrong side out.

Nobody bothered to ask if perhaps her britches were like that when she left, or, if not, what may or may not have occurred during the time of their transition. Who was to say that she hadn't stepped on a bed of red ants and wanted to make sure that any of the varmints clinging on had an opportunity to escape? And, hey. If alcohol is good for a snake bite, it might also work on ant stings . . .

Just getting expelled was the easy part. The worst part probably came later, when she had to explain to Daddy why she was back home with all her stuff . . .

ANOTHER OUTFIT with which I had former connections is also feeling the gales of change that somehow blew in from the lee side of its comfort zone. It was called the U.S. Army and its membership was not limited only to those who applied. I and many others like me got there by written invitation mailed out by a group called "Selective Service."

But membership was limited to males not romantically attracted to other males—not openly attracted, at least. Females were not allowed into the regular outfits that were available to do the work of "real" soldiers. A woman could be a WAC, where she would serve in roles that were important but totally different than—and removed from—the duties required of the guys.

Nowadays, women in all branches of service have been rewarded by getting to do all the fun stuff such as marching, crawling through mud and ice, firing and cleaning weapons, pulling guard duty and learning how to rid the world of all enemies, up to and including 3.2 beer and SOS.

Although I'm one of those old guys who goes into deep rhetorical lamentation at the collapse of any tradition, I'm not sure that having females doing real soldiering is a bad thing. I'm sitting here thinking about how much more tolerable my duties in the Alaskan cold could have been. For instance, instead of the bunk on the other side of my Quonset hut being occupied by a Yankee from Connecticut it had been, say, a real Peach from Georgia.

I guess they still put that stuff in your food . . .

FORTUNATELY, I had already given up cigarettes when the near-universal smoking ban was adopted. And my making a parallel out of smoking and cussing at the outset of this epistle was not a non sequitur or even slightly disingenuous.

Once you're accustomed to doing either, it's awfully hard to quit. I can easily relate a five-hour flight on our company plane where no smoking was permitted to the time I mashed my finger while my old-maid aunt and her entire ladies bridge club was watching me hang a picture.

Also earlier in this story I used two acronyms (WAC and SOS) without telling what they stood for. WAC stands for "Women's Army Corp" (which, Mr. Obama, is pronounced "Core."). The last "S" in SOS stands for "Shingle." The meaning of the first "S" cannot be written here. But if you may hear it if you're nearby when some junior high student asks permission to go to the restroom . . .

Suddenly, after all these tobacco-free years, I'm wishing I had a cigarette. But I'd have a tough time finding a place to smoke the &%*#@ thing . . .

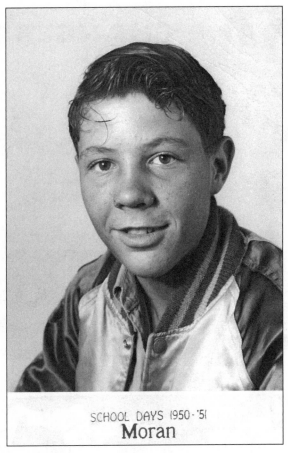

SCHOOL DAYS 1950 - '51
Moran

Burle at 16

# GAME CHANGERS

The Chapel at Fort Richardson, Alaska

## APRIL'S FOOL

AS APRIL SITS here today, taking its dying breaths, it occurs to me how much I always miss this month and, as well, how quickly it comes and goes. Of course, being a man of a certain age, I am impressed by the departing speed of purt near any month you can think of. February, for example, always leaves in a hurry because it spends fewer days on its getaway.

Unlike April, though, February is one of those months I'd just as soon skip altogether. It's too dern cold and, had the Super Bowl not been squeezed out of an overcrowded January, there wouldn't even be a football game to watch.

Some people are already wondering how I could hold in high esteem a month over which the Internal Revenue holds such domination. A valid question whose answer is simple.

By the time I was old enough to have much, if any, concern about things IRS, April was already residing in the positive channels of my very psyche. That occurred in and around Moran, Texas, back when a different world and a different time had their own set of priorities.

Being an irresponsible person works fine when there's really nothing to be responsible about. Moran's youth flourished in that environment.

IN THE EVENT that I haven't made this point clear in many previous etchings, I will attempt to do so now. That's because it is critical to the story at hand: If I could recapture my youth, put it into any setting during any era of history, it would be right back there in Moran, Texas, where and when the role of boyhood was played out with symphonic perfection.

Stated more clearly, it was simply the best place and the best time to be a kid. Period.

Much of that had to do with geography. From the front door of the pool hall you could hop on your bike and, within two miles of whatever direction you were riding, be splashing around in a swimming hole designed not by man but my nature itself.

Moran was surrounded by creeks, and two of them—Deep Creek and Battle Creek—ran deep and wide and were shaded by most any kind of tree you can name. Native pecans, cottonwoods, and sycamores were but a few that grew at the top of the high banks that defined the meandering streams.

If you wanted to go a few miles farther, you could swim or fish in Hubbard or Big Sandy. The creek nearest town was Post Oak but, not only was it the smallest of the bunch, it also was what went with whatever you happened to flush. Only that the indoor privy was in the minority kept Post Oak from being even deeper than it was.

But I digress.

WHAT ALL THIS has to do with my affection for the month of April requires more than a simple explanation but only a single topic: April was for me the Gateway Month.

For starters, its very first day was designed for frivolity, which took many forms. The obvious was the April Fools gags, which could be used to define two totally opposite personalities.

Group A consisted of those who spent the entire night of March 31 thinking up what all they could pull on who and how stupid they could make them feel. Group B consisted of those who spent the entire night of March 31 figuring out how to be compensated for having been the victim of Group A.

Little did we know that society its very self would someday be divided along those same lines and, furthermore, that would go on to become the respective philosophies of the two major political parties.

Is that not a Gateway or what?

AS A RESULT of a handful of senior students who devised and executed a plan that gave birth to an annual tradition, April became a Gateway Month for the entire Moran ISD.

The deal was that the entire high school student body would on April 1 assemble at a designated area far removed from the school grounds. It would be, effectively, a massive game of "hooky."

Obviously, there would be some logistic problems. A certain number—however few—of kids spent their every waking moment trying to please their teachers. You know the kind. Conviction without force was employed and, after several interviews with the most persuasive among them, even the reluctant eventually agreed that playing hooky would be a lot more fun than some of the other possibilities.

Another hurdle involved the kids who rode the buses. That worked out because the drivers normally let students off in town if they needed to buy school supplies. Hey, it was only a six-block walk and child abduction had not yet been invented.

April 2 that year was mainly spent explaining to parents and faculty about what happened the day before and, especially, who planned the whole thing. Nobody squealed.

The superintendent was on the one hand a disciplinarian but, on the other, was also a pragmatist. A year later on March 31, at a called assembly in the auditorium, he announced a new policy that would go into effect the next day. Instead of classes, we would have a school-wide field day. Classes would compete against each other in all sorts of sports events, complete with prizes.

The idea was so successful that it did become a tradition. While not as much fun as running up and down the creek banks, there were no repercussions.

The teachers' pets really loved it . . .

APRIL ALSO was the Gateway to spring by announcing its impending arrival through warm days, blooming plants, and a young man's fancy changing its course.

It was during that month when a school trip to Lake Cisco when a girl, whom he had never paid much attention to before, asked him if he would walk her through the hollow dam whose darkness and mystery added to the fame of that popular recreation area. As they walked toward the dam, she took his hand, which began to perspire in a pleasant sort of way. Once inside one of the lower and darkest levels, she stopped and gave him the first serious, down-to-business kiss he'd ever had.

It was a life-changing experience. Baseball gloves, bicycles, trading cards, swimming holes—they had moved into the farthest reaches of his thoughts, covered by the steam of hormones beginning to boil.

April is indeed a Gateway Month . . .

## SOLDIER'S CHRISTMAS

IT WAS A Silent Night that rolled on into morning and lasted throughout the day, decorated by the flashing brilliance of the Northern Lights and punctuated by the empty feelings of a homesick soldier far from home . . .

Although several feet of snow blanketed the ground from one horizon to the next, it was not the White Christmas that had inspired Irving Berlin a few years earlier; rather, it was a chilling reminder of the separation that marked an occasion dedicated to the love and warmth of family and friends.

It was an Arctic Christmas, my first away from home and, strangely, the first time I had ever really stopped and understood all the Christmases that had come before it. I then realized that the rewards of a close family could only be appreciated after that closeness of affection had been replaced by a distance in miles.

It was an irony that only added more weight to a joyous season turned heavy by all that was not there . . .

The day would come and go in a darkness that anchored a mood that was snugly tethered to the time. Winters in that part of the world came and went while the tilt of the earth kept the sun hidden around the clock. Then I realized that the light of day was another phenomenon that I had always taken for granted.

I LEFT CARR and Armstrong sitting on my bunk, sipping on a mixture of mess hall orange juice laced with vodka that had been smuggled in for an unauthorized party the night before. Perhaps because we were all good soldiers who worked hard at a mission that was at once critical and thankless, our off-duty antics were not closely monitored by those in charge.

Neither of my two buddies noticed that I had not returned from what they assumed was a trip to the latrine, which was a good fifty yards away. I walked instead down a trail leading to our battalion chapel, a picturesque little building whose prominence was highlighted by a thicket of aspens that surrounded it like so many sentries quietly standing guard.

I paused just outside the door, pondering on whether I wanted to go in and sit for a while, or just stomp on past, tracking through a layer of newly fallen snow. Then, to my surprise, the door opened and there stood Father Free, a major by rank and the battalion chaplain by assignment. Although he was a Catholic priest, he held services for all Christian faiths. He smiled and asked me to come in.

"Are you looking for conversation?" he asked, which was his way of asking if I needed to talk. My answer probably was puzzling, even to an educated man of God.

"No, thanks, Father . . . I decided I if was going to be lonesome anyway, I'd rather be doing it all by myself."

I turned and walked away, feeling foolish as well as lonely. The darkness now had become my friend.

Moving on deeper into the woods, I was stricken by a line from a Longfellow poem, the title of which I could not recall:

*The holiest of holidays are those kept by ourselves in silence and apart . . .*

MANY YEARS have passed since that lonely Christmas in an area whose distance has been shrunk by time and its effect on the travel habits of a highly mobile country. Alaska, which since has become a state and a popular tourist stop, was the last frontier; and, looking back on it today—only a few hours away from another Christmas—I am glad I was able to witness that territory as it had looked to Jack London some years before.

Unlike Longfellow, London's works did not cross my mind on that day, the bluest Christmas of my twenty-odd years on earth. Not only has Alaska since changed, so has Christmas . . . and so had soldiering.

Leaving a rural community in Shackelford County, I was exposed for the first time in my life to the diversity that I had read and heard about but had never seen. We were a totally protestant lot, there in Moran, and except for one Hispanic family that moved there to work in the fields and on neighboring ranches, we all looked alike, talked alike and, consequently, even thought alike.

What was different about Christmas back then was that it was celebrated by all Christians that I knew and respected by those of other faiths. It bothers me today that Christmas is not politically correct; that Merry Christmas and Christmas trees and even ol' Santa himself are being removed for fear of whom might be offended . . .

Burle on duty in the Arctic

BUT THE Christmas whose spirit I doused with my own tears of self-sympathy would look very, very appealing to any soldier serving in Iraq or Afghanistan. The only two perils lurking in my path that day were darkness and cold, and respite for either of them was but footsteps away. I think of the young men and women who, at the very instant I am typing this verbiage, have no assurance that the next step they take may be their last.

Sure, my folks back home missed me. My mom, who lost a son on Pelilieu just four days after the Christmas of '44, was now, one decade later, spending her first Yule season without her youngest child.

But she knew that I was safe . . . at least safe from anything not beckoned by my own reckless spirit.

A couple of years ago, I wrote about a girl named Amy whose husband had spent two years in harm's way, fighting in Iraq . . . a Christmas or two occurred in that span. She and her young daughter would have loved to have known he was in the Arctic . . . cold and blue—but safe.

CHRISTMAS IS, now as always, a special time for Christians and others who also get caught up in its spirit of giving, its premise that peace on earth is in the best interest of all, and that the love of family and friends is—if not a Divine Gift—a catalyst for universal tolerance and respect.

Beginning tomorrow, I will be surrounded by my sons and their families, my wife, and her mom in the serenity of our country respite, the peace and quiet interrupted only by the happy sounds of excited grandkids and the kibitzing of brothers, playfully enjoying their annual reunion.

As is my custom, I will be the last to turn in tomorrow night. On Christmas Eve, I typically spend an hour or so alone with my thoughts, enjoying the comfort of silence and surveying the pleasant memories of many Christmases past. I'll smile at the thoughts of that lonely Arctic Christmas all those years ago, then sober to the picture of those many young men and women stationed far away from all they love, thirsting for familial affection.

I will make it a point to remember why they are there and, in that same mood, take a vow to never allow the observation of Christmas to become a political casualty—not in my house, not in my heart—and certainly not in my greeting.

Merry Christmas covers it all . . .

## A SATURDAY ALMOST FORGOTTEN BECAME A SPECIAL DAY

THERE'S NOTHING particular to remember about that Saturday, all those years ago; but, based on our family's lifestyle and normal December weather patterns, certain assumptions can be safely applied. As a youngster halfway through my second year of grade school, I'm sure I was glad to have a day to do as I please. I didn't really mind school but, all things considered, I'd rather be at home.

Winters were different in those days. Houses were heated by wood-burning stoves and a fireplace that was the central gathering point for a family consisting of two parents and six siblings. Insulation had not come into common use and, on the coldest of days, any spot even a dozen feet away from a stove was uncomfortably frigid. I think of how it was to stand before an open fireplace, the front side of the body basking in the heat while the back shivered from the cold draft of a large room. But the aroma of burning mesquite provided a warmth all its own.

If winters were different, boyhood was much the same. Priorities started with plans to entertain myself: to go outdoors and walk on my stilts, play in the swing, or maybe help Ol' Tuffy scare up a rabbit.

For grownups in the family—my parents and four oldest siblings—Saturday was a workday. Weekends was a term not yet invented. Unlike today, Saturday was the big payday for retailers. That's when country folk came into town to shop. Moran stores stayed open late to catch those customers who worked their land up to last light.

IT WAS AN era of simpler times, of simpler needs and—perhaps the most significant of all—of simpler expectations. Success was not measured against what one owned but, rather, against what one needed. Food, clothing and shelter were judged only by their availability—culinary sophistication, lapel label, or height of roof peak were considerations for a day not yet imaginable, much less coveted.

*The Great Gatsby*, a story about a bunch of rich folks living in a mythical town, would've seemed to us as unbelievable as science fiction itself. Despite the popularity of the book, written two decades earlier, I doubt that more than a handful of people in our community had ever heard of F. Scott Fitzgerald. My library consisted of my Second Grade Reader. Period.

Although history now tells us the Great Depression ended in the late 1930s, that was not the case in rural Shackelford County, where drought plagued the farmer and the ending of the WPA and other similar programs left many to compete for jobs that were few.

Looking back on it from this vantage, I believe we were—as were all our friends and neighbors—impoverished. But we were not poor. Being broke was not the criterion for being poor. The poor were those unfortunate folks who recognized their financial situation and, accordingly, were guided by it.

My dad once proclaimed, "If the worst problem you ever have is a financial problem, you will have been blessed." By that decree, we were indeed a blessed family.

At least, we were on that particular Saturday morning...

SATURDAYS, AS we prepared to go into town, Bobbie and I sometimes had a dime each to "blow in," which was a popular adult term to describe money not spent on critical necessities.

My being the youngest in the family brought me some resentment from Bobbie because, until I came along, she was the "baby of the family." And, believe me, in a large family such as ours, that was an enviable status. And Bobbie did not let it go un-envied...

A dime went a long ways back then. It would buy a whole sack full of penny candy, purchase a show ticket at the Capital Theater (which actually cost only nine cents up to age 12) or, if you preferred, an RC Cola and a Moon Pie.

Just over the rock fence surrounding the Moran school campus, Mrs. Noland had a portable stand which she operated during the noon hour. Her hamburgers—I can taste them yet—sold for a nickel. If I had a dime for lunch—which was rare because Mom almost always packed ours to carry—I could choose between a burger and bottle of pop or, in my nearest imitation of Wimpy, could get two burgers.

For those who were not an avid reader of the funny papers, Wimpy was Popeye's rotund buddy who devoured hamburgers by the stack. Times at our house never got so bad that my Dad did not subscribe to the *Fort Worth*

*Star-Telegram*, which he read from cover to cover every night before bedtime. It was during those days that I became an avid reader of the comics, an addiction I enjoy today.

THAT TYPICAL Saturday mentioned at the outset as one whose significance, if any, has dissipated from memory. Whatever I did that day was easy to recreate in my mind because, as I said, most Saturdays for a second grader living in a rural area were typical, both in mode and behavior. But, as it turned out, it was a very special day.

That very Saturday would be the last of its kind.

It was Dec. 6, 1941, the last day of normalcy the world would ever know. The Japanese bombed Pearl Harbor the very next day. And even though WWII ended four years later, the world was changed forever.

So, that typical Saturday of my boyhood will forever remain silently significant as the country's last day of innocence. There had been many Saturdays before exactly like that one. But there would be none to follow.

I'm glad I was there for that one . . .

That Dec. 6. 1941, as a kid six months away from his eighth birthday, I had no idea it was the last day of normalcy I would ever see. Retrospectively, that part of that day exactly 74 years ago is easily remembered . . .

## LEE HARVEY OSWALD

WHEN I AROSE that morning and looked at my watch I was surprised to find myself so wide awake. Not only was it earlier than usual, but it had been well after midnight when I got home, and even a couple of hours later when I finally crawled into bed.

What was even more surprising was, after pouring my first cup of coffee, I walked into the living room to find my wife sitting on the couch, her eyes glued to the TV. It left me to wonder whether she had even gone to bed.

That was exactly fifty years ago today—and also a Sunday—and the both of us, along with the entire nation, was still in a state of shock. The events of two days before had altered the psyche, and the confidence, of a population that always believed it lived in the safest place on earth. Three rifle shots fired from a window of a building in downtown Dallas had thrown our country into a state of shock, stripped of its innocence and the naiveté that spawned it . . .

My wife, like millions of others, was stunned and hurt by the tragic event and the uncertainty that followed. And, because of my job and the improper decision of two universities, she had suffered through it alone . . . .

THAT PRECEDING Friday had started out on a cheerful note, an excited feeling about what had been a landmark in my career. By nightfall tomorrow, I would have completed my first season as beat man for Texas Tech athletics and, along with it, had begun writing the newspaper's lead sports column.

And what a year it had been! The Red Raiders were going into their final game of the season assured of at least a break-even season—a huge step from the 1-9 record from the year before. And, stocked with a crew of promising sophomores—led by Donny Anderson—things were looking up.

And, by day's end, I would be in Fayetteville, hearing for the first time the heralded "Hog Calls" in one of football's rowdiest stadiums. I made my way to the kitchen of our two-year-old home, poured a cup of coffee and joined my wife in the den. She was listening to "The Blue Danube" on our brand-new Curtis Mathis home entertainment center.

Little did I know that it would be the last time for several days that the Hi-Fi would be used . . .

I mentioned that my flight schedule would make it possible for me to join her in watching our favorite soap, *As the World Turns*, before leaving. As with all soaps, Friday is the day you don't dare miss.

It was about midway through that program when a CBS news bulletin broke in and announced that shots had been fired into the Presidential motorcade in downtown Dallas and unconfirmed reports said that the president had been hit . . .

HOURS LATER, while I was in Fort Smith, sitting in the hotel bar where all eyes were glued on the TV reporting all the happenings leading up to and following the assassination of a young and vibrant President, my wife was at home, dealing alone with all uncertainty that clouded the nation.

Assuming incorrectly that the Tech-Arkansas game would be postponed, as were the other four SWC games, I canceled my flight to Fayetteville. When Polk Robison, the Tech athletic director, called and told me that the Arkansas president had insisted that the game had to be played, I caught a ride on the team plane.

That meant I would be spending the night in Fort Smith.

As soon as I got to my room and pitched my luggage on the bed, I headed down to the bar, which had a larger TV screen—and, of greater import—other people. My need to be around others who, as I, were trying to sort through all the emotions that had set in like a fog, reminded me that my wife was at home with only two small sons who, even at ages five and three, sensed that something had gone terribly wrong. She sat on the couch, numbly watching the happenings and their aftermath unfold.

That's where I found her when I returned at midnight Saturday . . .

SO WHEN I walked into the den and saw her sitting in front of the TV set that Sunday morning—exactly a half-century ago this very day, I wasn't sure if she had gone to bed at all.

When I sat down beside her, she snuggled against me, rested her head on my shoulder, and said something like, "I'm so glad you are finally home . . . "

The TV camera was focused on the door of the aging building that housed the Dallas Police Department, explaining that at any minute Lee Harvey Oswald, the man who allegedly had killed the President, would emerge on his way to arraignment. In the meantime, the narrative of the telecast focused on what all, and what little, was known about this accused assassin.

Looking at the clock on the nearby kitchen wall, I was surprised that it was already 11:00 a.m. I had been sitting there for hours, staring hypnotically at the screen. About fifteen minutes later, there started to be some activity around that jail corridor.

Moments later, my wife nudged me and said, "Look, there he is! That's Oswald . . . "

Before she could finish the sentence, a man dressed in a dark suit and wearing a black fedora, came out of nowhere. One of the worst weekends of my entire life was punctuated by the unmistakable sound of a gunshot . . .

Jack Ruby was arrested on the spot. Lee Harvey Oswald died just under two hours later in Parkland Hospital.

That a crowd notorious for its noise sat in stunned silence from kickoff to final gun emphasized the obvious. Even Kenny Hatfield's game-winning punt return in the fourth quarter could not energize a crowd dealing with something even larger than Razorback football.

I don't know how long it will take to forget that dreadful weekend. Obviously, a half century was not enough . . .

## THE COLUMN WAS A CASUALTY BUT ITS MEMORY LIVES ON

I HAD JUST put the finishing touches on my daily sports column, pitched it to the desk man, and told him that I would hed it up myself . . . in newspaper jargon, that meant I would write my own headline. I sat down at my almost new Olympia standard and typed out:

"Walking on New Grass."

I looked at the clock on the east wall of the newsroom, and it was 9:35 p.m. I commented to Don Henry that I was waiting on a call back, but I wasn't going to wait much longer, that I was tired and hungry, and would soon be heading home.

My day had started early. My job, along with running the *A-J* sports department, was covering Tech football and writing a daily column. It was a great job. The Red Raider football program had rapidly matured into perennial title contention, and writing a column has always been fun. Running the department wasn't much of a challenge, what with a talented staff that included Henry, Randy Sanders, Walt McAlexander, and Jim Gintonio.

I liked the column I had just written. I had no way of knowing that it would never see light of day.

EARLY THAT morning, the late Ralph Carpenter, Tech's sports information director, and I had met at the Pancake House for breakfast, then headed for Jones Stadium, where excitement abounded. It was the day Tech would become the third school in the Southwest Conference to have artificial grass. The new Astroturf was receiving its final touches and being lined off for the Coaches All-America Football Game, which Lubbock had rescued from Buffalo, N.Y. and would be played right here just over a month from now.

Ralph and I were on the game's governing committee, our assignment being to host the flood of sports writers who'd be coming in from across the nation. We had a lot to do in preparation for that. The bright, green blades were covered with dew, which shimmered against the morning sun which was just clearing the bank of grandstands to our left as we strolled the length of the field.

Ralph suddenly "broke ranks" and ran over to a workman who had just stenciled a "3" instead of a "2" in marking the 20-yard line. The guy slapped his forehead, uttered an expletive, and trotted off hoping to find something that would erase paint from Astroturf. Ralph jokingly observed that, at least, the first mistake ever made on this new field couldn't be blamed on player or coach.

We both laughed and broke out in an off-key rendition of "Walkin' on New Grass," a Ray Price song that was popular at the time.

"Hey, Ralph," I said. "I think we just wrote my column for tomorrow." We laughed aloud again. It was that kind of morning . . . happy, carefree, and filled with promise . . .

BACK AT THE office that evening, I was filling my coffee cup and visiting with Wayne Panter, the night news editor and unofficial president of the office coffee club. Somebody looking over the weather wire commented that we were in a tornado watch. Panter, a real veteran of this craft, made an observation that would be a conversation point for days to come.

"You know, I must have been in a jillion tornado watches and warnings, but I've never really felt like I'd be in an actual tornado."

The reason I so clearly remember his comment is because it occurred to me that I'd always felt the same way.

The late Phil Hamilton, our night city editor and a close buddy, came over and told me that the fire department was having a barbecue and did I want to go. I told him no thanks, but as soon as John Mooney called me back, I was heading for the house.

IN THE WEE hours of May 12, teams of *A-J* newsroom personnel were still trudging through the death and destruction of a proud city brought to its knees by one of the most severe tornadoes ever recorded at that time. There were 26 fatalities, but the number could have been much higher. The crux of the blow struck in the downtown area at 9:50 p.m. Had the tornado sat down in a residential area, the number would likely have been in the hundreds . . . perhaps more.

The *A-J* building had taken a direct hit and, in the structural sense, had withstood the blow. The roof, however, was leaking and water poured down the south wall of the newsroom like a wide, flat waterfall.

Through some electronic quirk, a phone line connection between KFYO—then a part of the *A-J* family—and a Dallas TV station that had called to check on a reported tornado held through the storm. It was that line that provided our only connection to the outside world. The Dallas station somehow patched us to the *Globe-News*, our sister newspaper in Amarillo, and we dictated stories to their newsroom, allowing us to get an *A-J* on the streets by mid-morning. It was but a skeleton of our normal product, but it spoke volumes about the dedication of the *A-J* staff to inform its readers. It was that feeling of pride and accomplishment that helped salve the pain we all shared. Lubbock had escaped disaster for 75 years, then the string ran out in deadly fashion.

ONLY LATER WOULD I have time to shudder at how close I had come to being out in the midst of the tornado and, consequently, one of those grave statistics. I had told Don and Jim that I wasn't waiting any longer for the call, that I was heading out. Just as I got to the bottom of the stairs by the west door (which, at that time, opened onto the parking lot), the rain hit. My car was only about twenty yards away, and I already had made up my mind to dash for it.

"Hey," came a voice from the landing above, "Mooney's on the phone . . . " The remainder of Don's sentence was muted by a clap of thunder and what sounded like a series of explosions. We looked out the glass portion of the door just in time to see the carport whisked away. We rushed back up the stairs alongside a wall that was begin bombarded by debris of all sizes, propelled by the 200 mph winds . . .

Had Don not stopped me, I figure I probably would have been about halfway to my car when it hit . . .

THAT JONES Stadium also had sustained tremendous damage—its huge light standards were either fallen or badly skewed, looking like so many strands of steel spaghetti—attests to the width of the tornado's base. It would be days before the scheduled all-star football game would regain significance in the minds of a community struggling to regain its composure. That it did, however, attests to the spirit of its people.

Just a week later, Mayor Jim Granberry would address a luncheon of Coaches All-America officials and dignitaries who were in town to advance the game. His opening remark affects me still:

"The hand extended to you is bruised . . . and it's bleeding . . . but it's warm."

And the game did go on as scheduled, a proud testimony to the resilience of a town whose mettle had never before been tested so severely. The game not only went on as planned but played before a sell-out crowd for the first time in its history. It seemed to be a rallying point for a wounded but determined city.

I still think of that column . . . of that day . . . of Ralph himself, a friend whom I loved dearly.

I later located the column, still intact but never set in type. For years, I held on to it, knowing that I would never again submit it for print. The gaiety and spunk of the tone as it was written would never fit the somber reverence of all that had followed. Yet, in an ironic sort of way, "Walking on New Grass" could describe the attitude that saw this city not only rebound but replenish.

The tornado, with its tremendous jolt of death and destruction, did not make Lubbock a better city. But the way Lubbock responded certainly did. In so many ways, we've been "walking on new grass" ever since . . .

### SNEAK ATTACKS STIR PATRIOTISM, BUT DOES IT LAST?

WHEN I GULPED down the last swallow of coffee in a mug that had just been through its third refill, I looked down at my watch and began reacting to a mysterious sense of urgency.

I assumed it had to do with the busy week I had ahead of me, even though things wouldn't start until Wednesday when I had a six-something morning flight to Dallas and a late return that same day. Then I'd drive to our place in Fisher County where my sons and I would be hosting our 12th annual dove hunt. It would already be started by the time I arrived.

Wednesday itself would be stressful. I was a member of my alma mater's board of regents, and we had called a meeting in Dallas that day to make a personnel change at the very top of the university's flow chart. As chair of the committee that had recommended that action . . . well, it could not turn into a pleasant day.

And as I drove toward downtown Lubbock, my thoughts were of that flight at such an ungodly hour the next morning. I had no way of knowing that, at that very moment, four flights already in the air would change the world forever.

It was September 11, 2001 . . .

ALTHOUGH I had retired as editor-in-chief of the *A-J* almost exactly nine months earlier, I was enjoying idle time for only a few days when I was invited to come back on a part-time basis to assist the new editor and relatively new publisher in any way I could. Mainly, I would continue to write my weekly column, which had been a regular feature most of the forty years I'd been on the job.

During the drive downtown, my mind was bouncing back and forth between the two events that would round out the week. Ol' Red—my beloved pickup that was only three years old back then—had been fueled and serviced for the trip to Sylvester. My hunting gear was packed and placed in the back seat.

Then my pleasant musings gave way to more somber thoughts of the meeting in Dallas. Only yesterday had the board voted during an executive session via telephone to make the change. About now, the board secretary would be advising the affected person of the called meeting but not its agenda.

Having agreed it was something that had to be done somehow fell short of consoling a pang of guilt that I could cover only by looking forward to the hunt and the reunions it would provide. Thought diversion is a gift nature provides only for humans. Perhaps that's because humans are the only creatures that need it.

But I digress . . .

AS I PASSED through the lobby and headed for the stairs leading up to the newsroom, I saw two of my coworkers, Twila Aufill and Beverly Wilke, staring at a TV set in the comptroller's office. I asked what was going on.

"An airplane just crashed into this tall building in New York," Twila said. After only a quick glance I saw that the building was one of the Twin Towers. I stepped up my pace.

In the newsroom, the large screen TV was surrounded by reporters and editors. A second plane had crashed into the other skyscraper. Both of the Twin Towers had now been hit. Obviously, this was more than just a horrible accident. A few minutes later the Pentagon was hit. It now was clear that the U.S. was under attack.

But nobody knew by whom or for what . . .

Editor Randy Sanders, at the urging of managing editor Mel Tittle, began planning an Extra Edition, a rarity reserved for extraordinary happenings. This certainly was one.

Meanwhile, as the nation struggled to collect its thoughts, the President began preparing for the worst. Assuming that the devastating sneak attack might be the preparatory steps for a full-fledged assault, he ordered all aircraft to land immediately. All flights were cancelled for at least the next 48 hours.

Because that edict included my flight for the next morning, I quickly called our board chairman to discuss postponing our meeting. We agreed that the person most directly involved should not be left dangling, and made the decision to proceed as planned.

I made the two-hour drive to the ranch that night. The next morning I unloaded my hunting gear from the pickup and headed for Dallas. The dashboard clock read 4:05 a.m. That would put me there in time to further prepare for the meeting, which was set for noon.

My thoughts turned back to the day before.

Randy had asked me to write a column for the Extra, comparing the sneak attack of this day to the one staged by Japan almost sixty years earlier. I was the only one in the newsroom—maybe the entire building—old enough to remember Dec. 7, 1941.

The comparisons were valid, both in the sneak attacks and the nation's response. In fact, I closed the column with the observation that America may be caught napping now and then, "but its resolve never sleeps . . . "

Could I write that same closing today?

Let's examine that question: We've been shoved around by Russia, snookered and insulted by Iran, and baffled by ISIS. Our lines in the sand now become dust in the air. In short, we have lost our swagger.

Our two once proud and honorable major political parties have assured us that no matter who wins, we will have a sitting President who is detested by many, admired by few, and elected on the basis of the "lesser of two evils"—perhaps even more accurately, "the evil of two lessers . . . "

So the answer is "no." Somewhere, during these past fourteen years, that ever-alert resolve has dozed off. Someday, because of moral fiber that is residual, it will reawaken.

Hopefully, it won't require a loud explosion . . .

## Memories Born in September Will Forever Thrive

OF ALL THE months that cross my calendar each year, September may be the most special—and significant—of them all. That thought crossed my mind a few days ago while the haunting strains of "September Song" flowed from the inimitable voice of Frank Sinatra.

Perhaps that had something to do with my age. The song, introduced in 1938, was written to pattern the autumn years of one's life. Now being in my eighth decade on earth . . . well, autumn is upon me.

In life, there is always a special time that becomes a breeding ground for memories that linger and mellow and await an occasion to be brandished once more. For me, it has always been the arrival of September, not the cool breath of autumn, that brings forth the warmth of memories that defines the change of seasons.

But never more so than the one that lurks just five calendar days ahead . . .

AMONG THE many other emotional properties, September has marked a plethora of "firsts," the beginning of things long to remain to affect my very psyche.

There has been the arrival of football season, which affected me as a fan and, in junior high and high school, as a player of the game. In town for Homecoming a few years ago, I sat on the bottom row of the grandstands and could almost recapture a fleeting glimpse of that special feeling that came while standing on that very field preceding the game's opening kickoff. It was a mixture of nervous excitement and controlled apprehension that lasted through the school song and dissipated only after the initial contact.

Another first was in September, 1960, when the Red Raiders played their first game as a long-suffering member of the Southwest Conference. A dream of years standing had finally reached fruition. It also was my first year to cover that game and others as the newest member of the *A-J*'s sports department.

WHETHER FITTINGLY or by happenstance, September also brings an intertwined memory via an event that will be replayed less than two weeks from now. It will be the 28th Annual Dove Hunt—the capital letters well deserved—at our ranch in Fisher County. It was by the insistence of my youngest son, Scott, that the hunt was launched in 1989, when our ranch house was still a project in the works.

Scott was also born in September; the youngest of our three sons, he would become the most avid hunter in a family of gamers.

THEN THERE was the September that became, for me, a life-changing event. That's when, as a condition of our marriage, I enrolled in college as a 24-year-old freshman. By taking full loads each semester, summers and all, I received a degree in two years and eleven months. That took me away from working the oil fields and highway construction, and prepared me to step into a career I had dreamed of but had, before meeting her, given up as another of life's fantasies left unfulfilled.

Those always tough and often challenging times eventually became pleasant memories gilded by a feeling of mutual accomplishment. We took our degrees off the same stage the same day and carried them into professions that marked our efforts.

Years rolled by, our family grew and we had finally begun to enjoy the trappings of our efforts and our determination. While, as the song declares, the days may "grow short as you reach September," our pleasant memories began to lengthen. And so did our boys and our bank accounts. Although wealth was neither a dream nor a reality, we had arrived at a point where vacations and travel could finally become as one . . .

WE BEGAN TO take trips to interesting places, mainly domestic but always exciting and, in our bank of memories, quite productive.

And the month we set aside for our annual trips was ideally September. For one thing, school was back in session and transportation and hostelry became a buyer's market. Also, the weather was more suitable wherever we went. One of our first such trips was to Cancun which, fortunately for us, had not yet become the Mecca of tourism-gone-rampant that it is today.

There were the meals on the wharf at San Francisco, the beautiful view of dying foliage on a train trip through Vermont, the mansions around Rhode Island, the theaters and Broadway shows in New York, the auto trip to Florida and up the coast to Augusta, the thieving slot machines in Las Vegas, the food fare of New Orleans, the powdery sand of Destin (where I also landed a shark), the Smithsonian and other historical monuments of Washington D.C., and other places of a common product: memories in the making.

That does not include the nine Cotton Bowl games and one Gator Bowl I covered, and Frances made every trip. She often spoke proudly—she never boasted; it was not her nature—of the Cotton Bowl Ball when she danced with both the Governor of Texas and the President of Texas Tech.

And there were several occasions where we were in the company of Willie Nelson . . . and in Arkansas, where she went on daily "antiquing" treks with Edith (Mrs. Darrell) Royal and Mary Harmon (Mrs. Bear) Bryant.

I HAD HEARD Sinatra and others sing "September Song" many times; but for the first time, I actually heard the words. Suddenly, they were joined by the melody of memories that were already playing in my heart and mind.

A mood that was growing heavy suddenly became lighter and my thoughts moved instead toward a soothing realization: In a garden resplendent with pleasant memories, the pain of death will always survive but will never thrive. Now, almost three months after losing the most important person in my life, I am especially moved by the closing line of "September Song."

"... And these special days I will spend with you ..."

### BIRTHDAYS STIR MEMORIES OF LIFE'S MANY PATHWAYS

*On July 26, many years ago in a quiet rural setting, I began my trek down this journey called life.*

*My birth certificate says I was born six miles northeast of Moran, Texas, to John and Hazel (Hitt) Pettit, their seventh child in a marriage that had begun fourteen years earlier.*

*Despite the Depression that, in rural Texas, still stood between us and abundance, I was surrounded by love—a shroud those parents and siblings would provide throughout my formative years and beyond.*

*This weekend I am in rural Fisher County where two of our three sons, a fantastic daughter-in-law, and my beloved Princess Kendall have come to be with Frances and me during our birthday seasons (hers is the 28th).*

*I am not a Bible scholar, but the scripture that means most to me on such occasions as this is one Paul wrote to the people of Corinth which, paraphrased, spoke of Hope, Faith and Love, and emphasized that the "greatest of these is love."*

*Here on the eve of my birthday I realize the truth and depth of that etching. Love, when all else was meager, kept me in the clutches of its might. Thanks, family, for all you were, all you are, and all you will ever remain . . .*

I wrote the above exactly two years ago on my Facebook page. It reappeared Wednesday under the memories heading, again on Facebook. The column that appears in today's *A-J* was also written Wednesday, my latest birthday.

After reading that Facebook posting, I began recalling memories of birthdays past.

FOR A COUPLE of decades now, this is the time of year that my buddy Morris and I have exchanged gifts and jibes. With only two exceptions during that time, we have celebrated joint birthdays with dinner, beverages, and the kind of birthday cards found mainly at the local carwash.

Morris's birthday is July 20, mine comes on July 26, and my wife's two days later. So, it has always been a special occasion, with Morris pointing out each year that for the next six days he would be one year older than I, giving him the stature of superiority that comes with his being my elder.

Every year the gifts we exchanged represented more in thoughtfulness than in originality. We both bought cards from restaurants whose fares suited us all. That eliminated only Chinese, for which I never acquired a taste. Hey, I'm not going to eat anything without knowing what it used to be . . .

Morris Knox and Burle

Anyway, during the next week or so after the birthdays we two couples would cash in the wares. Amazingly, we never selected the same restaurants.

There were other birthdays that always remain within memory's grasp: My 21st, which was spent in the North Pacific aboard the *USS Funston*; my 22nd amidst an Arctic summer, wishing for a sunset that would not be coming; and others meaningful but not painted with such vivacity . . .

OUR COLLEGE years, if we were to have written them in story form, would appropriately been described as "Matriculation in Destitution." Overstated, obviously, but those times represented our most financially challenging days.

And it was during our last summer session prior to graduation that produced another memorable birthday. I had taken on an extra-heavy course load to meet the graduation requirements. We were broke; I needed to get out and get a job.

So, when I arose on the morning of July 26 it seemed like just another summer Tuesday morning. That is, until my bride came to the breakfast table, where I was feasting on a cup of instant coffee, my only available nourishment, and spoke a loud and cheerful "Happy Birthday!"

I unwrapped the box and found, lo and behold, a brand-new suit, an item I had not owned since my boyhood! Before I could ask how in the world we could afford such a lavish gift, she explained that she had, seven or eight months before, gone into the J. C. Penney store and placed it on layaway. Little by little, she had paid out the $24.99 it cost.

"You will need that when you report for your new job," which, she knew as well as I, wasn't yet on the horizon.

Then, fifty-one days later, I reported to work at the *Lubbock Avalanche-Journal*, wearing for the first time that brand-new suit! During the years that have followed I have been able to own such name brands as Burberry, Oxxford, HS&M, and others of fairly pricy ilk. But none could match the pride I felt in that dark suit labeled "J. C. Penney."

A gift born of the sacrifice from the one you love most has a meaning whose memory will never wane, no matter what subsequent years may provide . . .

TODAY, AS I write this for Sunday's edition, my birthday is much different than I have enjoyed for the past six decades.

The annual party won't be happening. Morris and Janice left yesterday on a three-week cruise. He texted me a day early because today they would be out to sea, beyond electronic range.

But most painfully, for the first time since 1956 I am spending this day without the love of my life at my side. I can imagine her being here, both sharing a laugh as I typed out the memory of the $25 suit. I would tell her that no matter what gifts, bought at whatever price, would ever match its meaning.

Frances passed away just over a month ago, leaving in my life an eternal void. As I prepare to leave on the morrow to be surrounded once more by my kids, my wonderful daughter-in-law and my grandchildren, she won't be among us.

But I will find solace as the warmth provided me; and memories of the brilliance of her sparkling smile will buoy me on toward another year, this one filled with wistful recollection . . .

My sadness will soon be overcome as I arrive at the ranch and dwell among the products of our mutual love.

And love is a gift of God that death cannot destroy . . .

Burle in his home office

# NATIVE TO TEXAS

Standing by the Moran city limit sign

### NATIVE TEXAN

AMONG THE MANY wonderful things my parents did for me was to see to it that I would be—then and evermore—a native-born Texan. That heritage is important to me, and to all others who get chill bumps when a horseman unfurls the Lone Star flag while galloping at full speed on the rim of Palo Duro Canyon or during the opening ceremony of the Fort Griffin Fandangle.

Native Texans are special and doggone proud of it.

As was the case with many rural Texans of those times, I was born at home. But what may sound a bit strange to some folks is how I was paid for. Once I'd been spanked and settled that warm July night, Dr. Henchmann headed back to Albany with a smile on his face and a right new shotgun in his hand. It was an engraved Ithaca, something to be proud of. And I'm sure he thought now and then about the unlikely manner that it had come into his possession. He not only hadn't expected to get it in lieu of pay, but he wasn't the one who was supposed to make the house call to begin with.

More on that part later.

I'm still not sure today whether that form of payment for my delivery was due to a cash flow problem common to most Depression era households, or whether it was because the good doctor had rather admired the shotgun and proposed the trade. Until somebody shows up to tell me different, I'll cling to the latter.

All that's really important after all these years is that I arrived safely and am, indeed, a native Texan.

TEXAS IS SPECIAL, and not only to Texans. Even the rudest of Yankees have long been treated to the music of Bob Wills and Ray Price and Willie, and cheered the exploits of such athletes as Bobby Layne and Doak Walker and Nolan Ryan and George Foreman and . . . hey, that list could run clear to the bottom of every page of this edition. But you get the picture.

There is so much supporting data. Like, for instance, among all the states in the Union, only Texas can fly its flag on a separate pole at an equal height to Old Glory, as well it should. And when Local Draft Board No. 77 decided I needed a break from college, I learned that even the U.S. Army has special feelings for Texans (jealousy is a close cousin to contempt, don't you think?).

One good example of that special esteem is that I spent most of the next two years going by the name "Tex." I'm sure that it was the same way with many other Texans, yet I never heard anybody call a Nebraskan "Neb." I believe it was the late author Boyce House who first penned that Texas fathers sent their sons off to the army with a common piece of advice:

"Don't ever ask nobody where he's from. If he's a Texan, he will have already told you. If he's not, there's no need to embarrass him."

THANKS TO that hitch in the army, an adventurous youth and a long period of covering football and basketball, I have seen every state. I closed it out a few years ago with a trip to Hawaii, where the bride and I celebrated our 50th anniversary. (I'm not sure I can count Alaska, either, being as it wasn't a state when I was stationed there.) Each of the states has something going for it.

But when I finished college, there was no doubt where I'd stay. When I was a kid, I heard a guy who'd just got out of the army say that if they built a barbed wire fence around Texas, he'd never rip his britches crossin' over it. In my youthful foolishness, I questioned his logic.

But I know now what he meant.

Several years ago, we had a corporate meeting in Snow Mass, Colo., right near Aspen. The wife and I decided to drive. Our company is made up of folks from all over the country. When we arrived, everybody seemed interested to learn how we'd enjoyed the drive.

I told them that for much of the trip the scenery was downright beautiful.

"But then we got out of Texas and we couldn't see the countryside for the dern mountains and trees."

I'VE HAD THE good fortune to be in Austin for a couple of gubernatorial inaugurations, the festivities of which always lump my throat. And seeing the governor of Texas sworn in does funny things to the hair at the nape of my neck.

Several years back, a couple that had just moved in from another state went down to Austin with us. They also were caught up in it all.

"Not only is Texas Pride very real," he said, "it's also contagious!" The next thing I know, he's buying a hat and a pair of boots, saying y'all and telling everybody what he's fixin' to do.

I'm very proud that my three boys were all born in Texas. And I'm very glad that their deliveries were covered by insurance. Even though I have more shotguns than I have sons, I don't have a single one I'd want to part with.

Except for a quirk of the weather, my dad might have still had that beautiful Ithaca for the rest of his life. For two days straight prior to my being born, it rained both hard and steady. By the time my mom was ready to deliver, Deep Creek had swollen out of its banks and across the only road accessing our house from Moran. Dr. Forrester, seeing that he was not going to be able to get to our place, somehow summoned Dr. Henchmann. The road from Albany was passable.

Being as Doc Forrester was our regular physician— ours and everybody else's in Moran—I'm guessing that paying for my arrival would have followed a more conventional method.

Obviously, I don't remember that particular shotgun. But, being something of a collector of firearms, I have seen that model. And it is one everybody would love to own.

If my dad regretted having given it up in the manner he did, he never once mentioned it. But one year at the start of dove season, I did catch him looking at me the same way he always looked at this horse he'd got in a bad trade.

My being born a Texan means a lot to me. But it didn't happen without a price . . .

## HANK THOMPSON

AT THAT TIME, it was about the farthest away from home I had ever been without knowing for sure when I would return. A few months earlier I was undergoing basic training at Fort Ord in California, which may have been equally far away. But I was relatively sure of at least a short leave before moving to a more permanent locale. So, when I talked some buddies at Fort Belvoir into going into town—town being the national capital—that night to catch a Hank Thompson concert, it was sort of like revisiting a piece of Texas.

Ol' Hank was a Waco boy.

I had been at Belvoir for only a week or so but I had already been nicknamed "Tex," a moniker that would be following me throughout my military career. That was partially because every outfit I served in would be uncomfortably short of Texans. But, mainly, it was because—then and now—I have always worn my Texas Pride on my cuff.

Now, a couple of the guys from rural Iowa already knew about Hank Thompson—one of them began warbling "Honky Tonk Angels" the instant I mentioned the name—but Allison, from Boston, only thought he knew the name. Turned out he had him mixed up with Hank Williams, whom he had heard of.

WHEN WE looked at the newspaper ad to find out the time and location for the concert, somebody mentioned that the guy opening the show had a band called The Texas Wildcats. I doubted aloud that they would actually be Texans and went on to explain how Yankees everywhere tried to capitalize on the draw of that name.

What I did see on the ad that really impressed me was that Hank's Brazos Valley Boys would be accompanied by Merle Travis, arguably the best guitar picker that ever lived. No argument about that would have come from Chet Atkins, who proudly admitted that it was Merle who taught him how to play in the style that would eventually make him famous.

But I digress.

Times were different back then, in the early to mid-'50s, and a major difference was the personal safety that everybody just took for granted. We caught a bus into town, then walked to the concert hall, passing through an area that nowadays not even a pit bull would dare enter after dark.

Another thing that was different was that very genre of music. It had not yet acquired the name, "C&W," but was called "Hillbilly Music," a term I was accustomed to hearing spoken with respect if not out-and-out delight. Now, here I was exposed to people whose own sophistication required that they not only look down on it, but to typecast negatively all who openly enjoyed its strains.

That flat floored me. Even the people in Moran—and their numbers were few—who preferred Popular Music (i.e., Bing Crosby, Dean Martin, Jo Stafford, etc.) had nothing bad to say about hillbilly. Those were the folks who, for reasons I could never understand, liked Hank Williams's stuff better when it was sung by Joni James or Tony Bennett or others whose nasal tones I found lacking.

A FEW DAYS later, just outside Cong. Omar Burleson's office, I met a cute little Texas girl who worked in the Agriculture Department. It was when I began keeping regular company with her that I began to learn which fork to use on which dish, that socks should sort of match up with your britches, and that the drink to your left belonged to somebody else. She, too, liked Hillbilly music but did so with a don't-ask-don't-tell strategy. Hey, closets can be used for things other than clothes . . .

I met her after the Hank Thompson concert had happened, and she said she would've loved to have gone. People in her office, she said, were more inclined toward a type of Opera that was of no kin to The Grand Ol' . . .

Later, I shipped out to the Arctic and she wound up marrying a lawyer from Houston. He probably didn't like Hank Thompson either, but at least I'll bet he knew who he was.

THAT NIGHT from all those years ago jumped back into my thoughts a week or so ago when Hank Thompson died at the age of 82.

We arrived at the concert in plenty of time to see the Texas Wildcats take the stage, tune up, and open the show. I looked at their leader, sort of a skinny blond guy, decked out like a dude cowboy.

"That guy's no more a Texan than you are," I whispered to Allison, the guy from Boston. "I betcha he's never been west of the Potomac. Looky at them boots . . . no Texan would get caught in anything like that."

It was the first cowboy boots I'd ever seen that had crepe soles. Between his act and the star's opener, I approached him, expecting him to sound something like Allison when he spoke. He didn't. He sounded a lot like me . . .

"What part of Texas you from?" I asked, exaggerating further my naturally exaggerated drawl.

"Plainview," he said, drawling right back at me. "I'm from Plainview . . . up close to Lubbock."

I rejoined my buddies at our table, bubbling with newly found excitement.

"Hey, I was wrong," I said. "That guy is indeed from Texas."

One of them asked how I could tell for sure.

"One reason is because he's friendly, another is that he doesn't talk funny."

A few months later, that same guy was knocking them dead all over town. He had his own television show in D. C. and, in a very short time, it had gone national.

TIMES CHANGE, people change, and the standards we set for ourselves are affected by those same shifting tides. There was a time when every Hillbilly singer included in his repertoire at least one spiritual song, perhaps just to assure his followers that his heart, albeit oft broken, was still where it belonged.

I hear the words used in the so-called Rap Music of today, and I am suddenly taken back to those times when every DJ closed his show with a hymn. Then I think of that guy from Plainview, whose signature hit had to be altered because the record producers feared its language was so offensive that radio stations would not dare put it on the air. The last line of the song originally said (Gasp!)

" . . . at the bottom of this pit lies a helluva man . . . " It was changed and re-released.

One but can imagine how the rappers of today would describe Big Bad John . . .

Now, Hank Thompson has moved on to that Big Opry in the sky, and the Texan who opened that show has pretty much retired. But the memories of that night all those years ago have burned anew, especially the most embarrassing part:

How could I have ever questioned Jimmy Dean's Texas heritage?

## DRUGSTORE COWBOYS

A FEW YEARS ago, a feller named Conway Twitty sang a song whose message was clear, both in its literal sense and in its other entendre. What he literally said was, "Don't call him a cowboy 'til you've seen him ride."

But what he really meant was, Don't call him a cowboy 'til you've seen him ride, uh, bareback . . .

That doesn't have a lot to do with the point I'm making except the part about people who start out playing cowboy as a kid and never outgrow it. Oh, they stop riding a stickhorse and brandishing a six-shooter loaded with caps, but they never quit dressing the part.

Now there's a little of that in a lot of us Texans. Shucks, that's part of our heritage. For example, in that hall closet right over yonder, I have several pairs of nice cowboy boots; and, down at the ranch, I have two hats—one straw, the other felt—that wouldn't look out of place sitting atop the most rustic of heads.

Every now and then, I like to lapse back into my boyhood fantasy of rounding up cows and shooting up owl hoots, Indians, and cougars about to spring on yon damsel. That happens most often when I'm down there in the privacy of my own pasture. Normally, here at home I mainly chase around in sneakers and jeans by day, a pair slacks for evenings out, and a regulation suit and tie for Sunday church, weddings, funerals and other similar obligations.

And, heck, I used to get as big a kick as everybody else around here come Cattle Baron time, dressed up like a freshly groomed drover as I moseyed around the V-8 Ranch, a taco in one hand and a sarsaparilla in the other, wishing I was brave enough to tell Nancy P. that she had her spurs on upside down.

But, come the next morning, I went right back to looking like I most generally do.

NOW, I GREW up in ranching country where, even today, cowboys ride the range, chase down dogies, and do brandings and dehorning and roundups and all that other stuff that made what they do both romantic and imitated. I never think twice when I see an old retired rancher dressing like he was still on the job, and, when forced by society to attend church or a funeral or something special, putting on his good boots, a dress hat and a suit tailored in a western cut.

What amuses me is to see grown men who've never ridden anything more contrary than a car with water in its gas tank, dressing like Ben Cartwright en route to Adam's recital. They seem to really like coming to church that way.

It's like my old man used to say: You can always spot the feller who knows which pile to kick and which one to step over. He was always amused by—yet politely patient with—what he described as "Drugstore Cowboys."

I don't know whether that term still exists, but the genre sure as yell does . . .

TEXANS ARE OFTEN amused, sometimes even bemused, by what Yankee folks think we're like. Last fall, the wife and I were in upper New England, spending equal amounts of time watching the leaves and trying to figure out what people were saying.

One guy in Vermont who almost spoke English pointed to the loafers on my feet and remarked: "Should I assume that you don't bring your boots when you leave Texas." (There is no question mark because Yankees don't *ask*, they *state.)*

Now, as I mentioned earlier, Shackelford County is ranching country and ranches are run by cowboys.

A few years ago, my sis and I stopped at a restaurant in Albany for lunch. We were a bit early, and there was only one couple in the place when we walked in. They obviously were traveling in the car outside that bore Ohio license tags. We took a booth right near theirs. In a few minutes, a bunch of cowhands from the Lambshead Ranch came in, walked right past the four of us, all wearing chaps, spurs . . . the whole bit.

The man from Ohio was obviously awed. He leaned forward and excitedly said to his wife: "Look, hon—those are REAL Texas Cowboys!"

She smiled knowingly, and responded: "They are not! They drove up in that truck . . . "

THERE'S A THIN line between those of us who keep our boots and hats and shirts with yokes and snaps in the closet along with our cowboy tendencies, and those who wear that garb around all day every day. It doesn't matter that they're heading off for work in an environment that doesn't require that they be careful where they step.

We Texans—most of us anyway—need to own at least one pair of boots and a pickup. When I go into Roby to coffee with my buddies, I sure don't want to have the only car parked out front.

For whatever reason, my wife of all these years hates it when I don my boots and hat, even when we're in the country. She doesn't care if my friends down there dress like that, I am to leave the house looking like what I really am—a guy from Lubbock whose only ornery steed is that 4-wheeler parked in the barn.

One of my sons guesses it's because she thinks dressing that way prompts me to break out in song, a la like Hank Williams.

Ironically, it seems nowadays that a lot of bona fide cowboys have gone to wearing ball caps and sneakers. I recently heard about a guy over in Guthrie who was approached by a stranger from out of state.

"What do you do for a living?" the stranger asked, looking first at the local's John Deere cap, then down at his sneakers.

"I'm a cowhand," he replied. "I work on that spread right over yonder."

"W-e-l-l," inquired the stranger, "if you're a cowhand, why aren't you wearing boots and a hat?"

"What! . . . And have somebody think I'm a *car salesman?*"

It's like ol' Conway said: A feller that knows how to ride can dress however he pleases . . .

## HAT ETIQUETTE

ROBERTA DOESN'T get out much anymore and, for at least a couple of reasons, that may be a good thing. That thought hit me a night or two ago when my wife and I were undergoing a delightful cholesterol restoration at one of our favorite rural eateries not far from our Fisher County abode.

Just as our waitress was placing my plate-sized chicken fried steak (gravy on the side, please) before me, I noticed something going on at the large table nearest our booth that, had Roberta been there, she would have found at once uplifting and disgusting. The guy who was the apparent father, husband, brother-in-law, and host of the eight or ten people in the party bowed to offer spiritual appreciation for the food placed before him.

Roberta, a lifelong Christian of strong Methodist leanings, would have liked that. But when he bowed, the wide brim of his big black cowboy hat not only was still affixed to his head, it was almost touching the ranch dressing that topped his salad. Roberta would have frowned at that and, judging on what happened at our country house a few Thanksgivings ago, she does not always frown silently.

More about that later.

I GREW UP in an area and an era when a man's hat was part of a special culture all its own. It had several canons, and my dad was a strict disciple of them all. To begin with, there was the style thing. After Labor Day, Dad put aside his straw and donned his felt. He wore it until Easter Sunday, when would again break out the summer straw.

I could not imagine my ol' man ever walking into a house without removing his hat, be it straw or felt. To eat with it on would have been unthinkable for any Moran male. And if such a breech did occur, it would provide conversation fodder for weeks to come.

Dad and his peers partook in another ritual that was so commonplace as to be expected. When passing a lady (all females of that era were presumed to be ladies unless proven otherwise), he would touch the brim of his hat and give his head a slight nod. That was called "tipping your hat" even though the tip was never completed.

Although not an exacting formula, you could often tell a man's occupation by the type of hat he wore. Moran being in the midst of West Texas ranching country, most wore western style in either straw or felt. "Cowboy hats" were their fitting description. Drummers, bankers, lawyers, doctors and such were more prone to fedoras. One storekeeper whose son would later become a famous sportscaster for Humble Oil and, later, CBS-TV, owned one of those Panama straws common to barbershop quartets. Moran had a barbershop but no quartet that I ever knew about.

Every café ("cow-fay" was the Shackelford County pronunciation) you went in had a hat rack or some other device designed to hold a feller's hat while he dined. It was so essential that it probably led to "something you can hang your hat on" becoming the best way to describe things of substance. And, in the absence of a hat rack or spike, a hat was placed crown down to protect the shape of the brim. Incidentally, most hats came with the brim, and often the crown itself, requiring "shaping."

Dad employed Mom's teakettle to assist him in fashioning the brim to suit him. No two hats you saw had exactly the same shape. Their commonality was that they expressed individual taste without compromising the dignity of the owners. Only ol' Hoss could get by with wearing a pushed-up crown without attracting a giggle.

FOR MOST OF my life there was a distinct difference between a *hat* and a *cap*. And I am convinced it was when culture began to blur that line that the long-held hat wearing etiquette lost its way.

A couple of decades ago, youngsters discovered what we old-timers used to call "ball caps." That discovery moved rapidly from being a fad to marking a society. Suddenly manufacturers in the cap racket sprang up everywhere. The old freebie "seed caps" morphed into something the youth of America were suddenly demanding. The crowns were lowered to the point that the little button on its top sat firmly against the bearer's scalp.

Girls jumped immediately into the cap brigade, bringing with them a revival of the pony tail. It was not necessarily the desired coif, but one that was necessary in order to join the culture. The ponytail was pulled through that little gap right above the fastener. Can you imagine that Lubbock waitress of a few years back who gained fame with her 'do wearing a ball cap atop that beehive?

Anyway, I believe it was the female's joining the craze that had wide-ranging effect on the nation's headwear conscience. As America has strained to de-sex itself (oops—make that read "de-gender" itself—the other sounds like something that would require a rather painful procedure), males adopted what had historically had been a right limited to ladies: They were allowed to—nay, expected to—wear their hats, bonnets, etc. indoors.

So, when the girls kept their ball caps on indoors the guys joined in. And, the cowboys, seeing that the other guys didn't unlid themselves, wondered why should they?

THE BALL CAP craze led to something else that I've (griped) about before. That is society's distinction between a cap and a hat having eroded to the point that we are now into a second generation of citizens who not only don't know the difference but don't care.

I walk at the mall fairly regularly and my ire over the name of a shop out there pumps my adrenaline to the point it hastens my less-than-Olympic quality pace. It calls itself a "hat" shop, and if there is one bleeping hat in there it's on the head of some cowboy who walked in without removing his.

I'm only going to say this one time: A hat has a brim. A cap has a bill. So dammit, if it has a bill it ain't no hat (grammar rules altered to fit the vernacular of the intended audience)!

WE HAD JUST sat down for our traditional Thanksgiving dinner that day. Roberta, the family matriarch, was seated in her special place. She was wearing her usual sweet smile prior to hearing the special blessing when suddenly she stiffened. Then, gesturing to one of her great-grandsons at the table, and—in a scolding voice befitting her school teacher's background—almost shouted:

"Take off that cap! You know better than wear a cap to the table!"

Both men of the two generations between her and the offender squirmed in the guilt of parental failure brought suddenly to light.

Two Thanksgivings and an equal number of Christmas dinners have passed since that day. And the next time we gather for our traditional turkey day feast, Roberta will be two months past her 100th birthday. Our table will be surrounded by five generations of very happy and hatless people.

Makes me wish the cowboy in the restaurant that night had brought his grandmother . . .

## BOOKS, MOVIES, AND THE HORNY TOAD RETURNS

I WAS LOOKING hungrily at a French grill that was idly serving as one of the features of an outdoor kitchen my son had added to our Fisher County retreat when my youngest granddaughter interrupted my spell.

"Look, Grandad!" Hayden exclaimed. "See what I found?"

When I looked into the box she was holding and saw a live, full-grown horny toad, I had the derndest urge to call my old friend Carlton Stowers and tell him he was off the hook.

Having spent her entire life in urban surroundings, Hayden had no way of knowing the significance of her find. Up until recently, it seemed that the great horned lizard was facing extinction—or, even worse, was already there.

But throughout the summer, I had been seeing them around the place, especially on the caliche drive leading up to the barn. But I didn't think of Carlton until Glenn Dromgoole sent me a copy of a book he had just edited. Its title was *West Texas Stories*, and it is about, as you may already have guessed, West Texas stories. It was published by the Abilene Christian University Press.

Among the stories making up the book was one that Stowers had written several years ago.

ALTHOUGH YOU don't have to be a longtime West Texan to appreciate its content, that region is the setting for yarns by A. C. Green, Elmer Kelton, George Dolan, and at least a couple of dozen others, most of whose names you will recognize, including Carlton's.

Heck, they even tossed in a piece I wrote.

Years ago, when Carlton and I toiled together in the *A-J* sports department, we spent considerable time swapping yarns about our respective boyhoods. Although Stowers was several years younger and many steps faster— he went to UT on a track scholarship as, of all things, a sprinter—our backgrounds were similar.

Now, his younger days were spent in Ballinger which, what with its rural motif, was somewhat like Moran, even though Moran never had a minor league team. It belonged to the Cincinnati Reds and produced a major league short-stop, one Roy McMillan. And, as I have already reported, Carlton's younger days followed my younger days by several years. Accordingly, I saw the Ballinger team—and McMillan—play. Yet he did play Little League baseball in that same park.

But I digress.

WE TALKED about what we did for spending money. I worked at the Myrick Dairy, milking cows then bottling and delivering milk all over town. Even before that, my friend Ray and I went into the shoe-shining business, charging a dime for shoes and fifteen cents for boots. That career was cut short by my Dad, who possibly didn't like us making our pitch to his friends and others. Probably wouldn't have worked out anyway, considering we didn't have any place for our customers to sit.

Carlton told me about his business, which was considerably more sophisticated. He rounded up horny toads and shipped them off to a distributor up north who paid him a dime a head for the little reptiles. Stowers sent them parcel post in shoe boxes with perforated lids.

That they got there alive would come as no surprise to people in Eastland, where a horned toad lived 31 years cemented inside the corner stone of the courthouse. The last time I was in there, which was nearly sixty years ago to get my marriage license, Ol' Rip's body was still on display in a miniature coffin made just for him.

Having a story in that Dromgoole book was no big deal to Stowers, who left the newspaper business years ago to become a full-fledged author. Obviously, he didn't make that change just to relax. He has since had more than forty books published and won a couple of national awards.

AMAZINGLY, West Texas, whose incognito comes from being on the wrong side of I-35, has suddenly taken charge of my entertainment pleasure. Shortly after receiving the Dromgoole book, I saw the movie, *Hell and High Water*, which was all about the part of West Texas with which I am most familiar (never mind that it was filmed in New Mexico, even though the Post scene looked a lot like downtown Post).

Then right after that, here came another Stowers book. It is titled—doesn't it bug you when somebody says a book is "entitled," which means something altogether different? You can find it in the dictionary under Hillary— *On Texas Backroads*, and it is about columns and articles Carlton has written through the years.

Which brings us back full circle to the original topic . . .

SEVERAL YEARS after he had told me about his days of rustling horny toads, the delightfully ugly creatures had begun to disappear. Nobody knows why. Everybody had an opinion—pesticides, a lack of red ants and, I'm sure, climate change.

In a column he wrote for the Dallas paper Stowers took full blame. He said he sent too many of them up North. Could it be that a species that can survive being sealed up in a cornerstone for going on forty years just couldn't handle being surrounded by Yankees?

The important thing is they may be making a comeback.

After hearing my story about Carlton believing he may have caused the shortage, Hayden immediately set her new pet free . . . near an ant bed I had considered eradicating. But, because it was in the edge of the pasture, I decided to leave it alone. Hey, if the horny toads disappear again, it ain't gonna be because I starved them out.

I like it better when Carlton takes the blame . . .

## BIG RICH

I JUST FINISHED reading *The Big Rich*, a book about four Texas oil jillionaires who made money faster than even Obama could spend it. The book, written by a displaced Texan named Bryan Burrough, wasn't exactly a page-turner, but it did hold my interest.

For one thing, I have grown up reading and hearing about the Cullens and Hunts and Richardsons and Murchinsons and, like most people whose lifestyles have been somewhat more pedestrian, I have been intrigued by them and their doings.

I did have the good fortune to become personally acquainted with the late Lupe Murchison, who was married to John. Lupe, who was one of the classiest, most charming and delightful people I ever knew, was appropriately treated kindly by Burrough who, incidentally, seems a better fit for New Jersey where he now lives than the Texas he left.

But I digress.

What follows is something that may be unfair to Bro. Burrough, being as I have never undertaken such a comprehensive project as the one he turned out about these folks. His research on those four families—along with a few others, such as the colorful Glen McCarthy—represented a monumental task.

That I'm about to be critical about at least part of his epic effort might be a bit unfair, except for the fact I shelled out the better part of thirty bucks for my copy which, as I later learned, would have been considerably cheaper at the on-line Barnes & Noble than it was at the checkout counter of the local Barnes & Noble.

WHAT LITTLE I already knew about those four families was that H. L. Hunt was once considered to be the richest man in the world which, among other things, allowed him to afford two wives and two sets of kids. I knew that his son from his primary wife, Lamar, launched the American Football League, and that his own Dallas Texans caused the NFL to plant the Cowboys in Big D to protect the market.

Fittingly or otherwise, those Cowboys belonged to Clint Murchinson.

It's difficult to tell what Burrough set out to do with all that work. If the intent was to make a couple of bucks by essaying a colorful era and the history it produced, he was very successful. If it were to pick up where Edna Ferber left off with *Giant*, portraying wealthy Texans as a bunch of blowhard, bigoted, anti-Semitic right-wingers . . . well, he did a little of that, too.

Yet it was a very interesting read.

I DID LIKE the fact that he treated Lupe kindly. He recognized her as a person of wit and charm and class which, as I said above, she certainly was.

When George W. Bush, the governor, appointed me to the UNT board of regents, one of the first persons to greet me there was Lupe. When I called her "Mrs. Murchison" (thankfully, I did correctly pronounce it Murkison) she corrected me.

"I am just *Lupe*," she said, "and I am going to assume that you are just *Burle*."

I had news for her: I was already *Just Burle* long before I met Mrs., er, Lupe . . .

Shoot, I could spend the remaining space in this piece I'm writing just talking about Lupe. She not only was kind but generous. (The next time you're going up I-35 which splits the UNT campus through Denton, take a look at the Lupe Murchison Performing Arts Center—There's a reason it bears her name.)

Once my wife questioned my driving up for a board meeting in my pickup. But it was a brand-new, bright red Dodge, and I wanted to see how it did out on the road. I pulled into the regents parking area at the same time Lupe was being dropped off, and she waited for me to climb out of my truck. She walked around it a couple of times as though she might want to buy it, boasted about its beauty, and we walked together on into the ad building.

The commencement exercises were being held on another part of campus, and when the board broke up to head in that direction, the Chancellor offered Lupe a ride.

"No, thanks," she said. "I want to ride in Burle's new truck."

En route to the coliseum, she patted my shoulder and said, "How's that for inviting myself?"

"Fine," I said, audibly. "Damn fine" was what I was really thinking . . .

ALL OF US regents were thrilled when Lupe insisted we hold one of our annual retreats at her ranch near Athens. We guys were housed in the big house whose long hallway was covered with pictures of presidents, kings, politicians, senators—all the persons of clout Burrough described in his book. It was a great three days of working, relaxing, eating and strolling the grounds, which—as the sign at the gate had informed—were patrolled by armed cowboys on horseback.

As I said, I don't know how accurately Burrough portrayed the other characters. Lupe is the only one I ever met.

Again, I have never undertaken the writing of such a complex matter. But I have spent considerable time in the oil patch, and I was around when WWII kicked off.

So, while his research seemed to be thorough and comprehensive where the family biographies and holdings were concerned, he didn't spend enough time learning more about the workings of the oilfields themselves. And they played such an intertwining part of the book.

If he writes another book about Texas oilfields, he needs to know that roughnecks don't lay pipelines; roustabouts do that. Roughnecks work on rotary drilling rigs. Tool-pushers aren't part of a cable tool drilling crew. Those guys are tool-dressers. Tool-pushers are the bosses of all drilling crews, each of which answers to a driller.

And, hey Bryan: There was no need for additional *jet* fuel when WWII started. That's mainly because there were no jet planes.

I have to confess that I enjoyed the book. And I did learn a lot from it, mainly about the four families he featured. But I also learned something about money:

I should have bought the dern thing at Amazon .com . . .

On the job at the *A-J*—only in Texas

# TEXAS TECH
# AND SPORTS

Burle with Donny Anderson and Tom Wilson

## WHY '48 WAS MORE THAN A BASEBALL MEMORY

THE MAIN difference between the World Series just completed and the one played in 1948 was that this time I was not emotionally invested in its outcome. But, World Series titles aside, the difference between now and the year 1948 exceeds my ability to measure.

Cleveland having won that one was just one of many things that seemed to be going my way in '48—and I'm not talking wealth, either. The fact that a brand-new Ford DeLuxe sold for $500 didn't mean that everybody in Moran could rush right out and buy one. Dollars meant a lot in those days, as did the way of life itself. But the latter fell victim to changing priorities that stripped a nation of its innocence and replaced its comfort zone with skepticism, and dampened its faith with the louder voice of cynics.

But, for me personally, 1948 was a great year to be a boy whose naiveté served as a catalyst for a belief that everything would always go his way. And Moran, Texas, a town whose 1100 or so souls who were as close to the earth as the soil they tilled, offered nothing to impede, much less dispel, that outlook.

Bankers loaned money on a handshake, people bought groceries on credit and paid cash for everything else and—of frequent importance to my buddies and me—the local sheriff was more interested in keeping boys out of trouble than he was in making arrests.

And, in the eyes of my dad and most others of his ilk, the measure of a man was how hard he worked and whether he paid his bills.

ASK A HISTORIAN about the year 1948 and he'll likely bring up how LBJ stole the Senatorial race from Coke Stevenson; or, equally likely, chortle over how Harry Truman's upset victory over Thomas Dewey shocked the GOP and left the storied old *Chicago Tribune* with egg all over its masthead. The *Trib*'s morning editions had announced in type four inches tall that Dewey had won. The picture of Truman holding up the front page of that paper got worldwide play.

That may have been the last year in which everything—from the school house to the White House—seemed to go just to my liking. Now I must inject right about here that I grew up in a household, a town, a county and a state where almost everybody was a Democrat. Accordingly, not realizing there were other states with different outlooks and moralities, I often wondered why they even held a General Election. All Shackelford County races were settled during the primaries.

But I digress . . .

It was also the time that I developed a set of criteria for my heroes, and that measurement follows me yet. In '48 my idols were Bobby Feller, Doak Walker, Bob Richards, and others who starred as citizens as well as athletes. That criterion has not changed for me through the years; accordingly, I have had few heroes, although Craig Biggio comes quickly to mind.

IT WAS IN the autumn of '48 that I entered high school, which in itself would begin a four-year journey that, even now, I recall as one of the most meaningful experiences of my life. With no exceptions that I can now recall—I likely would have named several had I been asked at the time—my teachers were strict and demanding, but they knew how to impart knowledge. And had it not been for an English teacher and an ag teacher, I might today be an idled octogenarian roughneck hoping that the oil prices would soon surge so I could go back to work.

It also was a time when my favorite teams were the Moran Bulldogs, the SMU Mustangs, and the Cleveland Indians. In '48, that the Bulldogs won district, the Mustangs won the Southwest Conference and Cleveland won the Series was no surprise to me. To my way of thinking, that's the way it would always be: My teams would win, my heroes would be recognized.

And, hey, didn't Walker win the Heisman, Feller pitch the Indians into the Series, and Richards become only the second man in history to clear fiftteen feet in the pole vault? No further convincing could I have needed . . .

AND MORAN, Texas, itself was a great place to be a kid. It had everything a boy could want—especially a boy who'd never been more than 120 miles from home, had no idea that fish or steak could be cooked any place other than a cast iron skillet, and who assumed all cow feed was selected not by its ingredients but by the pattern on the sack.

Hey, we had a pool hall, a drug store, a café with a jukebox, and a number of deep swimming holes in all three creeks surrounding the town.

That was about the time I began to transition from my regular buddies toward friends who were softer of touch, sweeter of smell, and a whole lot easier on the eye.

That's also when Garland Shelton, our barber, would get closer instruction on how I wanted my hair to look when he finished. Shooting a game of Snooker with my pal Rabbit suddenly paled in comparison to accompanying a Moran cutie to Doc Martin's soda fountain.

And if the girl really liked you, she didn't mind that you ordered one drink and two straws. Either germs had not yet been invented, or maybe they just hadn't found their way to Moran . . .

DUE TO THE outcome of last week's Series finale, the year 1908—worn into time by frequent mentions as the last time the Cubs won the series—will fall out of prominence as it yields that position to 1948. That will be remembered by baseball enthusiasts as the "last year the Indians won a World Series."

But to me, 1948 will mean much more than that. It will indeed be forever remembered as a great year to have been a fourteen-year-old boy in Moran, Texas.

It doesn't get any more meaningful than that . . .

## WINNERS ALL

A NUMBER OF years ago I was sitting with a couple of sports legends, sipping ice tea and talking about, of all things, Little League baseball. That nobody at the table had anything much good to say about it is, I suppose, why that conversation of yore came flashing back today.

Now here I am this day, having spent much of an entire week sitting at chair's edge, hanging onto every pitch, every swing of the bat of a bunch of twelve-year-old kids involved in a serious flirtation with a world's championship . . . not just any kids . . . Lubbock kids . . . OUR kids!

We adults hereabouts should have learned something from this bunch of youngsters, whose bright eyes stayed focused, who seemed unperturbed even when the games would take an erratic turn. They seemed to know they would regain control, and they generally always did.

It was a team that every dad wanted to toast, every mom wanted to hug. It wasn't just Lubbock that got involved with this team. I spent much of the week in the Metroplex and was delightfully surprised by the number of people thereabouts who were caught up in the Series. Which proves another point:

Texas Pride is far too boisterous to be constrained by the bounds of a single city . . .

LITTLE LEAGUE baseball has been a popular target for critics through the years, especially those whose image of the organization was one of parents out of control, of zealous fathers trying to bury their own athletic frustrations vicariously through their sons, of coaches with a Vince Lombardi complex, etc., etc.

In fact, back in the mid-1970s, when a group of us from the Monterey Optimist Club launched the MOB basketball program, our first stated goal was to "not become like Little League baseball." What that actually meant had naught to do with Little League baseball itself but, rather, a perceived need to devise regulations that would provide control of parents and proper behavior among our coaches.

Several of our board members were involved in both sports. Kids were never the problem; they just wanted to play. Adults were the concern.

GETTING BACK to the conversation mentioned at the outset, I was in the company of one of baseball's all-time greats, Mickey Mantle, and football legend Bobby Layne, who had invited me along.

Mantle brought Little Leagues into the conversation sort of obliquely. He was talking about what country kids used to do for pastime.

"At Commerce (Oklahoma), we'd find us a vacant lot or a cow pasture or any open space and play baseball from morning until it was too dark to see the ball," he recalled. "I think that's really how I learned to hit.

"And that's my problem with Little League baseball. It's too regimented. A kid might get to bat, what? Once or twice a day . . . three at the most. Hell, we'd bat twenty or thirty times a day."

I mentioned Joey Jay, who was the first Little Leaguer to make it to the majors.

"Yeah," Mantle acknowledged, "but Joey's a pitcher."

THOUGHTS OF THOSE old images of Little League baseball stormed back into my mind each time the TV cameras would pan the crowd of Lubbock parents, all seated together, cheering and laughing and enjoying the game. What impressed me most of all was their behavior in general, their demeanor in particular. The fantastic ambassadorship being displayed by the Lubbock kids on the field was mirrored in the stands by their parents.

It occurred to me that I was the only person I saw yelling at the umps and using words unbecoming of the occasion. Fortunately for Lubbock's image, I was looking *at* the TV, not vice versa . . .

Today (this is being written shortly after the third-place game), the only ill feelings I am harboring for LLB is the 85-pitch rule and what it cost Garrett Williams . . . not once, but twice. The entire world shared his pain today when one fouled-off pitch cost him personal claim to a no-hitter. And young Garrett likely was the least demonstrative of us all, when he simply ducked and lifted his head in a motion of temporary exasperation.

Had one pitch not been fouled off, he would have been allowed to face another batter.

Earlier, the pitch limit had no doubt cost him at least a share of the World Series record for strikeouts. The rule itself is a good one, devised to protect youngsters from the perils of overuse. But, on each occasion, I found myself hoping that the commissioner would appear out of the stands to grant an exception.

Obviously, it didn't happen. Even so, Garrett was clearly the best pitcher in the Series which means, essentially, the best in the world. Not bad for a Lubbock kid, eh?

THE LONG RANGE benefit this city will receive from these youngsters is that, no doubt, many of them will grow up and take their place in its midst.

It gives me a great feelings nowadays when my everyday activities . . . everything from walking in the mall to trading cars to doing my banking . . . brings me into contact with kids that I either coached or got to know during my dozen years of involvement with MOB basketball. Tired though it may be, the assumption that sports participation builds character is frequently upheld. And those seven boys who just completed a fantastic performance on a worldwide stage already personify that very trait.

So do their coaches . . . and their parents.

I wish I could have seen this far down the road the day I sat with those two Hall of Fame athletes, conversing about Little League baseball. Both have since passed on. And the restaurant itself, which bore Mickey Mantle's name, was destroyed in the tornado of 1970 and never rebuilt.

Meanwhile, Little League baseball has survived and thrived and flooded the rosters of every major league team. And this group of Lubbock kids, their parents, their coaches are not left to lament all the things that might have been.

They've only to bask in the glory of what they have done.

Winners, all . . .

## CHRISTOPHER

IN THE FIRST place, Christopher shouldn't be old enough for college to be a consideration—not this guy, who only a short while ago sat perched atop my shoulders spinning a ceiling fan, and, shortly after that, roused me from a filling Thanksgiving meal for what he called "our traditional game of catch" with the football he kept there at the ranch.

I looked at him, sitting there in the chancellor's office, confident and poised, listening intently to every word. He's a young man, now, I thought, silently wondering what gives Father Time the right to steal the very things a grandfather cherishes most.

My mind was brought back to the present, beckoned by what I was hearing Kent Hance explaining to Christopher.

"You are coming to Texas Tech," he said. "You don't even need to look in any other direction. This is where you belong."

Hance sells Tech the very way the Watkins man used to sell liniment . . . let the product define the need. That, plus his unyielding confidence in the direction the university is headed and, of even greater import, Kent's sincere conviction of what his university is all about.

In reality, it was I who was being sold. Christopher was already there . . .

I WAS DEALING with a very private fantasy about having one of my grandchildren attend the university where I not only did my undergraduate work but, in addition, served two hitches—twelve consecutive years—on its board of regents. Christopher, who attends Plano West High School just a few miles down the road from UNT, was the most likely candidate. It's a great organization, the UNT System, whose anchor university is the fourth largest in the state and rapidly closing in on the University of Houston as No. 3, behind only UT and A&M.

Still, that fantasy was admittedly driven by ego. A part of me liked the thought of someday having a grandson wandering through campus buildings whose cornerstones bore my name and his. During my term, at least eleven buildings were erected, each having the members of the board of regents prominently displayed. When the first such building was completed, I remember joking to my wife that it felt sort of good, seeing my name on a school building where I hadn't scratched it there myself . . .

Even my affection for my alma mater diminishes against the thought of having Christopher in Lubbock for four years . . . even longer, given his chosen field of study.

THERE WERE MANY things about Texas Tech that Christopher found impressive . . . the awesome beauty of the campus . . . the friendly and helpful nature of a student body busily loading cars to head home for the summer . . . the academic and athletic facilities that commanded the landscape . . . the lore and traditions of the institution itself . . .

It was not Christopher's first time to see Tech. He had been on campus a number of times before. But this time it was special: This was Christopher's official visit, a two-day excused absence his high school makes available for students to visit universities they are considering. That visit had started the day before in the office of Rob Shindell, who heads up Tech's recruiting. He explained the mechanics to Christopher, answered critical questions, and set up the campus tour.

Over the past four decades, I have spent considerable time on the Tech campus, both as a graduate student and as a sports writer who spent a dozen years covering Red

Chris, Nana, and G'dad

Raider athletics. But I had never had an actual tour of the place. I found it both interesting and enlightening.

Busy as they were, the students we encountered went out of their way to be friendly and courteous and helpful to this group of highschoolers making up the tour. Directing the walking tour was a sophomore student whose last name I remember because it's the same as my home county—Shackelford.

I already knew that rearmost orifice of Will Rogers's horse could be used as a compass to locate College Station, but this was the first time I had heard it mentioned in such an official forum. I also learned that this sweaty guy who breezed past us was a regular at what he was doing. It was quite warm at the time, but he zipped by like a campus streaker who'd forgot to take off his britches.

"That is . . . was . . . Pat Knight, our basketball coach," Ms. Shackelford explained, watching him zoom past. "He jogs around the entire campus every day."

Christopher was sort of impressed when I told him that his own dad had been a ball boy for Gerald Myers during one of Gerald's championship years as the Red Raiders basketball coach. That awe diminished some, though, when I explained that Scott had served in the old Coliseum, not the stately United Spirit Arena where Pat Knight operates.

BY NOW, I should be past being amazed at Kent Hance. But watching and listening to him converse with a potential student gave me a little more insight into a man who has enjoyed success as a teacher, a congressman, a statesman, and even a lawyer. I watched the years separating this man of sixty-something and my sixteen-year-old grandson peel off as Hance revisited his own freshman year on a level that resonated immediately.

"I was an eighteen-year-old freshman living in Bledsoe Hall when I met some of the best people I ever knew and some of the sorriest; some of the smartest people I ever knew and some of the dumbest," Hance recalled. He then paused, and added ". . . and I learned something from all of them."

He gave Christopher advice on how to behave, how to study and—with surprising effectiveness—how to learn.

Hance had served in Congress with the colorful Charlie Wilson, who was his friend. Chris wanted to know whether the movie, *Charlie Wilson's War*, was an accurate portrayal of the East Texas politico. Christopher was openly amused by Hance's anecdotal description of where the movie both overstated and understated the personality and behavior of Wilson.

"He invited me to make that trip (to the Middle East) with him, but he was going to be gone longer than I could be away."

En route to the airport, I asked Christopher what impressed him most about Tech. He listed off a plethora of things that made him fall in love with the place. Then he mentioned what *intrigued* him most: The big guy at the top.

"I never would have thought somebody that important could also be cool . . . "

In the autumn of '09, Christopher will enroll here, having chosen Tech and never really considering UNT. His reasoning smacked of logic.

"Tech is to an architect what UNT is to a musician."

My little grandson of yesterday is indeed all grown up . . .

It will be fun having him constantly around . . . even if we no longer play with the ceiling fan. We can still have a game of catch . . .

## TECH—THE OLD DAYS

I'M SURE THINGS are better now—salaries and facilities certainly are—but the recent passing of Jess Stiles ended the last mark of a comfort zone that once defined Texas Tech athletics.

It was my good fortune to arrive on the local sports scene the very year the Red Raiders would be playing their first season in the storied old Southwest Conference. Tech sports had just moved into "town," so to speak; but, like the country boys of lore, it was slow to adapt to "city ways."

Covering the Red Raiders in those days had to be the easiest job on the planet. I had full access to the facilities and everybody who worked there—from Luie the groundskeeper to Polk Robison the athletic director—it was, as the old sit-com used to say, actually going someplace where everybody knew your name.

A coffee pot in the northwest corner of the athletic department lobby was always full, and the round table next to it was a favorite gathering place for supporters who would wander in and make themselves at home. They would be joined intermittently by JT King or Gene Gibson, the head football and basketball coaches, respectively. Polk was frequently there, and assistant coaches from all sports often stopped by to chat. I could always count on seeing either Chuff Benton, Bob Fuller, my boss Parker Prouty, Buster Hicks, or any number of other high-powered benefactors sitting around the table when I would arrive to make my afternoon rounds.

I FIRST MET Stiles during a Red Raider Club golf stop in Borger, where he was coaching at the time. Jess had built a reputation at Wichita Falls Hirschi, a brand-new school when he took over the head job. Previously, he had been on the staff of the legendary Joe Golding at Wichita Falls High. We were in the same foursome that day and by the time the round was over I felt like I had known him for years. And, looking back on it, his ability to build relationships was the skill that brought him success at every job, at every level.

Although Stiles was a graduate of Midwestern, his heart and soul were converted to Tech. He was one of three members of King's staff that survived the change when Jim Carlen took over the football program. And, perhaps because of that, there was a special bond among the holdovers, Jess, Tom Wilson, and John Conley. It's my guess that for the remainder of his life, Wilson remained his closest friend. That assumption is based on his moving to College Station to join Wilson's staff when Tom was named head coach at A&M.

"Wilson was the only person who could have got me to leave Tech," Stiles told me at the time. "When he called, I asked him if he really felt like I could help him. When he said yes, we started loading the car."

That relationship never waned, even after Wilson moved back home to Corsicana and Stiles returned to Lubbock, where he pulled his red blazer out of the closet for good.

PAY CHECKS were another facet of the 1960s that, along with easy access to coaches and players, was different from today. Darrell Royal, arguably the best coach of his era, retired in 1976 without the kind of financial security he no doubt would have accumulated in today's college football market.

After back-to-back bowl appearances in '64 and '65, King's pay was in the $20,000 range. And when he was able to convince the Tech administration that John Conley, his top assistant, was worth $16,000 a year, the published report caught the attention of Gibson.

"That's the amount I'm going to be asking for," Gibson told me. "I think the head basketball coach should get at least as much money as the highest paid football assistant."

Gib didn't get it. But, when he was fired a year later, that's the exact amount Tech paid Bob Bass, his replacement.

However, it must be pointed those were the days when you could get a pretty good seat in Jones Stadium for less than $5, and for four bits you could get a burger with fries and drink purt near anyplace in town . . .

TOMMY DOYLE, one of a large number of players from that era who came in for Stiles' funeral, told me a story that brought home just how long ago the '60s had been. Donny Anderson noticed among the other passengers on a plane he had boarded was Sheryl Swoopes, the all-America star of the national championship Lady Raiders basketball team.

"Donny went over, introduced himself, and told her how much he appreciated all she had accomplished and all the attention she had brought to Tech," Doyle related. "She thanked him, then as he was about to return to his seat, she said:

"By the way, Donny, did you go to Tech?'"

STILES' FUNERAL brought together scores of former Red Raiders and, along with them, renewed memories of those days of yore and the cast that made them indelible . . . Robison, King, Berl Huffman, Conley, Gibson, Bill Holmes, Ralph Carpenter . . .

Jess was indeed special to Don King, an all-everything guard in the '60s. Don had been an all-state performer on Stiles' breakout team at Hirschi. But it wasn't only players and fellow coaches who filled the sanctuary to pay final respects. Through his personality and helpful nature, Jess had somehow touched the lives of everyone who came to pay tribute. All, however unwittingly, were also there to witness the end of an irretrievable era. Stiles' relaxed nature mirrored those days when Tech athletics were all about fun and fellowship. Funding, although critical, was a byproduct not yet a consummate force.

I think back to those days each time I cross paths with my friend Buddy Forbess, one of the throw-backs. No matter what twists and turns our conversation takes, Buddy always closes with the same observation: "I still miss that old coffee table . . . "

He never bothers to say which coffee table; he doesn't need to.

I miss it, too, Buddy. And all the times and personalities its memory represents . . .

## Jack Dale Era

ALTHOUGH IT'S tempting to say the passing of Jack Dale marked the end of a sportscasting era, it wouldn't be accurate. That era ended at least a generation ago—or whenever it was that Exxon (nee Humble) decided to get out of the broadcasting business and focus on pumping gasoline.

I don't remember the exact date even though I have been grumbling ever since.

The change, which was drastic, came when colleges borrowed a page from the NFL and set up their own networks, hired their own broadcasters who, if they wanted to keep their jobs, were expected to hooray the wins and put a positive spin on the losses. And objectivity wasn't the only collateral casualty.

During the years when Humble ruled the Southwest Conference airways, every member school's game was broadcast every Saturday. No matter where you were in Texas and no matter which was your favorite team, you could eventually find a station that was carrying its game. Nowadays you don't have to be far from home to be out of touch with your Red Raiders or Bears. In fact, there are spots in Lubbock where the Tech game fades out with the sunset, or however soon after dark the station has to cut its power.

But I digress.

JACK DALE WAS first and foremost a basketball announcer whose love for that game was the engine that drove him upwards to a level above all others in the field. But he also blossomed as a football sportscaster when he was added to the Humble team.

It was during his time doing color alongside the game broadcasters that Dale honed his own play-by-play skills and, of lasting import, the discipline of objectivity. Both were mainstays of his long and productive career.

It wasn't long until McKinn-Ericson, following a recommmendation by its lead announcer, Kern Tips, moved

Dale into a play-by-play role. During much of that time, he was assisted in the booth by another Lubbock sportscasting legend, the late Ray Boyd. That relationship also revealed a lot about the character of Jack Dale.

Ray, who had been crippled by polio as a child, could maneuver with a pair of canes, but only barely—certainly not well enough to handle a briefcase or anything that had to be carried by hand. So at every airport stop, Jack would see to Ray's luggage, then get a wheelchair and push Ray through the terminal and onto the plane. And he did so with that trademark smile glued to his face.

Jack didn't preach the Christian ethic; he just practiced it . . .

AS THE AGENCY representing Humble Oil throughout its sponsorship of SWC football, McKinn-Ericson not only established the standards for the broadcasters (i.e., no "homing," no trite phraseology, no criticism of game officials, etc.), they had a representative in the booth at every game. Because all the above had been Jack Dale's practice during his years at courtside in basketball, it wasn't much of an adjustment. But it did engrain the tenet even deeper which, in later years, made it difficult for him to look kindly on the generation of broadcasters that followed.

"I don't like it a bit," he once intimated to me after I had asked him about working with cheerleaders at the next mike. "It just goes against everything I was ever taught."

The problem for Jack and other objectivity purists is that the fans love it. They want the announcer to yell "way to go" and question every call that goes against Ol' Siwash.

Hey, you want objectivity, read the accounts in tomorrow's newspapers.

When Tips retired as lead announcer, he was replaced by Connie Alexander, Jack's closest friend in the business. Jack was paired up with Frank Fallon of Waco and took over Connie's No. 2 spot (Did I not mention that Alexander was my old schoolmate at Moran High? Probably just as well that I didn't . . . )

Shortly afterward, the network disbanded and the broadcasting world changed forever.

DURING MUCH OF the 1960s, I spent most of the winter months with Jack and his sidekick Bob Nash, traveling with the Tech basketball team from the Southwest to the Midwest, from California to Kentucky, and many stops in between. Cooped up hours at a time in the confines of a 1940s vintage DC-3, the three of us had lots of time to get acquainted. It didn't take long to know everything there was to know about Nash and me, both being a bit on the talkative side. Jack mainly listened, more amused than interested.

It was the nature of that airline charter service—now long out of business—to foul up, sometimes harmlessly, other times not so much . . . like the time when we were heading for Houston and the port engine went lame somewhere above Spur. And again when we were seven hours late arriving at (then) Lubbock Municipal Airport after leaving Lexington, Kentucky, early that morning. That last one led to a wire service reporting that a plane carrying the Texas Tech basketball team was hours late and presumed lost.

Actually, we had to put down at an abandoned Air Force base near Gene Autry, Oklahoma. It wasn't a mechanical thing that time: The boss had radioed the pilot that an FAA inspector was at the Lubbock airport and they were to set down somewhere until after he had left. Nash and I grumbled for the entire time. Jack walked around the desolate premises, perhaps thinking of his days at Altus, wherever that was from wherever the yell we were.

TUESDAY, AT Jack's memorial service, I was amazed but not surprised at the turnout. The large sanctuary at Trinity Church was practically filled—not only by sports figures whom you would expect to be there, but by fans who had spent much of their lives listening to that magnificently clear voice and his stylistic delivery.

When his sons were talking about their dad's one byword ("Ke-rap") I thought about that for a while and later determined it must have been a familial thing. During my years of traveling with Jack, the closest thing to profanity I ever heard him utter was that same word, but spoken without the "e" sound and preceded by the word "well."

Jack Dale left behind many friends and a multitude of admirers. I never heard anybody ever criticize Jack, but it's my contention that he would have handled criticism much better than he did praise.

When he was elected to the sportscasters hall of fame, I called with the intention of complimenting him and offering congratulations. I couldn't get it done because he kept changing the subject.

He's gone now, and Lubbock has lost another legend. But his craft lost even more.

Jack Dale was the lone survivor of sportscasting done right . . .

## SPIKE WAS A CLOSE FRIEND TO EVERYBODY HE KNEW

EXCEPT THAT it's probably one of the largest such venues in town, I have no idea how many people can fit into the First Methodist Church auditorium. What I do know is I arrived there ninety minutes early for Spike's funeral and it was already about two-thirds full.

You note that I did not use Spike's last name; few people do. And if it hadn't rhymed with "Spike" that number might be even smaller.

By now—a day shy of two weeks since his shocking death—everybody with a computer and an audience has written endlessly about this fantastic man whose life was a legend unto itself. That he was a dern good football coach had little to do with the void created by his departing wake.

Now it's my turn to speak . . .

I FIRST MET Spike in 1971 when I was a sports writer covering Southwest Conference football. I was in Darrell Royal's office when Spike stuck his head in the door, perhaps to ask a question. When he saw that Darrell had a guest, he turned to walk away. Royal beckoned him back, introduced us, and told Spike he'd see him in a few minutes.

Obviously, I knew who Spike was. Having by then spent more than a dozen years covering Texas football,

I—like everybody else in the craft—knew of Spike Dykes as a successful, and much travelled, high school coach.

It was at least a year later before I would see Spike again. That was when it first dawned on me that this guy with a pleasant smile and a ready quip had an uncanny memory for names and faces. Just as I started to introduce myself, he interrupted. "I know you," he said, extending his hand. "I met you in Coach Royal's office. You're from Lubbock, where I was born, sort of accidental."

He went on to tell the story, which I would hear many times in the years to come, about how his dad and his pregnant mom were simply passing through Lubbock when she went into labor. Spike's dad whipped into the old St. Mary's Hospital where she gave birth to a bouncing baby boy. She couldn't have been aware that this infant someday would become an indelible legend in that very town.

BY THE TIME Spike joined the Tech coaching staff, I had been out of sports writing for several years. But joining the management team at the *A-J* had not diminished my interest in college football, especially the Red Raiders.

I was at the press conference announcing his promotion to head coach. I stood around and waited to offer congratulations. As I shook his hand, I looked closely to see whether having just been handed the reins to a highly respected college football team would show up in his demeanor. Nope. He grinned that same old grin and asked me if I shouldn't be back behind my "big desk" at the paper trying to figure out who needed yellin' at.

.   We didn't visit all that often but on the occasions I did send him a note he always fired one right back. The difference was, his were usually funny. Our conversations normally weren't football related, except when it involved my alma mater, UNT. More on that later.

Spike, at least to me, not only would never criticize one of his players, but would come to their immediate defense if I did. One quarterback used to really get under my skin. He had a cannon for an arm, but it seemed to me his bad plays came at the worst times possible.

"He doesn't know one jersey color from another," I lamented.

"He's gonna throw interceptions," Spike said. "That's because of the way he plays. But he's a dern good quarterback and I'm glad he's ours."

That very quarterback went on to play several years in the NFL.

Then he had a defensive lineman who went out of his way to get roughing penalties that not only were unnecessary but often affected the outcome.

"Why do you keep playing that guy?" I asked.

"He plays with emotion. He can't always control it but it makes him a good player."

ONE OF THE most pleasant visits I ever had with Spike was in January of 1996. He showed up in my office with a smile that was even wider than ever. After an exchange of pleasantries, he reached into a bag he was carrying and pulled out a football. It was addressed to me and had been signed by the entire Red Raider team, coaches included. Tech had finished 9-3 that year, including a win over Air Force in the Copper Bowl.

It was, indeed, a special memento. One, it represented the last ever Southwest Conference season. But, mainly, it was because Spike had hand-carried it to me.

"You can put it up there on that shelf, right in front of that green and white one," he quipped, pointing to a football on which was printed, "North Texas 21, Texas Tech 14."

It had been dropped off by UNT coach Darrel Dickey after the 1999 game, one of three losses Spike suffered at the hands of my old school. Even though I was proud of those victories, I felt bad that they were bringing Spike much grief. I never once needled, or even kidded him about them.

AS THE FUNERAL ended and the overflow crowd began to disperse, it occurred to me that every person there probably considered Spike as his friend. And, most likely, he could have called each one of them by name and, equally predictable, would have had something to say with each handshake.

He was a special coach. Unlike those who followed him and set up schedules to assure a bowl bid, ol' Spike took on them all—USC, Ohio State, whoever he could get.

Spike never took himself seriously, and he never had to work hard to sustain that "ol country boy from Ballinger" persona. Whether he ever gained his due recognition as a great football coach, Spike long had been toasted as a great human being.

Two weeks ago in Lubbock he was honored as both . . .

## TOM WILSON

ONE ASPECT OF being an old guy is the accompanying realization that, under our very sun, nothing is really new.

Oops . . . I wrote that sentence while only considering such things as cars that recently introduced push-button starters and full-sized spare tires. Only later did it occur to me to compare something of yore with the iPads, iPods, iPhones and all the iWhatevers yet to come. Couldn't do it.

Yet one thing is for sure: Almost anything that happens nowadays reminds me of something that occurred at least once before. And anytime it does, it kindles the urge—actually, the necessity—to run tell somebody about it. Like the other day when Tech's AD rushed out and hired the Aggie offensive coordinator, who happened to be a former all-conference Red Raider quarterback.

That immediately took me back to 1977 when a Tech AD almost rushed out and did the exact same thing, right down to it involving the sitting Aggie offensive coordinator, who also happened to be a former all-conference Red Raider quarterback.

The difference is that Kirby Hocutt hired Kliff Kingsbury with full administrative support.

J. T. King hired Tom Wilson, but the administration made him renege on the deal.

That was, in my opinion, an administrative double-cross that left one party embarrassed, another devastated, and put a good man's word in limbo.

ANYWAY, THIS old story popped up in my mind due to the circumstance which, at first thought, was not at all unusual. Hey, lots of offensive coordinators get head coaching jobs, some were former quarterbacks and, I'm guessing, some even go back to coach their alma maters. But, considering how close it came to Kingsbury's hiring being a repeat of what had happed exactly the same way once before . . . well, I decided it was a story worth telling. First, though, I decided to call Wilson and see if he'd thought about the same thing.

Turned out he hadn't. At the time his cell phone rang, he was lining up a twenty-foot putt that he felt very confident about making. We visited a few moments before he excused himself, said he'd be right back to me after "I knock in this putt." The phone lay silent on the frog hair and, not hearing the "S" word, I figured he must have made it.

"Nope," he said. "Left it two inches short."

Remembering Tom as I do, he wouldn't have uttered the "S" word if it had rolled clear off the green. Not necessarily because of the purity of his vocabulary, it's that I never heard him say it when he overthrew a receiver, which would have been more perplexing and, I'm guessing, less frequent.

But I digress.

ACTUALLY, WRITING a story was the last thing on my mind when I called. I hadn't talked to him in a while and, mainly, I wanted to catch up. Much has happened to Tom since that disappointing day in 1977 and—greatly to the credit of his own character and talents—most of it has been good.

A year after the Tech job backfired, he was named head coach of the Aggies, where he served for the next three seasons. That tenure ended not because he was fired but, instead, because Bum Bright, the jillionaire who at the time was chairman of the A&M board of regents, went out on his own and hired Jackie Sherrill away from Pittsburgh. That caught not only Wilson but the university president by surprise.

Also notable, that made Sherrill the first college coach in Texas to sign a million dollar contract.

Wilson did return to Tech as Jerry Moore's offensive coordinator but, after Moore's firing, Tom decided to retire. But, before that, he closed out his coaching career by taking Corsicana—his old high school team, to the state finals—and spending the next few years as the CISD athletic director.

Then came politics. He ran for, and won, a seat on the Corsicana city council, where he continues to serve.

NOTHING EVER came easy for Wilson but somehow he always made things work. To begin with, he wanted to go to Baylor but couldn't. Baylor had a rule against married players and he and Dawn, his girlfriend since junior high, got hitched as soon as they graduated from high school.

At Tech, having already landed Brownwood High superstar Ben Elledge and Monterey's James Ellis, Tom was taken almost as an afterthought. As a sophomore in 1963, he played just enough to waste a year of eligibility.

Come spring training, his fortunes changed. Whatever team Tom was on always won. Coaches notice such things. When King told me that summer that Wilson would be his starting QB come fall, I thought he was joking. King justified his decision with a single sentence:

"The kid's smart and he's a winner."

Wilson took practically every snap for the next two seasons, both of which ended with Tech in a bowl game. His senior year, he made the all-conference first team, an unknown kid from Corsicana having beaten out a bunch of guys everybody had heard of.

AFTER TALKING to Tom—I had to get his cell number from Donny Anderson, his closest buddy in college and beyond—I called Don Williams and told him about the comparison. Don was snowed under and barely had time to say hi.

I typed up some notes and emailed them to Terry Greenberg, the editor, figuring he could decide what, if anything, to do with them.

To my surprise, those very notes showed up Sunday morning under my very mug. (Yes, I still look somewhat like that picture which was made sometime after Wilson graduated.) Not that I minded, but if I had known it would be appearing in print I would have changed the ending, which said he didn't want to discuss that old issue any further. That left the impression he was bothered by it.

Truth was, he didn't want to discuss *anything* any further. He was on the 18th green, the press was on, and he had a putt to make.

I didn't even get to listen for the "S" word . . .

## COTTON BOWL '09

BY THE TIME this appears in print, I should be back home preparing, perhaps, to write about only the second Cotton Bowl game I ever watched from the stands. I'm hoping—nay, counting on—its having left me in a better mood than I was in after watching the first one I saw there. That's the time a whole bunch of us watching USC play football were joined by the Raiders themselves, who also were watching USC play football . . .

Anyway, I am writing this piece in anticipation of being there for the last Cotton Bowl game ever to be played in that storied old arena, long known as "The House That Doak Built." The stadium's first major expansion was made necessary by the ticket demands influenced by Doak Walker, the three-time SMU all-American and, in my humble opinion, the best collegian ever to play the game.

Until Walker came along, the Mustangs played snugly if not smugly inside Ownby Stadium, right there on campus.

Without a Doak Walker or, for that matter, even a Pete or Sam or Johnny Walker, SMU several years ago downgraded itself to, of all places, Ownby Stadium.

But I digress.

THAT TECH-USC debacle was the first Cotton Bowl *game* I watched from the stands. I had seen a lot of other football games—including a couple featuring Walker— in the Cotton Bowl stadium. But the ten or twelve actual Cotton Bowl games I had previously watched were from the press box which, come to think of it, is the second-best place to watch the game.

The best place—especially for a guy of my age and intolerance for cold weather and yelling seatmates—is right there in my kickback chair, comfortably positioned in front of my HDTV and within easy range of both coffee pot and bathroom. That's without mentioning access to a pause button in case the bladder gets out of sync with the called timeouts . . .

Obviously, I will not mention that part to my son, who thought he was doing something special when he gave his mom and me these game tickets for Christmas. And maybe I'll get lucky and the weather will turn out warm and I'll be seated behind somebody who realizes you don't have to stand up to see the game and next to somebody who's medicated by Prozac instead of Lasix . . .

COVERING THOSE Cotton Bowl games was a lot of fun, especially since that was happening during a time when I was younger and before I had severed my relationship with adult beverages. Now don't get me wrong: I know that a feller could have just as much fun when he's sober. But he probably won't. Hey, who wants to face the next morning remembering everything he did the night before?

I have many memories of Cotton Bowl Week—sports writers always went in a week before the game to keep the folks back home informed about team activities, preparations, and how the game itself was shaping up. It was not all about partying, even though the Cotton Bowl Committee's press hospitality room was seldom poorly attended. I

Covering a Cotton Bowl game

don't remember covering a single one when the workload was slack.

In fact, the first one I worked was after the 1963 season when Navy's coach Wayne Hardin was questioning whether UTexas and not the Midshipmen was the legitimate national champion, never mind that the Longhorns were undefeated and that Navy had lost an early season game to SMU. That's when I first learned to appreciate Darrell Royal's strongest quality, which is Class.

Sports writers that we were, we couldn't wait to run to Royal to get his response to Hardin's daily doubting of who should be No. 1. Instead of saying something steamy that would prompt us to trot back to Hardin for further comment, all Royal would do is shrug and say, "He may be right. But we'll know for sure right after the game."

Texas beat Navy, Roger Staubach and all, 28-6, in a game that was never actually that close.

IN THOSE DAYS, the toughest ticket in Dallas was the Cotton Bowl's New Year's Eve Ball, held in resplendent elegance in a luxurious hotel. Its prestige was further enhanced by the attendees, who included governors and educators and financiers and whoever else was of sufficient prominence to swing an invitation. There by default were sports writers who, among other things, were thinking up ways to get tux rental onto their expense accounts.

Our wives loved that party—at least, I know one who did.

I recall one year when we were seated with Gov. and Mrs. Preston Smith, Tech president and Mrs. Grover Murray, and one or two other similarly distinguished couples. It's the tradition that each of the guys dances with each of the ladies at the table. The good news was that my wife got to dance with a governor and a college president. The bad news was having her learn that some men dance without pumping their arm and swayin' their hips . . .

Another time, we sat at the table with Darrell and Edith Royal, the Hayden Frys, and a guest of the Royals, Willie Nelson. Now, to give an idea of how long ago that was, ol' Willie had short hair, was clean shaven, and looked plumb nice in his tuxedo.

ONCE WE GET into the stadium come Friday, I will glance toward the press box, reminiscing about those days of yore and wondering if I would know a single soul other than the *A-J*'s reps. I doubt it.

We'll be riding with my son, so we'll be getting there very early. Being as the game kicks off at 1:00 p.m., we'll probably leave the hotel at 10:00 that morning. That means we'll likely have a lot of time to spend, looking around at all the other folks clad in red to see who all we recognize. At least, it will give me time to locate the handiest concession stand and closest restroom.

One reason we will be getting there that early is because my son remembers riding with me for Tech-USC and by the time we got to our seats, they'd already been playing for three minutes. What made that so regrettable was that we missed the best part of the game. I believe it will be much different this time.

And by the time you read this, you'll already know the score.

That's something some of us never really learn . . .

## Dawn's Early Light Dims as NFL Leaders Turn Away

FOR A COUPLE of reasons, I probably shouldn't be writing this on this day, in this mood. Actually, I believe those two reasons actually blend into one: Patriotism and religion. That's because in the home of my upbringing they demanded equal respect. And, of all things, they both were intertwined in the educational process of my schoolhouse where the American Flag was raised daily, assemblies were opened by a prayer, and patriotic songs were the feature of my music class.

In my home is where my exposure to the importance of patriotism and religion began, my dad teaching the former and my mom keeping the latter in the forefront.

Beginning at that tender age, I always get a tingle when the National Anthem is played at any venue. Miss Lola Baughman, our fourth grade music teacher, taught us to stand, hands over hearts, as we all joined in to sing, "Oh, say, can you see . . . " Then, years later, as a third generation of my family to serve in the U.S. Army, I stood and saluted proudly each time the song played. I frequently thought of my two brothers and my father who had soldiered valiantly before me . . .

THAT HAVING been said, it's no surprised that I— and, I'm guessing—most of the country not bound by the so-called laws of Political Correctness and beyond are appalled at the National Anthem becoming a tool of protest by the NFL . . . that it has dribbled on down to the colleges and even the high schools.

Incidentally, I proudly salute the Houston area high school coach, a former Marine, who kicked off his team several players that failed to respect the National Anthem. Because youngsters have always tried to emulate the college and pro stars on the playing field, I suppose it's no surprise they'd try to follow them down less honorable paths.

A friend of mine, an intelligent man, once told me that criticizing PC was to admit to racism, however oblique the stand. To him and others I still contend that PC is BS. Fact is, it has done more to attack the very values that have governed us so well, both as a nation and individually.

Racism does exist, no doubt. And it's probably a violation of PC law to point out that all racists are not white. Black racists, as well as white racists, fuel the problem at every opportunity.

Every person is guaranteed by our very constitution to have equal rights; none is guaranteed special rights . . .

ALONG WITH everything else that put me is such a mood today is the indiscriminant removal of symbols that represent our history. PC should stay obnoxious enough trying to change things as they are; now they attack history itself.

News Flash: The Civil War happened and all its significant players should be remembered. The statues, names and markers represent those events. Now, to top it all off, Six Flags Over Texas announced it will remove the Confederate Flag from its trademarked identity. So, will it now be "Five Flags Over Texas"? Er, uh, no, responded its leadership. We'll just take down all the flags except one.

Okay. So now Texans must get used to the fact they were never an independent nation, never were owned and operated by Mexico, did not participate in the Civil War, etc., etc.

Bet you'll never again hear the late Johnny Horton's song, "You fought all the way, Johnny Reb, Johnny Reb . . . " Remember, it also had a line saying President Lincoln at the ceremony marking the war's end asked the band to "play the song, Dixie, in honor of Johnny Reb and all he believed . . . "

GETTING BACK to the NFL, its management and owners, and the disservice it is allowing to every man and woman in uniform whose honor and deeds are marginalized each time the flag is desecrated or the National Anthem's very meaning is compromised. Despite the conservative political leanings of owners—including Jerry Jones—they have effectively endorsed the demonstrations. Why? Because their fear of reprisals by the players trumps the anger of the fans which, history has shown, is addicted to the sport.

I wanted to inject along about here the name of a football player who, during a campus riot at San Diego State circa 1970, stood alone to prevent a mob of protesting students from taking down the flag. A rather imposing figure with an even more imposing determination, he held them at bay.

Even though I interviewed him in Lubbock a few months later, I cannot remember his name. I tried unsuccessfully to Google it. Alas, none of the search engines I tried had any recollection of the event. Bravery and gallantry are among the victims of PC running rampant.

I'm sure he wouldn't mind his name being forgotten but likely is saddened that what he stood for has become meaningless . . .

WHERE FOOTBALL was concerned in those school years mentioned earlier, Moran had no rival they detested more than the Strawn Greyhounds (and that included Albany, a cross-county rival). And no one disliked that Strawn team more than I, who had a big brother playing for my beloved Bulldogs.

On this Thanksgiving Day, as the two teams—both undefeated—were meeting to determine the district championship, I looked across the field at the visitors' sideline. There stood a Marine in full dress uniform. Suddenly I was smacked in my very psyche by the realization that Strawn, as terrible as it had always seemed to be, was on our side in this fight to maintain our freedom. When it came to this battle against the Nazis and Japanese, we all were on the same team.

His proud salute as the soloist sang "The Star Spangled Banner" changed my entire perspective. Football, I realized that November day, is just a game . . .

And the National Anthem was not then, and never will be, just a song . . .

Although Moran and Strawn, once powerhouses in the old Class B designation, were relegated by dwindling populations into the six-man game, what I felt that day watching the salute of that Marine lives on in my mind.

And, also, in my mood . . .

Burle's retirement party

# SCHNOPPER

Schnopper hard at work

## THEN HERE CAME SCHNOPPER

What began as a response to a miffed Lubbock city politician took on, literally, a life of its own. The councilman had ended his remarks about one of my commentaries by suggesting: "You should just let your dog write your column!"

Due either to the public response or my own enjoyment, I decided to continue a regular piece under Schnopper's byline. I was both amazed and delighted by the result. Almost at once, Schnopper not only had generated his own following but developed his own writing style. His sophisticated tastes in music, art and literature; his aloof attitude; and his disdain for the unpolished provided him with a personality all his own. I truly believed that persona worked because of Schnopper himself. He was, in real life, unlike any common dog. I believe fully that the words that appeared in print fit the guy himself.

Not only did he attract a local following, he gained some renown across the country. A *Fort Worth Star-Telegram* feature on Schnopper was picked up and distributed nationally. I received clippings from Scripps newspapers in several states.

And Schnopper's celebrity locally extended beyond his writings. He made several public appearances at schools and clubs, and was the "Mystery Roaster" at the League of Women Voter's roast of Texas Tech chancellor David Smith. He received several write-in votes in the local mayoral race, floods of greeting cards at Christmas and his birthday and, after undergoing back surgery, was flooded with get-well cards. One elementary school declared a "Schnopper Day" and classes were dismissed for his appearance.

His untimely death was marked by scores of messages of sympathy.

Even though I soon acquired another miniature dachshund, whom I named Deuce (he was registered as Schnopper II), there was never any thought of having him start a column of his own.

There has been only one Schnopper, and only I never considered his work to be make believe . . .

## 'He's Only a Dog' Is No Way to Console a Man in Pain

THE FIRST time the sentence really stung me, I was sitting on my bunk in a Quonset hut far away, surrounded by the cold darkness of an Arctic afternoon and fighting against the tears that blurred my mom's handwritten words.

As close a friend as Armstrong had become, it took all the strength I could muster to keep the fist I had so tautly formed from heading for his chin. It occurred to me just in the nick of time that he was expressing his own relief when he said it.

He walked in just as I had read that ol' Tuffy had died and that Dad had taken him out to the home place to be buried.

Tuffy was seventeen, three years my junior, and he had been by my side through every crisis and every joy I had ever known. I remember when my brother was killed in the South Pacific and, not being able to comprehend all that was going on around me, I sat on the back steps, stroking Tuffy's head. Seemingly realizing how much I needed him, he positioned his large and strong body into his own version of a snuggle. We stayed just like that throughout one of the most horrible evenings I would ever spend.

As a teenager, when most of the family found me to be, very often, much more trouble than they could withstand, ol' Tuffy was there, presumably just for me. The morning after my first date with that special girl, I sat with Tuffy, my hormones still at full stir, and talked to him about all I was thinking and feeling, and, of greater import, that I would not dare say to anybody I knew without the risk of ridicule. Tuffy understood . . . perhaps not exactly what I was experiencing, but certainly what I was needing from him.

The day I left for the Army, I spent several minutes with ol' Tuffy, and I still believe he sensed that I was going away. Maybe we both knew that it would be the last time I would ever feel his special warmth, which ran to the depths of his soul. When I hugged him goodbye, he turned and walked slowly to the porch. It was the first time in my life that I noticed that Tuffy was getting a bit feeble.

Almost two years later, with all those memories running through my mind, I did not need to hear anyone, friend or foe, say, "He's only a dog . . . "

WHEN KEVIN, my first-born, brought Schnapps to the house, the last thing I believed that we needed was a dog. With three boys, ranging from barely above toddling to pre-teens, there already was enough around there to attend. And here was this dachshund pup, perhaps seven or eight weeks old, looking like more of a mouse than a dog, worming his way into my life. My firm "you can not keep him" mellowed as I recalled my own boyhood with ol' Tuffy who, for all those years, went where I went and did what I did.

And, as the years passed and the boys grew, Schnapps had charmed himself not only into my home but into my heart as well. We grew very tight, as he stood by my own sons through their highs and lows, supporting them at whatever risk it might put his own family standing. That he seemed to rally to the side of whichever of the boys seemed to be in the worst trouble would begin to peeve me. But then, I would think back to another dog, another boy, another time, and my anger would give ground as the tears began to well . . .

Schnapps was the happiest I had ever seen him that Christmas season of 1984. This was the first year that they boys had all departed, pursuing their own lives and dreams, but were home for the holidays. Again, his own gift was on the tree, and he had his whole family around him. I had begun to notice that Schnapps, just like ol' Tuffy years before, had begun to gray and that his gait had started to slow.

But not that night, two days before Christmas, as he romped with the boys and was energized with the returning spunk and spirit that had marked his puppyhood. Later, after we had all gone out to eat, we returned to the house and a ringing phone. It was the emergency veterinary clinic calling. The spirit and laughter of Christmas was doused in tears . . .

Again, just a few days later, I would be reminded by an insensitive outsider that he was "only a dog . . . "

AND NOW COMES Schnopper, who may be the most remarkable of the three dogs who've anointed my life with their special personalities. It was last Saturday morning, while speeding toward Lubbock, that all these memories came rushing back.

Schnopper was seriously hurt earlier that morning, having made a bad landing on a fall from a bed. His back . . . a very vulnerable part of the dachshund anatomy . . . had been injured, and here we were at the ranch, more than 130 miles from our team of vets.

I must inject here that the prognosis is good. Schnopper faces a long and perhaps slow rehabilitative process, but Doc Farley, his lifelong pediatrician, expects a full recovery.

I sped across the countryside with one eye looking for State Troopers and the other watching Schnopper look at his closest friend with eyes that pled for help and reassurance. My foot pressed even heavier on the gas pedal. Both Tuffy and Schnapps died out of my view, and now I found myself preparing for the worst. Schnopper was cradled in the arms of his Mom, whose tears fell unashamedly.

It was between Snyder and Post that I saw a State Trooper, but he was in the process of stopping another car as I sped past. I wasn't concerned about a ticket . . . that was the least of my worries. It was what would happen after the Trooper asked what they always ask: "Is there an emergency?"

Obviously, I would answer yes, then hurriedly explain. I don't know where I would be writing this from if his response to that would have been, "He's only a dog . . . "

That's one sentence I hope to never hear again.

## DOG'S PURPOSE WAS CLEAR; NOT SO WITH THE CRITICS

MAYBE THE critics didn't like the movie because they didn't think it made sense, never mind that they gave five stars and an Oscar to one that really didn't. I saw both movies with the same friend.

When *Moonlight* ended, we looked at each other blankly, both offering the same unspoken question: "What was the point?" Conversely, when *A Dog's Purpose* ended, we joined in on the round of applause that erupted throughout the theater. Yet, it was a movie that even my favorite professional critic gave a paltry three stars . . .

*Moonlight* was a narrative about a guy going through several stages of his life. The other was about dogs going through several stages of other people's lives. And he had dramatic effect on each one.

I left the theater after *Moonlight* thinking about what I'd have for supper. I left the theater after *Purpose* thinking about Tuffy and Schnapps and Schnopper and Deuce. That thought lasted through supper, on into the night and for several days to come.

Heck, I'm still thinking about it, which is what brought me to this very keyboard.

MY METHOD of judging a movie lacks the sophisticated and complicated calculus required to determine how many little stars to place beside the title. My approach, which would get me expelled immediately from the critic's union, is quite simple: Did I enjoy sitting there watching it?

Given that criterion, my choices among the last eight or ten picture shows I have seen would be something like this:

One, *Hell and High Water.*

Two, *Purpose of Dogs.*

Three, an unbreakable tie among *Fences*, *Hacksaw Ridge* and *Hidden Figures.*

There would have been very little separation among the five movies, all of which I enjoyed *sitting there watching.*

During the past four of five months I have seen more picture shows than I had seen in the past two years put together. Going to the movies is a little like exercising or going to church: All three are easier to do once you get in the habit. There's no connection between my increased movie attendance and my slacking off on both my physical and spiritual calisthenics.

But I digress.

*DOGS* WAS the story about a dog who would join a family through one means or another and stay there until he died, which happened only when he had served his purpose. His next stop would find him joining another household and looking nothing like the dog he used to be. Even as another breed, his psyche, his very soul—actually, his very Being—would transition without a hitch. He'd simply make himself at home and go on with his life's (lives?) work.

Now, that didn't mean he was a little four-legged angel. He got into the same sorts of trouble that follow all pups. One of the best scenes came when his best buddy, the kid of the house, spilled his dad's rare coin collection. Thinking it was a morsel of goodies, the pup swallowed the most valuable of the lot. The funniest part came when the boy was trying to coax him into passing it, and his remarks while the kid was recollecting the priceless coin.

Anyway, the dog's commentary throughout the movie ranged from funny to poignant to downright sad. It was audible only to the theater audience which, despite its paltry three-star rating, loved every minute of it.

BEGINNING before I ever started to school, four dogs would play important roles in my life; each served a purpose.

First, there was Tuffy, who protected me from rattlesnakes and other hazards when I was little more than a toddler; was the only family member who liked me as a teenager; and was my only friend when I was being shunned by everybody in the household after having eschewed a college scholarship to take a roughnecking job.

The night before I left to go into the army, Tuffy and I sat until the wee hours of the morning, silently pondering what both of us knew would be our last goodbye. I would be gone for two years and Tuffy had already lived at least five years beyond his life expectancy. He moved very close to me, almost in my lap.

I sat there and rubbed his head. It was a melancholy time. The dreaded letter from Mom came a few months later: Ol' Tuffy had died. He had served his purpose . . .

But had he?

SCHNAPPS CAME into the family quite accidentally. He allegedly "followed" my ten-year-old son home. Our other two boys were eight and four. Only now has it occurred to me that Schnapps came there to see that all three were both entertained and, when the need arose, corralled.

Shortly after the last of the three boys had left the nest, Schnapps uncharacteristically wandered out into street and was hit by a car. He had served his purpose . . .

But had he?

SCHNOPPER CAME into the family as a Christmas gift from my wife to me. Recently weaned, he appeared in a stocking with only his head and front paws protruding. He came straight to me as soon as he hit the floor. We bonded at once.

I don't know whether I needed an alter-ego, but Schnopper took over that role. He took over my column-writing duties one Sunday each month. I expect nobody to believe this, but I know deep down it was his idea. And he could get by with statements that I wouldn't dare print under my name—he once explained a vasectomy: "The lightning still strikes but no damage is done."

Schnopper died of complications from back surgery. He had served his purpose . . .

But had he?

DEUCE, OUR third dachshund, required a trip to a kennel in Goldthwaite. He came into a family consisting of a seasoned couple, the mom of which became his instant soul mate.

Deuce and Burle

As her health became an issue, he was a great comfort to her as we transitioned from our long-time home into the OFH. Once we were settled in, Deuce died an untimely death. He had served his purpose . . .

But had he?

After all, he, Tuffy, Schnapps, and Schnopper were all dogs of purpose and they served them well.

See the movie before it leaves town.

It has a purpose.

## SCHNOPPER'S EXPERIENCE WITH MARCH MAKES HIM EAGER FOR APRIL

THE ONLY THING I know about the Ides of March is what I read when I was into Shakespeare, and I haven't personally witnessed the comings and goings of this month for enough years to testify to the old saying about the lion-lamb entry-departure. But I do know one thing. March has been a tumultuous month around our house. Or, make that houses: It has been much the same when we were out in the country.

Hereabouts, I had a very busy time a couple of weekends back. Both of my folks came down with that respiratory thing that people get. I don't know exactly what it's called but it sounds a lot like distemper.

He had it worse than she did; or, more accurately, he made a bigger deal of having it than she did. I think that's a guy thing, the need for pity and consoling and the exaggerated noise he makes when he sneezes and coughs. And nose blowing . . . a disgusting habit that thankfully is limited to people . . . he does with the subtlety of a foghorn. Now, to her credit, she mainly wipes her nose quietly and even uses a different tissue to muffle her coughs.

Not only did he feel rotten, he seemed to resent her illness as an intrusion on his personally deserved down time. Like, how dare she be too sick to pamper him with the sort of sympathy and constant attention he always gets when he catches this thing they call a "cold."

Being the only objective observer in the house, it was clear to me that she felt worse than he did. Not only was she running a higher fever (I peeked at the thermometer which humans get to place in their ear . . . but I digress), she was on a guilt trip for not feeling up to pampering him.

A FEW DAYS before that, while we were down at the ranch, I was introduced to a critter I knew only from watching cartoons. The roadrunner. Only we have a whole flock—actually, I think the term "herd" more aptly describes anything that mainly runs around on the ground. I tend to think of a "flock" as a bunch of birds flying around from one tree to another (and, in the case of those stupid grackles, leaving behind one big flocking mess!) and hanging out together through it all.

Now roadrunners, though, can drive you batty, even if you're not a wily coyote.

We have become, unwillingly and unwittingly, hosts to a whole roadrunner family. Last year, evidently, two of them set up housekeeping in a brush pile just across the fence in the edge of our pasture, right behind the play-house where she attends her hobby involving crafts and things. That's on the opposite side of the yard from where he keeps his 4-wheeler, tractor, welder, cultivators, shred-ders, and all sorts of toys that look rugged to him, junky to the rest of us.

To the roadrunners' credit, they picked the better neighborhood.

A PROBLEM I will have now and forever when I see that cartoon will be the way it depicts the roadrunner as crafty and intelligent. You see, in real life, the roadrunner has a brain the size of an M&M, and it has the capacity to issue only four commands: Run. Turn. Stop. Jump. That it repeats it over and over would madden one who allowed it to.

I must admit, I made the initial mistake of barking at one, then taking off after him. Unlike the dumb coyote in the cartoon, I saw immediately how fruitless it is. Heck, you can't even cut across and head off somebody who has no inkling himself of where he's heading. I'm serious. Roadrunners take off at full speed with absolutely no destination in mind. They zip around at breakneck speed and, were it not for their uncanny leaping ability, would likely trash their bods against all sorts of unexpected objects laying in their path.

There was a time, I am told, that the Texas Chaparral was almost extinct, and may still be in some areas. But not Fisher County, I guarantee you. But one might wonder why they aren't. Anybody who spends every waking hour skittering aimlessly about is heading for extinction at breakneck speed. Or so you would think.

But, at the end of my short chase—hey, I got the picture early on—I took to watching them very carefully. Between heavy panting, that is. Whew!

WHEN A ROADRUNNER does hone in on something, he doesn't have to think. He just lets the flying grasshopper, the scurrying mouse, the skittering lizard or slithering snake set his course. In very short order, he overtakes him, then brings the meal home for all to share. Most of us born hunters work from a game plan, a strategy that maps out in a scientific manner our quest for food or sport.

Not the roadrunner. He just sets his little beady eyes on their butts, takes off, and matches them move for move, zip for zip.

I guess I should go ahead and confess that I didn't just willingly give up that chase. My experience with that roadrunner came to a painful ending, much like something that happens to the coyote mentioned afore.

Now, to be short of leg and strong of heart, I move pretty swift myself. And here I had this creature, who must be half bird, half gazelle, on a dead run in a straightaway toward the playhouse steps. Actually, I was gaining when we got there and, to close the deal, I had just put on a burst of additional speed as we approached the steps from the side. Then, at the last fraction of a second, the roadrunner jumped up on the porch and I crashed headlong into the riser. My neck is stiff to this day, and there's an ugly knot violating the smooth landscape of my skull.

Literally adding insult to injury, I later read where the roadrunner is a member of the cuckoo family.

Well, at least the Ides of March has passed. Now . . . et tu, yon lamb?

## SCHNOPPER HAS SOME DOGGED OPINIONS ON HOW TO SELECT NAMES

What's in a name? That question, although often asked rhetorically, deserves an answer, which I can supply in two words: A lot.

Or, in the vernacular of the Moran native who lives hereabouts, three words: A ho lot.

So, while you grammarians out there are pondering whether the article A should count as a word, I will proceed without waiting to count the votes.

A person's name is very, very important and can, in some instances, actually shape his future. Parents, puh-eeze use your heads instead of your emotions when you are about to hand junior a name that will honor some old relative or uphold a meaningless tradition. Sure, it might bring you some nods of approval from a generation whose head pats still warm the cockles of your self-image, which is most likely anemic or you wouldn't be needing such emotional reinforcement.

Get over it. You do that by projecting your thoughts down the road your offspring will be traveling. With a moniker that his peers find humorous, such a trail can be long and rough and lasting. That's without even mentioning embarrassing. Also, keep in mind what the proposed name might rhyme with. Even a kid with such a great name as Art may one day come in from his first day of school crying and announcing that he's going to start going by Arthur . . .

A YOUNGSTER, whether kid or pup, may have his entire future shaped by the name he was either hastily or thoughtlessly handed—remember the guy in the old Johnny Cash classic . . . ?

For example, if you named your pup, say, Rover or Pooch or—perish the thought—Doggie, you are telling him right off the bat that you don't expect much of him. Give somebody a name to live up to and they probably will. Conversely, give them a name without imagination or spark, and they will spend their lives the same way: No imagination, no spark.

Dogs have it even worse because they often get names for reasons that are so obvious that they rank right along with puns when it comes to drawing groans. Take Spot. I know a Dalmatian with that name. You know what his owner told me? He chose that name because it was the name of one of the main characters in the first book he ever read. I resisted the temptation to surmise that it was also probably the last . . .

Another dog I know is named Blackie; then there's old Snowball . . .

Down in Moran, there was a poor pup called Diddiebitechee. Here's how that name came about. He snapped at a toddler, whose frantic mom blurted out the question, "Did he bite you?" From that day forward, the kiddo called the dog Diddie-bite-chee, which is exactly how that question would be pronounced by a certain guy who lives at my house . . .

And after hearing that question posed almost daily, what's a two-year-old to think?

DOGS CAST AS the canine versions of Super Heroes were given some great names, but some others that were quite questionable.

When I was a puppy, I sobbed my way through the movie *Lassie, Come Home*. And to this very day, I believe anybody who could watch that whole flick and leave with dry eyes should be watched very, very carefully. But imagine my shock to learn that the Lassie part was played by a male actor. Can you imagine how much money it took to get a proud Collie to compromise his very gender? Maybe a Yorkie or a Pug . . . but a Collie? Wow!

Another of my heroes was the star of *Old Yeller*. I'm glad I saw that when I did because nowadays I would pass it by, figuring it was about a dog of French descent . . .

My all-time favorite novel (obviously, other than the Classics, which I greatly prefer) was Jack London's *Call of the Wild*. You want heroic dogs with names to match, you read that one!

Rin Tin Tin was a name that worked okay for that role, except I will admit cringing a bit every time that kid called him "Rinnie."

THE GREAT WILLIAM Shakespeare, whose genius was both creative and prolific, is among my lifelong heroes. His senses of romance and tragedy and comedy are lasting influences on all of us whose appreciation of classic literature drives us to composition. Even though I have never been tempted to emulate his style, my motivation can be greatly credited to the thought processes you are now following, word by word.

I don't write like the Bard, but I certainly think like he did. The plight of King Lear, the frustrations of Romeo and the complexities of Hamlet occupy my daydreams and imagination and, yes, even my trespasses into daily mischief.

But, alas. He did the world no favors when he dared reckon that the rose would not have changed had it been called by some other noun. Not that he wasn't absolutely correct. Hey, a rose by any other name would still have the throny appendages that make its bushes the favorite escape route for yon neighborhood cat who is oft to befoulest my territory.

While Shakespeare was obviously speaking of the inanimate traits of this majestic flower, it has unwittingly lured people into a state of nonchalance when naming their offspring.

ON A PERSONAL note, I have always credited much of my own self-esteem, which is considerable, to the distinctive originality of my own name. The guy at my house who christened me "Schnopper" is not given to great fits of creativity. But when he picked a name for me, he hit one of his home runs, however rare. It is a name that is totally unique to me. (Yes, I know, "totally unique" is a redundancy in the purest sense.) In fact, I have thought about getting it copyrighted.

But there is a downside to that: It's my own ego, which also is considerable. Think about it from this angle: Any dog anywhere that shows up with the name Schnopper will be my namesake. It will have been named not only *after* me but *for* me. And if that doesn't give him enough to live up to . . . well, forget it!

Just as the name may inspire the pup, I have to believe that, in my case, the pup may have inspired the name. It was a case of a very ordinary person being moved to properly christen an extraordinary pup.

Truth should never be cloaked in obligatory modesty . . .

## Schnopper Wonders Why People Need Such Big Houses

I'VE BEEN LYING here in my crate, looking out across the den and into the kitchen and thinking how much different life would be if people built houses the size they really need to be. They do that for their dogs, you know. Hey, how many dog houses have you ever seen that had more than a single room? And my crate where I sleep, and where I lounge like I am right now, is big enough for me to stand up, turn around two or three times, and lie back down.

What else do you need?

Just look at this house! It is no mansion, by any means, but like I told that census taker, it's cheaper than many but nicer than the national average in some countries. (Government people *love* sentences like that!)

Seriously, why do people need so much space? There are three of us living here, and if some giant picked this house up and shook it, we'd be rattling around like three BBs in a Prince Albert can.

GRANTED, THEY BOTH spend a lot of time walking around on their hind legs. And, though he's pretty tall, our ceiling is so high that he couldn't touch it if he jumped. Why is it so high? Because everybody else's is, I suppose. It's sure not because anybody needs all that room above his head.

Maybe it's because I'm short, but I think there's something to be said for smug.

And why so many rooms? I guarantee you, there are floors in this house that would never be stepped on if Yolie didn't come to clean or the grandkids didn't drop in to join me in an occasional game of chase. Even then, there are rooms that pups and kids are forbidden to enter.

Like the living room. Who needs it? In the 1½ years I've lived here, I have never seen those couches and chairs sat upon. The dining area is the same way.

But I have to confess something: When The Princess Kendall comes, she and I love to sneak into the living room, get so quiet that we attract immediate attention, and then see how much time elapses before one of them comes in yelling for us to "get off that couch and out of this room!" The record, as of this writing, can still be measured in seconds!

REALLY, I THINK it all has to do with the economy. If houses were built to their required proportions, a guy with a hammer, saw, and a bundle of kindling could knock one out in half a day. Consequently, there goes the labor market and, along with it, the plumbing, furniture, and clothing business.

Some people may think that I'm coming up with all this because of my pet peeve, which I've aired here on several other occasions: That being that I am the only one who has to go outside to potty.

It does irk me that our house has enough bathrooms that we could easily have one apiece. But, really, unused bathrooms are just a small part of this structural overkill that people not only practice but embrace. Besides, I have a strategy that may someday allow me to do my number someplace other than the back yard.

Ever since I was a small pup, I have insisted that one of them stays out there with me until I'm through, come rain or sleet or dark of night. If they go in the house, I jump against the door and start barking at the top of my voice. They either let me in or come back out here with me. And sometimes it can actually be fun.

Like that time last winter when he was standing out there with me in his pajamas, robe, and house shoes when SWISH!—sprinklers came on at full force and he was straddling one when it popped up.

Such language!

It didn't help when she asked how come he was so soaked and I was so dry. Her poorly stifled giggling didn't help much either . . .

ANOTHER THING that smaller houses would alleviate would be his bellyaching about the local tax appraisal system. His view is that the folks over at city hall do a lot of chest-thumping about not increasing the tax rate when, all the while, everybody's property tax bill is going sky high. They generate much more revenue by jacking up everybody's evaluation.

I saw a story in the paper the other day that said in the period 1990–1999 there was not a single million-dollar house in Lubbock but there are now thirty-four of 'em. When he saw that, he scoffed it off, saying that those houses weren't built as million-dollar houses. He bets they went on the tax rolls in the $100,000 range.

"Leave those folks at the appraisal office alone," he said, "and there'll be another thirty-four next year."

He really gets lathered up over that. For a while there, I thought I was going to have to lead him back across that sprinkler.

PEOPLE, DUE TO the keep-up-with-the-Joneses mode they are programmed in, would never consider even a mild stage of downsizing. And our guy wouldn't consider anything that didn't allow his chair to sprawl forward halfway across the room in the direction of a TV whose screen is bigger than the Moran picture show in his belabored days of yore.

He's not bothered by the fact she hates that chair and, come to think of it, seldom speaks highly of the TV. She says neither looks good in that room. I'm never sure whether she's talking about the *TV* and the chair or *him* and the chair . . .

I could see it either way.

Along with the size of houses, there's clothing. Every house I know about has closet after closet, and they're all full. He has both a "fat" closet and a "thin" closet, the contents of the latter showing little evidence of wear. Nobody needs that many clothes. In fact, if you are among those who wonder why it is that people, among all God's

countless creatures, have to wear clothing, I can show you
the answer:

Someday just hide and watch one of 'em get out of
the shower.

## A MAN SHOULDN'T BE KNOWN BY THE DOG HE KEEPS

STANDING THERE in Love Field, having just got off a
flight from Lubbock, I noticed this very attractive flight
attendant sort of looking me over. And, when we made
eye contact, she smiled warmly, reminding me that maybe
I had better turn the charisma down a notch. That would
be later. Right now, I chose instead to look approachable . . .

It was Monday, and I was in Dallas as part of a stretch
of moving about Texas that had me in San Antonio Friday,
Saturday and Sunday, and would have me in Seagraves
Tuesday, back in Dallas Wednesday, Thursday, and Friday
before stopping off in Sylvester the following Saturday and
Sunday.

Each stop had presented an interesting array of people, but the two most intriguing came in that Dallas airport and on a grocery store parking lot in Sweetwater . . .

*Southwest Airlines really knows how to hire, them, I
found myself thinking, as this young woman clearly was trying to decide how to approach me. She was blond, petite,
and had a friendly smile that I thought had retired with June
Allyson.*

San Antonio is a delightful city, clearly my favorite
among the state's metropoli (Fort Worth is a close second,
Austin a clear-cut last), and it's also where I go each year

to watch The Princess do her dance recital. Seagraves was a lot of fun, the audience there so pumped by recent rains that even my jokes didn't hamper the jovial mood. But it was during a side trip from Sylvester to Sweetwater that I met an interesting man with an intriguing comparison of women and trucks.

*The young airline lady finally decided to make her move, and I greeted her approach with a sly grin that got away from me, turning into a smile that not only widened but gaped. Her demeanor sparkled as she pointed at me with a curled index finger and said, "I think I know you." An old line. But, heck, it was working.*

I HAD DRIVEN to Sweetwater very early last Sunday morning to pick up a copy of my favorite newspaper and to draw five gallons of water from a coin-operated machine. I was driving the old Ranger pickup I keep at the ranch. It's fun to drive and, besides that, my wife has a thing about my taking her car over a caliche road.

Daybreak was sill nearly an hour away, and I was surprised to hear a voice wishing me good morning. I turned to face a man standing with an empty bottle in one hand, several quarters in the other. He had parked his shiny, late-model pickup beside my truck, whose beige tone looked dull in comparison.

"That's a good-looking truck," he said. "What model is it?"

"It's a '90 model," I said, "but it runs good. But, hey, your truck is really neat looking, and it's a lot newer."

Even in the semidarkness I could see his expression sadden.

"No, it's not a good truck," he said. "I had another of the same make that wasn't much to look at, but it sure ran good. Then I married this lady who couldn't work a standard shift and she asked me to trade it for this one, which has an automatic transmission and is much prettier. I've had nothing but trouble ever since."

*It was clear to me that this flight attendant had been pondering what to say and that was the best she could come up with. I was tempted to go along and say, yes, I know we must be acquainted and I am also trying to remember where I know you. That surely would help her along.*

THE FELLOW BY now had moved into the light. He was a slight man, very pleasant, but the sadness that crossed his brow seemed deeper than a bad truck-trade would cause.

"What's wrong with the truck?" I asked.

"One problem after another," he replied. "First, the computer went out. Then the fuel pump, which they had to drop the gas tank to replace. Those things happened back-to-back."

I mentioned having a pretty good idea what those two repair jobs must have cost him. but that wasn't all.

"The marriage didn't work out either," he said, "and all I have to show for that is this truck that I didn't want to begin with."

Not knowing what to say, I dropped another quarter into the machine and watched the stream that would finish filling my bottle. We both were silent until I pulled my bottle back and was replacing the cap.

*It's good that I didn't yield to the urge to make up some place that we probably had met, because the next thing I knew, this delightful lady was finishing her sentence: " . . . you are the guy with the dog that writes a column!"*

AS I WAS lifting the heavy water bottle to put it in my truck, my new friend followed me around to the tailgate.

"If your truck runs good, you keep it," he was saying. I told him I had no intention of trading it, ever, and he seemed pleased.

"Trucks and women are a whole lot alike," he said. "You tend to get caught up with what they look like and it's only after you leave the lot or the church that you learn what you really have. Looks don't mean much if what's inside them is bad. And in both cases, it causes pain and costs money."

All the way back to Sylvester, I thought of this man and what he had said. Driving back, I wished for a moment that I had spent some time assuring him that there are other women and other trucks. Then, realizing how dumb that would have sounded, I was pleased that I hadn't. I already felt guilty enough thinking how good-looking his truck was and wondering what his wife had looked like . . .

BACK AT LOVE Field, the flight attendant was explaining that, no, she had never met me but recognized me from my picture because it runs with Schnopper's column.

"That Schnopper is delightful," she said, explaining that she also has a dachshund and that her parents, who live in Plainview, send her every one of his columns. "I just love to read them," she kept saying over and over, until finally, I interrupted her momentarily, saying rather meekly that, ahem, I also write a column.

"They never send me those," she said. Then, apparently seeing my chin heading toward my chest, added: "But I'm sure they're good, too . . . " She then smiled, waved, and dashed off to catch her flight.

Meeting such delightful people is the best part of travel. Back at the ranch, I told my wife about what a great guy I had met at the water machine.

I've decided not to tell her about the flight attendant . . .

# THE NEWSPAPER INDUSTRY

Interviewing a player at a Coaches All-America game

## AUGUST 29, 1960

I KNEW ON that day—Aug. 29, 1960—that I was walking into a life-changing experience, that whatever awaited me at the top of those two flights of stairs that were gaping out before me would be different than anything I had ever experienced.

It was a new job in a new town in a new profession. Driving in from the apartment we had moved into just a day earlier, I thought about my first day on a variety of jobs . . . the one on a rotary drilling rig, where "weevils" (rookies) were normally preyed upon, rarely in good-nature, by veteran co-workers . . . my first day of infantry basic at Fort Ord, California, back when Drill Instructors' modes and manners would have been outlawed by new CIA interrogation standards . . . and the crusty foreman who greeted me on a highway construction site where I had hired on as a heavy equipment operator the day after my discharge.

Sure, I had been nervous about other new challenges. Like the day that I, at my new bride's urging and encouraging, had given up the highway gig to enroll in college. I was a bit nervous again, that time as a rather seasoned freshman about to pursue a degree in one of the most exacting journalism schools in the state. Strangely, being nearer the age of some of my professors than I was to my fellow students gave me more comfort than concern . . .

But today, this hot August day, was different. This job, I had counted on becoming my life's work. I had to get it right.

NEWSPAPERING was much different back then. And so was Lubbock.

My drive to work had taken all of seven minutes. You could drive ten miles in any direction from downtown and be totally outside the city. A loop being planned would circle all areas, residential and commercial, and those who didn't want to pay bootlegger fees for adult beverages could drive to Nazareth or the state line.

As I neared the top of the staircase, I could hear the sound of dozens of manual typewriters as writers and reporters were already busily preparing copy for the next morning's editions. At the first landing of the staircase, a reporter dressed in slacks and a blazer sped past me and out the door.

I looked at my watch, which I had routinely wound that morning, and noticed that I was a half-hour early for my 4:00 p.m. appointment. I already was feeling a bit awkward, dressed out in the black J. C. Penney suit my wife had scrimped to buy for this very occasion. All the other guys I had caught a glimpse of were wearing blazers or sports jackets over their white shirts and dark ties.

I decided to do my waiting outside, so I walked back down the stairs and out the south door. I lit a cigarette and walked down the sidewalk on the east side of the building. It was there that I noticed that the *A-J* building, like a number of others downtown, sported a Civil Defense logo, meaning that it was a certified bomb shelter, complete with emergency supplies of water and food, along with a Conelrad radio.

Incidentally, the designated Conelrad radio station was KFYO which, at the time, was owned by the *A-J*. In fact, until the paper sold a dozen years later, the KFYO logo appeared on the front page of the morning paper.

Morning paper . . . another term of the past. Up until 1990, the *A-J* published morning and afternoon newspapers, and printed two editions of both.

I HAD ACCEPTED this job over the phone. Jay Harris, the managing editor of the morning paper, had called and made the offer. I had also been contacted by the *Fort Worth Star-Telegram*, for whom I had done some work, and the *San Angelo Standard-Times*. All three were sports writing positions. Lubbock had two advantages. One, Jay, acting under the insistence of Chas. A. Guy, outbid the other two by $5 a week. Two, I would be able to help with the coverage of Tech athletics.

It was a Monday afternoon and, as I would soon discover, Monday was always payday. For years, newspapers everywhere paid on a weekly basis, and it was always Monday. Later, Mister Guy would explain to me that it was a practice made necessary by the raucous and nomadic nature of the old-line reporters.

"If (newspapers) had paid on Fridays . . . hell, there wouldn't have been anybody available to put out the weekend papers," he explained. It was an era he obviously knew well . . . and, for whatever reason, clearly missed . . .

Payday was one of the questions I had forgotten to ask about, and learning that I wouldn't have to wait long for my first check was a relief. The move, the deposit on the apartment, and a wife looking for a new prenatal doc was, well, financially stressful.

BY THE TIME I had finished my preliminaries and paperwork with Harris—who had been almost two hours late, a trait I would later learn was a part of his persona—I was finally meeting the fellows in the sports department. Joe Kelly, the sports editor, showed me my desk, exchanged a few pleasantries, and headed home for dinner.

The other two staffers, the late Ken Estes and Bill Hart, were about to head out for Pete's Café, the only eatery within walking distance that served the evening meal, and they invited me along. Thankfully, neither asked why I didn't accept a menu. I went ahead and lied about not being hungry. In truth, I left home without a dime in my pocket.

It was clear that I had arrived at an exciting time. In a couple of weeks Tech would be playing its very first football season as a member of the Southwest Conference. I would be doing a sidebar. Estes, who had the Monterey beat, was excited about a couple of new coaches just joining the Plainsmen, Gerald Myers and Bobby Moegle. Conversation also included the Dallas pro football situation. It would be the first season for the Dallas Cowboys, which would be playing in the established NFL, and for the Dallas Texans and the league its owner, Lamar Hunt, was instrumental in starting.

Hart and Estes then got into a friendly argument over whether John F. Kennedy could be elected President. Ken, an avowed Democrat, hoped he could.

"The country will never go for a Catholic," Hart opined.

Bill proved he was more adept at handicapping football than politics when he said he believed DeWitt Weaver would step down at the end of the season.

"He wants to coach this first season (in the SWC) and that'll be it."

IT WAS well after 1:00 a.m. when we closed out the paper and I headed home. My wife, who was eight months pregnant and anxious to hear about my new job, had waited up for me.

"It's a good job and a good newspaper," I said, replying to her obvious question. "It's a place I think I'd like to stay for a while."

I am writing this on Aug. 29, 2009, which is forty-nine years to the day later.

I'm still trying to get it right . . .

## DIRK GENESIS

DIRK WEST WAS both an ad guy and a sports nut. Because of the former, he spent a lot of time in our building. Because of the latter, he spent a lot of time leaning over my desk, telling me what I needed to be telling those (pick an adjective) charged with directing Tech's football fortunes.

All the while, three things began to occur to me.

One, Dirk looked at football through the eyes of an unwashed fan. He admittedly knew little about the complexities—if complexities do indeed exist—of the game itself. But, like so many others in a community that had used up its patience during years of waiting to get into the Southwest Conference, he couldn't understand why the Red Raiders weren't beating up on Texas, Arkansas, and the others like they used to the HSUs and Texas Westerns of the old Border Conference.

Two, he was a gifted cartoonist.

Three, maybe he could bring to our sports pages some of what the late Bill McClanahan did for the *Dallas Morning News*. McClanahan did, among other things, weekly previews of the Southwest Conference games, using cartoon characters to depict each school's mascot (I particularly liked "Ol' Sarge," who represented the Aggies).

Over coffee one morning, I tossed the idea to Dirk, showing him a copy of what McClanahan had done that very week. Dirk barely glanced at it, shoved it aside and said:

"If I do something, it won't be like that."

Hello, Dirk. You just set the tone for the way our relationship would go for many years to come . . .

THAT McCLANAHAN had intrigued me was a logical byproduct of a lifetime admiration of the newspaper business. I fell in love with newspapers somewhere beyond the reach of my memory's span and, looking back on it, I realize that cartoons were the likely catalyst for that attraction.

Even during the toughest of times, the one thing that survived every budget cut imposed on the large and struggling Pettit family was the *Fort Worth Star-Telegram*. It was Will Rogers who once said, after watching first-hand some phenomenal event, "I won't believe it until I read it in the paper."

It was Will Rogers who *said* it, but I believe it was my dad who thought of it first. With a world about go to war against the same Germany he had fought against just two decades earlier, Dad believed that whatever he needed to know about what was happening in that arena (and with his beloved Boston Red Sox) would be best presented by the ol' *Star-T*.

I honed my reading skills through the bubbles above the heads of Dick Tracy, Smilin' Jack, Tim Tyler, and all the other heroes of the *Star-Telegram* comics. And it was the intrigue of those characters that caused me to park daily on the editorial page, where Hal Coffman depicted in cartoon form his opinion of local, state, and national events.

Coffman was a pioneer of editorial cartooning and, even though I was too young to grasp his issues, his work was what moved me from the comic strips to the news itself. And, indirectly, to someday approach Dirk with the proposition.

I DON'T REMEMBER the idea I tossed out for Dirk to use on his first cartoon, but it was not the one he brought back to me. And, through all the years ahead, it never would be.

Once, somewhat irritated that Dirk had scoffed at one of my suggestions, I asked him why he so adamantly rejected suggestions from me or, for that matter, anybody else.

"Can you write a column that somebody else suggests?" he asked.

I thought about it for a few moments, and the answer was . . . not really. I have tried it, and it just doesn't work right. I don't know why it doesn't, it just doesn't.

So the groundwork that was laid in our agreement pretty much laid itself. The only editing I did on Dirk's cartoons was getting him to come over—he officed across the street in a building he owned ("no other landlord would tolerate my housekeeping")—and correct a spelling error. For some reason he always left off the second L in Darrell (Royal). He grumbled about it, but he would always fix it.

I think, deep down, that Dirk believed it was Royal who spelled it wrong.

Through the years, Dirk and I developed a special friendship. Every morning of the work week, we ate breakfast together in the *A-J* coffee shop. Our discussions ran the full gamut from sports to politics to city issues to plain ol' gossip. And, both being very generous with our opinions, our arguments were frequent.

Something I learned, long before Dirk's distaste for city hall drove him into running for the council, was that Dirk West was not just a gifted artist with a sense of humor. He was intelligent and incisive which, come to think of it, made his stubbornness all the more difficult.

Dirk made, in my opinion, one of the most effective officials we've ever elected to either office. His wit and pragmatic outlook simplified much of what the bureaucrats preferred to keep as complex as possible. And he took the same approach to the football coaches he parodied. An example was the delight Dirk got out of a former Chicago Bears quarterback's remarks about how coaches loved to pretend that football was a very complicated game. The quote went something like this:

"If the game of football was all that complicated, most of the guys coaching it now would be out of work."

That supported what Dirk once told Jim Carlen who, smarting from a cartoon that had stung him where it hurt, told Dirk that he didn't know anything about the complexities of offensive football.

"Hey," Dirk replied. "I don't know anything about the complexities of my TV set, but I know when it ain't workin' right. And what I know about your offense is that it ain't workin' right!"

I SHARED IN the delight that went along with seeing the evolvement of Dirk's cartooning prowess. I loved that very first cartoon which, looking back on it over stacks of his later works, was relatively pedestrian.

Somewhere along the way, his characters took on personalities that were both delightful and relevant. Aggies hated the Aggie Dirk drew but, as several of them admitted to me, it did accurately (and painfully) depict the way non-Aggies loved to view them.

Grant Teaff, who miraculously coached Baylor football from its lowest point in history into a championship team, is the only coach I ever knew to affect Dirk's work. Dirk's Baylor mascot, all during the preceding coach's regime, had appeared as a little Teddy Bear with an ever-present tear dangling from the corner of his eye.

After Baylor began winning, Teaff asked Dirk if he didn't believe that Baylor's Bear deserved a little toughening up. The result was a growling, grossly mean and filthy

Bear that stood a head taller than all the other mascots in the picture.

The Aggies and Carlen would have loved to have had such influence!

And, at times, so would I . . .

## COMICS KILLER

AMONG THE MANY things I learned while occupying the corner office of my favorite newsroom was that the people who respond to surveys ain't the same people who read the funny papers. And, akin to that, the biggest enemy of the cartoonists who draw up the strips is the PC crowd. That came to light when I foolishly decided to survey the readership to learn which of our comics might need to be reevaluated. I had been unduly influenced by a piece I had read in one of the trades about how the tastes of readers had changed, most noticeably in their preference of cartoons.

The social climate is changing, it read, and comics should be selected in concert with what the sophisticated reader will soon be demanding. Hard as I tried to picture a Mensa qualifier peering learnedly at our comics page and nodding approvingly, it just wouldn't come into focus. To me "changing social climate" translated into somebody handing a kid a trophy he didn't earn.

Being, to put it mildly, no fan of Political Correctness to begin with, I not only resented their often misguided behavior but also, to an even greater degree, the war they were waging against humor. My recommending a good laxative went unheeded.

But I digress.

My own personal interest in the comic strips was at once deep-seeded and influential. As a pre-schooler, perhaps even a pre-toddler, I was attracted to the funny pages of the Fort Worth newspaper that was part of our daily lives. After all the older sibs—I was the youngest of seven—had gone off to school, I would perch in Mom's lap while she read the funnies to me.

She would start reading at the upper left and finish at the top right, which is the same reading pattern I follow today (incidentally, when I come to a strip I don't like, I don't simply skip over it—I pause and glare at it for a few seconds, hoping it will go away; it never does).

In later years, Mom told me that the first complete sentence I ever uttered was "Read Popeye." It was some-where along about then that I decided I wanted to be a newspaperman.

AT THE TIME I decided to launch a comic strip survey, I should have known better. That's because of an earlier one that we performed out of necessity when we decided to eliminate our afternoon paper.

Among the necessary casualties of the move were a full page of funnies. Despite each strip's individual popu-larity, two pages of comics wasn't a practical offering. In order to make the best decision possible, we turned to the readers to assist in the culling process. After the tumult and the shouting, we finally selected the survivors. Obviously, every strip that didn't make the cut was somebody's favorite . . . seemingly, *everybody's* favorite!

It was several years later that I read that stupid article and thought, hmm, it's probably time that we checked in with our readers about our current fare. A short memory is no sin but it sure can be troublesome . . .

Only after I had pulled the trigger to launch the survey did I slap my forehead with the heel of my hand and utter expletively, what in the yell have I done!

IT SHOULD BE pointed out along about here that the removal of a certain strip is often beyond the editor's control. Cartoonists sometimes thoughtlessly die or just stop drawing.

Among the most significant of the former were Al Capp and Charles Schulz, creators of Li'l Abner and Peanuts, respectively. Capp went so far as to mandate that, after his death, his strip was not to be continued, either in re-runs or drawn by another artist. The Schulz estate did not forbid the former.

Some of my favorites were stopped simply because their respective cartoonists grew tired of deadlines and/or other drudgeries that go along with the rigidity of the practice. A few examples were Calvin and Hobbes, The Far Side and Rick O'Shay, to name a few.

Those aren't the changes you have to spend a lot of time explaining. Or, trying to explain. No matter how sincere I sounded in telling an irate customer why his favorite didn't make the cut, nothing I could say would make a difference. And it was the long-running strips that stirred the loudest outcry. That's also when it comes clear that, despite having published the survey for several weeks, most complainers swear they never saw it, that all they read is the front page and the comics.

Now, because of my disdain for the PC, it didn't bother me to tell the women's group that started a letter-writing campaign against Andy Capp that, yes, I know he is a lout, a cad, a drunk, and a womanizer. But he's funny and, after all, this is the funny paper, not scripture.

Years later, ol' Andy wouldn't survive the cut. But I did get him about a thirty-year stay of execution . . .

ANDY WASN'T THE only strip to get mixed reviews. The Far Side, which I mentioned earlier, was drawn by Gary Larson who, not only was a stylistic cartoonist but a guy with a weird sense of humor. Some of his offerings required several reads before I could get it. And—I'm confessing here—I sometimes would laugh along with everybody else just to hide my density . . .

Probably my main rationale for keeping Andy Capp was due to reader complaints that our comics lacked humor.

"Hey, I've seen funerals that were funnier than your funny pages," is how one guy put it.

And if I thought the complaints about comics changes would soon die down and eventually disappear, I was wrong on both counts. Recently, at a social gathering, a friend of mine was about to introduce me to a rather distinguished looking fellow.

"Yeah, I know who he is," the man said. "He's the SOB that killed Dick Tracy!"

NEWSPAPER SALE

*Editor's Note: The recent sale of The A-J to Gatehouse Media stirred memories of an ownership change in 1972.*

WHEN I LEARNED that the newspaper had been sold, I was in Austin, and I couldn't have been more surprised. As I recall, Texas was about the third stop on the Southwest Conference press tour, meaning it would be several more days before I would get back to Lubbock to greet the changes sure to come . . .

That was almost exactly forty-five years ago, my twelfth year with the *Avalanche-Journal*, and I wasn't at all excited at the thought of working for a new outfit. Hey, I already had what I considered to be the best sports editing job in the state, and for two very important reasons:

Chas. A. Guy and Parker F. Prouty.

Although the Whittenburg family of Amarillo was the principal owners of the *A-J*, those two men ran the paper with total autonomy. Not only were they my two biggest bosses, they were my best advocates. I just didn't fathom the idea of working for a company whose methods of measurement might involve a different yardstick.

In fact, those two men were the very reason I was still working at the *A-J* at the time of the sale. Because newspapering jobs were then a buyer's market, I had received several decent offers. I had never given more than passing consideration for any of them. But three years before, I was offered the position as sports editor of the *Houston Post*. After having me down for an interview, the *Post* flew my wife in to look at houses. We both thought it might be the thing to do.

To make a long story short, those two men improved my situation considerably. I suddenly had become a very happy camper. Only upon learning that the paper had sold did I second-guess that decision.

THE FIRST TIME I met William S. Morris III was a couple or three weeks later at the Lubbock Club, where the new owner had a reception to meet with his newly acquired leadership team. When I introduced myself and referred to him as Mister Morris, he corrected me. "Call me Billy," he said.

I liked that. Hey, after all these years I could never bring myself not to say *Mister* Guy and *Mister* Prouty.

For reasons obtainable only by visiting a shrink, I've always had trouble messing with something that's working well. I went through the same thing when we changed football coaches before my junior year, or the time we got a new company commander when I was in the army. Anyway, I did hear myself saying I should have taken that dern Houston job . . .

It never occurred to me that after the changes of football coaches and company commanders, my situation actually improved. I doubted that would be the case this time.

The title "Executive Sports Editor" might not carry the same weight in Georgia as it did in Texas . . .

I HAD MANY reasons to love my job as sports editor, not the least of which was the position's high profile in a community where Red Raider athletics was the most discussed topic on any street corner in town. And then, in the heyday of newspapering everywhere, the sports columns often kicked off those conversations.

It also helped that one of Tech's most ardent supporters, vocally and financially, was Parker F. Prouty. And, until I had taken over the Tech beat, he didn't know me from a sack of potatoes. Mr. Guy, who promoted me into the position, liked my writing style. That did not mean that I was immune to his corrective measures, which often lacked sensitivity.

Ironically, it was a former Southwest Conference coach whom I credit for getting me on the good side of Mr. Prouty. Blair Cherry, a hall-of-fame coach, was not only a good friend of Mr. Prouty, Cherry was his idol. During my first season of covering Tech football, Coach Cherry bragged to Mr. Prouty about my sports writing abilities.

That's all it took. I don't like to think what would've happened if the old coach had become a critic . . .

HERE, MORE than four decades after Morris Communications bought the paper, I find myself shuddering at the thought of where I would be had the Whittenburgs never made the sale.

My accomplishments as a sports writer—writing awards, professional recognition, high offices in state and national organizations, and the high regard from my two most powerful bosses—served both my ego and my comfort zone.

What it didn't do was provide for my future.

Despite the efforts by Mr. Prouty and Mr. Guy, the Whittenburgs refused to provide any retirement program.

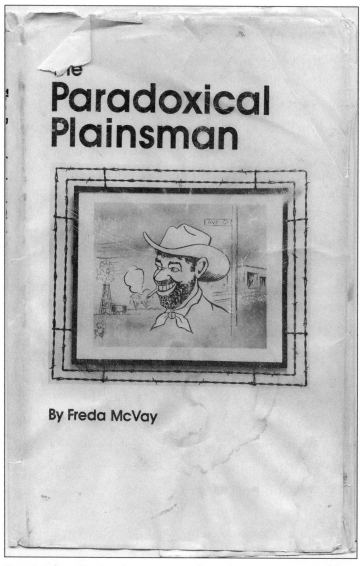

Drawing from Guy's column

They supposedly believed reporters to be a nomadic group that would never stay any place long enough to retire. Immediately following the MCC purchase, *A-J* employees became participants in a number of perks. Suddenly we had great insurance plans—health and life—and a retirement program that was based on profit sharing at a time when newspapering was a very profitable business.

ALTHOUGH I was correct in my assumption that being a sports editor was not nearly as impressive to the new ownership as it had been under my old bosses, that soon became a moot point. Less than a year after the sale, I was moved into management and began a climb up the ladder that culminated in my becoming only the second editor-in-chief in the newspaper's long and storied history.

Although each time I walked in and took my seat in an office built to the specifications of the late Chas. A. Guy, I never felt totally deserving. The standards he had set were insurmountable. Yet today, seventeen years after retiring, I am far from being a person of wealth. But I am living comfortably in the city's premier retirement community and wound up my career working for an outstanding corporation.

Each month as my Social Security check shows up on my bank statement, I credit that sale all those years ago for it not being the only entry in that account.

Thanks, Billy. It's been a great ride . . .

## PC Policeman

A READER, WHO I am tempted to say is obviously two steps to the left of reasonable, just took me to task.

I'm no newcomer to criticism. Having been laying my opinion out there on a regular basis for more than a half-century, I've been called about everything from an idiot to a city snob. Hey, lots of people have been called "idiots" but, as far as I can tell, I'm the first person from Moran, Texas, ever to be called "a city snob."

But I digress.

What put a scorpion in this reader's drawers was my having panned an Academy Award winning movie. Now I have done that before, at least twice. Once was when *One Flew over the Cuckoo's Nest* won, and the second time was whatever movie beat out *Dr. Zhivago*.

Anyway, this reader took me to task for doubting the Oscar credentials of *Moonlight*. An apparent member of the PC Police, he busted me on several charges, the major two being (1) a racial bigot and (2) a homophobe. He did cut me some slack, being as I "lack the experience of being black, gay and on the wrong side of Segregation." He also mentioned, or maybe just implied, that I also knew nothing of poverty.

I will confess to being neither black nor gay, but I am offended that he put me on "the wrong side of Segregation."

If he had been reading me in the early '60s he might remember that I was hammering my friend J. T. King to sign James Ray Jackson of Lubbock and Junior Coffey from Dimmitt, two great high school football players and a pair of outstanding citizens. They both were black.

I was a student at UNT when it integrated and was a staffer on the school paper which strongly supported the move.

Being the seventh kid born to my parents, and my arriving at the beginning of the Great Depression, I may not have been a close friend of poverty, but it and I did become well acquainted . . .

AS A MODERATE who does generally walk a couple of steps to the right of center on many issues and lean left on a few others, I used to be put out by both the Far Left and the Far Right. Now, neither puts me out—instead, they both scare hell out of me!

That reader's comments on the movie *Moonlight* emphasize the negative impact the social phenomena, "Political Correctness," has had on our country, our beliefs, and—perhaps worst of all—the hindrance of freedom of speech. Maybe freedom of thought will come next.

A friend of mine—himself an intelligent guy—once told me that the people who lashed out at Political Correctness were probably at least somewhat bigoted. I disagree. My contention is that simple human decency provides what PC demands. The difference in the two is that the former requires that every person is entitled to EQUAL treatment. The latter often requires certain persons to receive SPECIAL treatment.

For his information, I did get what the movie was about. And I never said it was a lousy picture or that I didn't enjoy it. It was, to me, underwhelming—unlike two of the ones I mentioned in that same column as being among the very best. One was *Fences*, which was about the complex dynamics of a black family. It was a story of great depth that inspired both empathy and illusion. Guilt and pain were vividly presented. The other was *Hidden Figures*, the true story of black women mathematicians whose work at NASA had a prominent—perhaps the most prominent—role in the success of the U.S. space program, which not only was falling behind the Soviets but was floundering in its own state of confusion.

I got no flak over thinking, like *Moonlight*, two other nominees were over-rated: *La La Land* and *Manchester by the Sea*.

THE NOMINEES did include an unusually large number of movie and acting candidates that featured black stories and starred black actors.

That followed a year when the Academy was criticized—even chastised—for not including either among the candidates. At first blush, one might wonder whether the drastic turnaround was an attempt to make atones for the perceived shun.

I find that very unlikely. Given the liberal sway of the Academy voters, I doubt the previous omission was for any reason other than available product. And, considering the quality of the movies and casts, the black themes and black stars were among the best of the year.

And I am sure that the PC cop who busted me is convinced that I selected *Hell and High Water* as my favorite was because it carried a theme about Honky robbers and Honky sheriffs. I did like it because it cut a trail across towns that were a part of my life. Even though it featured some great acting, none of it—in my opinion, at least—rose to the quality of Denzel Washington in *Fences*.

THE MAIN THEME of that column was my method of judging which movies were great. If I enjoy watching every scene, that's a GOOD movie. If I enjoy watching every scene then continue thinking about it all the way home and beyond, then it is a GREAT movie.

A *Dog's Purpose* fit both criteria. Heck, I still think about it now and then. And only when my liberal critic explained it to me, I didn't really know why. It's all because of my "Lubbock attitude" that I "enjoyed a panned film about a dog who learns to emphasize more than (I) would enjoy a film about segregation, bigotry and racism . . . "

But, conversely, could it be that I judge movies by the content of its message and not the color of its actors? Obviously, that was a play on one of Martin Luther King's greatest speeches. It seems to make my case.

Unless, of course, the PC filter keeps clouding the view . . . for not liking a movie for all the wrong reasons . . .

## OLD NEWS

THAT PARTICULAR newspaper was originally delivered one week shy of forty-seven years ago. But only when re-reading it last week did it occur to me that what separates then from now is not time alone.

The city itself has changed; the world has changed; I have changed; and, most obviously, the newspaper itself has changed.

The paper was brought to me by a friend who ran across it while cleaning out his files. Actually, it wasn't the entire edition, just the sports section. He was about to toss it when he noticed my column. Perhaps because he was amused at how young I looked in that picture. Hey, even if I had worked out daily—which I have not—I would have changed somewhat during that forty-seven-year span.

But I digress.

LUBBOCK'S CHANGES during that almost half-century span have been awesome, both in population and infrastructure. And, in some cases, in attitude and expectations.

The 1960 census showed the city's population at just over 149,000, compared to today's count estimated to be a quarter-million. Loop 289, which encircled the entire city in 1970, is now considered to be in central Lubbock. The Marsha Sharp Freeway now moves traffic from I-27 to a flourishing Milwaukee corridor. None of the three was even in the thoughts of the town's most liberal visionaries.

The freeway was named for a Tech women's basketball coach whose national championship ratcheted up the challenges of all future teams and the expectations of every year's fan base. Milwaukee Avenue resulted from one of Lubbock's visionaries, former mayor Tom Martin. And, as is the way of many visions, Martin's plan drew skepticism from many, including the *A-J* editor who at the time was I.

A development that had been started out there several years before had not blossomed. There were those of us who were influenced by that. Martin, despite losing his bid for re-election, was kept in charge of that project by his successor. Driving down it, one readily experiences a farm road gone urban. Martin beat his successor to win another term as mayor, only to lose out again in his final bid for reelection.

Again, success often begats expectations.

ANOTHER THING made painfully clear by scanning the old newspaper was the effect of inflation.

Seeing only those ads that were targeting those most apt to be reading the sports section, the prices of the day were—by current standards—almost unbelievable. Sears, Wards, Globe (remember Globe?), Firestone and Goodyear all would gladly sell you a set of four tires for under $100.

A pair of Freeman shoes was offered by S&Q (remember S&Q?) for $28. And for fisherman, Sears was selling a ten-foot jon boat for $58—if you wanted to paint it yourself. Otherwise, you'd have shell out another $3.50.

Inflation also had impacted the newspaper industry which, back then, only gave token attention to the price of newsprint. I noticed that when I opened the old paper and it seemed to spread out forever. Actually, it was about four inches wider than every paper to hit the nation's doorsteps this morning. Sadly, that's not the greatest impact change has had on the industry. In fact, it by comparison, was insignificant.

When I started my journalism career as a sports writer in the late '50s until I retired as editor-in-chief in 2001, newspapers were the nation's primary source for information and advertising. Ours was no different.

Then came the Internet. It was embraced by a generation of people that didn't read, period, and which was immediately caught up in the unbridled and often nonfactual output that was the lifeblood of the electronic maelstrom.

Newspapers were knocked out of their comfort zone. After having done the same things the same way—and enjoying uncommon wealth in the process—they found themselves having to adjust to compete. What long had been a single-barrel volley of printed verbiage now was a multimedia output. Online editions with sound and motion gave new breath to a process suddenly overtaken by age.

BUT THE MAIN thrust of the news published that day—May 14, 1970—revolved around the most trying and disastrous event in Lubbock's history. It was the third day after an ultra-large tornado had ripped the heart out of the city, leaving twenty-six dead, thrice that many injured, and millions of dollars in damages.

Despite its pages being illustrated by pictures depicting the destruction of the largest-size twister measurable, there was about the news more uplifting than brooding, more of hope than despair. A good example was a headline over a story in which J. T. King, then the Tech athletic director, assuring one and all that the Coaches All-America game slated to make its first Lubbock appearance, would go on as scheduled.

Obviously, that would take some doing. The light standards surrounding Jones Stadium were either on the ground or standing like so many twisted wires protruding from the ground. He was speaking from his office whose window framed a picture not only of damaged light poles but of destruction as far as the eye could see. Trees were gnarled and limbless, buildings were piles of rubble, and cars throughout the area were crushed and battered wads of steel and broken glass.

"We'll get it done," was King's only answer to the obvious question.

WITH THE resolve of a wounded eagle refusing to allow a broken wing to ebb her determination to fly again, Lubbock gave birth to an attitude of virtual reformation.

Not only did the All-America game go on as scheduled, it played before its largest crowd in history. Then, even more amazingly, a city known for its fiscal conservatism, pulled off a bond election that resulted in a new and modern library; a civic center whose size and amenities rivaled any in the state; and an airport with major league boarding gates, a restaurant, newsstands and the "feel" of a metropolitan facility.

The Lubbock of today is, indeed, a very different city from that one portrayed in the 1970 newspaper. But one has to wonder what this burgeoning country locale would have been like had the leadership of forty-seven years ago failed to respond as it did. Tragic though it was, that 1970 tornado spawned a determination that turned success into expectation, vision into a catalyst.

A mere drive down the MSF displays the results.

## 50 YEARS LATER

*(Published Aug. 29, 2010, exactly 50 years from the day I began my A-J career)*

GRACE KELLY WAS off someplace exotic, honeymooning with Prince Rainier, and Richard Nixon had just taken a two-week hiatus from his Presidential campaign to enter a hospital with a knee infection.

The Dallas Cowboys were in their first NFL preseason ever, and the American Football League was looking forward to its maiden campaign. The New York Yankees and Pittsburgh Pirates were leading their respective American and National Leagues, both of which consisted of eight teams.

Nixon would be off the stump for two weeks, but why worry? Despite John F. Kennedy's charm, the country was not about to elect a *Catholic* to the most powerful job on earth.

Closer to home, the Red Raiders and their fans were agog over the approach of their first ever Southwest Conference football season, and there was talk about a loop that would encircle the entire city, residential areas and all. That, however, was a few years away, and I had my head full just dealing with today . . . that day.

It was a hot August afternoon, and I had just paused at the top of the stairs to take in the surroundings, hoping to get all those butterflies flying in formation before I stepped on in to begin a new job in a new profession in a new town.

IT WAS TWO flights of stairs that got me to the spot where I was standing; but it was a long, winding road, often filled with bumps, curves and detours, that had brought me there. I don't know whether I did, but I could have uttered under my breath, "After all these years it is really going to happen . . . "

Back in Moran Grade School, it was Miss Baughman who asked the boys in the class what they wanted to be when they grew up. That the girls were not asked the same question says more about the times than it does about the teacher who had posed the question. And that the girls themselves were not offended was because they had not yet been taught that they should be.

But I digress.

Carl planned to be a mechanic. Jack said he would be a truck driver. Cuz wanted to be a carpenter. Miss Baughman nodded politely after each of those responses, perhaps even commenting that the country, then at war, needed mechanics, truck drivers, and carpenters.

It was when I said I was going to someday be a writer for a newspaper that her tempo changed.

She stared at me awhile, trying to figure out where I was coming from. For all her good qualities, Miss Baughman always had a feeling that I was up to something. She didn't say "Posh!" but I could feel her thinking it.

"You would have to go to college to do that," she said, then went right on back to whichever of the Three Rs that were the original topic.

I did not take her remark personal at the time, nor do I now. Moran boys didn't go the college. They became mechanics, truck drivers, and carpenters.

WHAT MISS Baughman had no way of knowing was that I had not simply blurted a quick answer to a simple question. Rather, I had bared a long-harbored dream that she had taken as an impulsive fantasy. Even though there was nothing impulsive about my response, the time would come when I, too, would accept it as just a fantasy. But not yet at that juncture.

The school years rolled on, the war ended, and I had moved on up to high school.

Meanwhile, I would read the *Fort Worth Star-Telegram* every day, cover to cover, wondering what it was like for those people who wrote the stories. I envied what I figured to be their lifestyles—especially the sports writers who got to speak daily with such college stars as Doak Walker and ballplayers like Ted Williams and Bob Feller. It wasn't that most of my friends didn't take my dream seriously; they simply didn't know enough about the subject to even wonder if I could do it.

Then came Marguerite Haggard, who not only knew exactly what I was talking about but was excited by the thought.

Miss Haggard was our new high school English teacher and, of greater import to me, a former newspaper journalist. Although I'm sure she often wished that I was as interested in serious matters as I was in football, girls and mayhem, she never stopped encouraging, urging, and coaching. In my senior yearbook she wrote a nice note, saying I had "a fantastic flair for writing," and how she expected great things for me.

It was Miss Haggard who convinced me I *could* do it. My problem was deciding that I *would* do it.

SEPARATING THAT high school graduation day, when Miss Haggard told me she also was leaving MHS, and the day at the top of the aforementioned stairs, a lot more things than passing time breezed through my life.

With Miss Haggard's prodding no longer available, my aspirations lapsed back into the reality of my surroundings. College would mean—despite my scholarship offers—financial hardship for my folks (who, unbeknownst to me, were very eager to make it) and a rather pedestrian, literally, lifestyle for myself. My friends had taken roughnecking jobs and actually had bought their own cars! Hey, no guy's charm could persuade a chick to go to a movie if it meant walking to the bleeping theater!

I tucked the dream away, decided it wasn't my lot to begin with, and took my life down a different route. After stints in the West Texas oilfields and highway construction, I was drafted and spent two years in the Army. Shortly after my discharge I met a pretty co-ed, fell in love and—only after my having agreed to join her in pursuit of a college degree—we eloped.

Encouraged by her persuasion, financed by the GI Bill, and motivated by the need to get out of there and get a job, I completed my bachelor of journalism degree in two years and eleven months. Sorting through several job offers that came as a result of that J-school's reputation, I told my wife that I thought we should go to Lubbock, where they wanted me to write sports.

"Lubbock?" she said, sounding reluctant. "That's way out in West Texas . . . "

"Listen, it's a very good newspaper and a chance to cover the Southwest Conference. And we'll probably just stay there for a year, two at the most."

WHILE STANDING at the top of the stairs that day, my thoughts could have reflected on those two

schoolteachers—Miss Baughman and Miss Haggard—
and how both, quite paradoxically, had accurately assessed
my aspirations.

Not much happened during the years since both
those amazing women passed through my life that the
both of them did not somehow affect. Miss Baughman's
dogmatic pragmatism and Miss Haggard's unspoken permission to dream and to aspire were permanent residents
of my psyche.

Today, the 50th Anniversary of my walking up those
stairs, I knew I was allowing a boyhood dream to culminate.

But I had no idea that the company I was about to
join back then and the town I had just moved to would
become more than merely an occupation and a place of
residence.

Both institutions would come to define me. It took a
while for me to do that for myself . . .

# INDEX